BORN TO REIGN

Born to Reign

Nicholas Campion

CHAPMANS

Chapmans Publishers
A division of the Orion Publishing Group Ltd
Orion House
5 Upper St Martin's Lane
London WC2H 9EA

A CIP catalogue record for this book is available from
the British Library
ISBN 1 85592 640 7

First published by Chapmans 1993

Typeset by Deltatype Ltd, Ellesmere Port, Cheshire
Printed in Great Britain by
Clays Ltd, St Ives plc

For Wendy

Acknowledgments

I owe deep thanks to Wendy Buonaventura and Beth Shaw for their assistance and ideas, Marjory and Ian Chapman for their enthusiasm and my agent, Doreen Montgomery, for her support over the years. I am also indebted to Martin Harvey for his many articles in *The Astrological Journal* and *Astrology Quarterly*.

Data

The birth times and dates for the horoscopes of the British monarchs are available from the data collection of the British Astrological Association. All timed data for the European monarchs is taken from André Barbault's collection in *La Prévision Astrologique*, Éditions Traditionelles, Paris 1986, except Napoleon II and Louis XVIII, available from the Astrological Association.

All dates before 1752 (1582 in Catholic countries, 1918 in Russia) are according to the old-style calendar. Under this system, the Sun changed zodiac signs as much as ten days earlier than nowadays.

Contents

Introduction

The use of astrology by the crowned heads of Europe is one of the great untold stories of history. For thousands of years, practitioners of what was known as the 'Royal Art' were welcome at court. Their advice was often invaluable, and their access to their kings and queens frequently unrivalled.

When it was revealed in the spring of 1990 that Princess Diana had for years secretly been visiting astrologers for advice and guidance, few eyebrows were raised. Most of the press comment even seemed to be respectful, perhaps because of an instinctive realisation that there were ancient and venerable connections between the monarchy and astrology. The new royal astrologers were erudite and sophisticated in their use of astrology, skilled in the art of relating the steadily changing patterns of the planets to the ebb and flow of emotional and psychological cycles. One of Diana's astrologers, Penny Thornton, was the author of several respected books and was, like another, Debbie Frank, a highly qualified and experienced counsellor. They, together with Felix Lyle, the third astrologer named as having helped Diana in the late eighties, provided her with personal self-understanding, showing her how to make the most of gifts which until then had never been properly developed. According to reports which surfaced in 1992, Diana's astrologers showed her how her horoscope, based around her compassionate Cancerian Sun, offered her the opportunity to take a serious involvement in charitable work. This she has done very successfully with her work for the hospice movement and with AIDS patients.

More than this, though, Penny, Felix and Debbie were the latest in a long line of royal astrologers which in former times included some of the greatest philosophers of the western world. Astrology was originally an exclusively royal preserve, and the first astrologers, who lived and worked in ancient Sumer (southern Iraq) about four thousand years ago, provided their advice and forecasts for the king alone. Although horoscopes were cast for individuals after 400 BC, astrology retained its popularity at court. Kings, of course, wanted their astrologers to predict the future and give them advice on the most auspicious time to be crowned, to fight battles and generally outwit their rivals. However, there was more to the links between astrologers and the court than mere self-interest.

Monarchy was once a divine institution. From ancient times until the eighteenth century kings and their queens were seen as the earthly representatives of divine power: God ruled in heaven, and in the palaces and castles of medieval Europe a succession of emperors, kings and princes carried out His will. This, at least was the theory. The legacy of these ancient ideas is still evident in the splendid ritual of the coronation, in which the blessing of God is called down upon the new monarch. In return, the sovereign utters a solemn oath to protect God's church, justifying the title, 'Defender of the Faith'.

The survival of these ancient myths and their attendant rituals into modern times partially explains the dilemma of the British royal family today. Its privileges are based on the idea that it is special, and, although few people talk in such terms, the British monarchy is still regarded as a semi-divine institution. Legally, the Queen's religious duties are concentrated in her role as Head of the Church of England. Yet the feelings of awe and reverence with which the monarchy is regarded by so many go far deeper than the simple legal situation would suggest, and are rooted in archaic reverence for the divine king. We have moved on less than we imagine from the worship of the Egyptian Pharaoh or the Roman Emperor. The glittering spectacle surrounding monarchy, the belief that the king or queen is a special person quite unlike the mass of the population, and the symbolism and religious ritual of the coronation ceremony derive directly from these ancient beliefs. Even the raised throne from which the Queen addresses the House of Lords is a relic of the ancient relationship of the monarch with the stars. The throne, it was thought, should raise the monarch above everyone else to make the point that he, or she, was closer to heaven – and the stars – than anyone else. This is why it was so important to have astrologers close at hand.

A Simple Guide to Astrology

Astrology is the art of interpreting celestial patterns in relation to life on Earth. Broadly speaking, the astrologer examines the movements of the planets as they progress through the zodiac and then relates their cycles and the patterns they form with each other to changing events in human existence. A general misunderstanding is that astrologers believe that the planets influence life on earth. In fact, only the Sun and the Moon exert a measurable influence. Astrology works through the comparison of cycles; cycles in the solar system correspond to cycles on earth, and by looking at the larger, planetary pattern, we can gauge the state of earthly developments.

Astrologers usually cast horoscopes for the time of birth, from which they both interpret character and assess possible future events. There are also other applications of astrology, and in former times the royal astrologers spent much of their time reading horary charts, which were horoscopes calculated to answer specific questions, and estimating the most auspicious moment at which to inaugurate new enterprises. Altogether ten planets are used:

 THE SUN

Strictly speaking, the Sun is a star, but in astrology it counts as one of the ten planets. Its position in the zodiac reveals a great deal about our character. This is why we refer to ourselves by the sign of the zodiac which the Sun occupied at our birth – the Sun sign. To be a Taurean or a Sagittarian, for example, means that the Sun must be in Taurus or Sagittarius at our birth. According to ancient tradition, the Sun also represents the monarchy in general.

 THE MOON

Like the Sun, this planet also reveals much about our character, and the sign of the zodiac it occupies at birth is always important. It shows the manner in which we express our feelings and our attitudes towards our home and family. It also often indicates our relationships with our mothers.

 **MERCURY**

Mercury describes our minds. It indicates the way we think, talk and communicate, the choices we face and the decisions we take.

 **VENUS**

This is the planet which indicates our inner female nature, regardless of our sex. It also shows the kind of woman we are attracted to as friend or lover, as well as our capacity for enjoyment and our aesthetic sense.

 MARS

Mars is the opposite of Venus. It reveals the inner male nature which we all possess, whether male or female, and indicates the kind of men we find attractive, whether as friends or lovers. It also indicates our general energy level and how good we are at accomplishing practical tasks.

 JUPITER

This is the planet which rules the principle of growth and expansion. It has a great deal to do with ambition and the attaining of major goals. It is also associated with greed and carelessness.

 SATURN

Saturn is the opposite of Jupiter. It indicates self-discipline, self-control, order and limitation. It is also closely associated with our ability to work and bring routine but necessary tasks to a successful conclusion. Saturnine people are usually convinced conformists.

 URANUS

Uranus signifies all unusual people and objects. It indicates originality, a desire for independence and a love of change. Those who have this planet strongly placed at birth often go their own way or defy convention.

 NEPTUNE

Intuition, imagination and dreams are all symbolised by Neptune. This is a wonderfully helpful planet for artists, mystics and dreamers, but people who are born under powerful Neptunian patterns often find it difficult to cope with practical work.

PLUTO

As the ancient god of the underworld, Pluto has acquired astrological characteristics closely connected to strife, struggle and confrontation. It has often brought critical moments to those in power.

Particular combinations of planets in an individual's chart also tell us a great deal about them. For example, Saturn (which indicates inhibition) together with Venus (indicating feelings) points to emotional inhibition. Mercury (the mind) combined with Neptune (the imagination) lends a poetic quality. The precise distance between each pair of planets adds further variety to the manner in which each planetary cycle is expressed.

There are two further points of great significance in every horoscope. One is the **Ascendant**. This is the degree of the zodiac rising over the eastern horizon at the moment of birth. It is also known as the Rising Sign, and has profound significance for the character as does the Sun sign. The **Midheaven** is the degree of the zodiac culminating which, broadly speaking, means it is the degree of the zodiac occupied by the Sun at noon on any one day. It is less important than the Ascendant. It has a great deal to do with the career and, according to ancient tradition, is also the part of the horoscope especially associated with monarchy.

The best general description of character is to take three signs of the zodiac together – those containing the Sun, Moon and Ascendant. This combination allows much greater depth of analysis than the Sun sign alone, while the next level of detail requires deeper technical analysis.

Astrology has been used by royalty for thousands of years, and its use in guiding people through their lives has been proved time and time again. But can it truly predict the future? Forecasting with astrology is extremely complicated and fraught with uncertainties. In this it shares much with economic forecasting and weather prediction. However, astrology has proved its ability to pick out both the time and nature of future events. For the evidence, we should look to Roger Elliot's 1977 book, *Astrology and the Royal Family*. On page 185, Roger looked at what 1992 would bring for the royal family, and it's well worth quoting his words in full, for they show how the astrologer works through a reasoning process to arrive at a final forecast: 'This is the crucial year for the Prince of Wales and, by implication, the whole royal family. He will undergo a deep and important change due to Pluto moving from a square aspect at birth to an exact conjunction with the Sun. This was the transit that accompanied Princess Margaret's declaration that she would not marry Group Captain Peter Townsend. Some similar kind of sacrifice may be required from Charles. That, or a calling to some ineluctable destiny.'

In December 1992, after months of speculation, Prince Charles became the first heir to the throne to separate legally from his wife, provoking the worst royal crisis since the abdication in 1936. Even *Old Moore's Almanac*, containing predictions written in December 1990 and published in June 1991, forecast that the position of the monarchy itself would come under question in October 1992. Prediction of the future is not an end in itself, however. The point, in a personal situation with a client, as when Penny Thornton was advising Diana, is to increase awareness of possible future choices and courses of action. The fact that precise forecasts such as Roger Elliot's can be made is, on the other hand, convincing evidence that there are cycles operating in both the monarchy and the nation as a whole. Astrology is the best – indeed, with our current knowledge, the only – way of measuring such cycles.

Astrologers at Court

The history of astrology is as old as the history of monarchy itself. In

The Signs of the Zodiac

Aries

Taurus

Gemini

Cancer

Leo

Virgo

Libra

Scorpio

Sagittarius

Capricorn

Aquarius

Pisces

England our story begins a thousand years ago, when William the Conqueror defeated Harold at the Battle of Hastings on 14 October 1066. Nobody who followed the stars was surprised by that year's tumultuous events as, for months before William set sail from Normandy, Halley's Comet had been attracting attention in the night sky, causing consternation among those who believed it was an evil omen. The greatest intellectuals of the time believed that the comet was a warning from God of punishment and retribution for the wicked, and it was thought to portend invasion and the death of kings. This is why a section showing the comet was included in the Bayeux tapestry, and why the faces of the people looking up at it reveal such anxiety. Years later the comet's appearance was still remembered with awe, and in the middle of the following century the chronicler Otto of Freising wrote of how it had coincided with the Norman conquest. In his epic work, *The Two Cities: A Chronicle of Universal History to the Year 1146*, he wrote that 'in the one thousand and sixty-sixth year from the incarnation of the Lord, a star of the sort that is called a comet is said to have been seen and failed not to have its effect. In the same year William, Count of Normandy, conquered Greater Britain, which is now called England, killing Harold, its King, and, after reducing the entire province to slavery and settling the Normans there, ruled himself as King'.

William selected Christmas Day for his coronation, an act which some historians interpret as a simple piece of convenience. He had to be crowned quickly, they say, to reinforce his power. But why on Christmas Day? In those times, to be crowned on the anniversary of Jesus' birth sent a clear message to all God-fearing people that here was a man whose rule was ordained by God. Yet Christmas Day was also close to the winter solstice, when the Sun reaches its lowest point on the horizon, before commencing its return to summer (the early Christians had adapted the old Roman feast of the Sun God, 25 December). This sent out an additional message – namely, that William's rule was also sanctioned by the cosmos. Anyone who stood in his way was also standing in the way of God, nature and the stars. We don't know what time the crown was actually placed on William's head, but some say it was at noon, just as the sun reached its highest point in the sky. If anybody had missed the significance of a Christmas

Day coronation, the time, noon, would at the very least make them realise that they were witnessing an important event.

Henry II was the first king known to have used astrologers on a regular basis, and he planned the various stages in his rebellion against King Stephen by consulting one of the most notable astrologers of the day, Adelard of Bath, his former tutor.

Not all kings approved of astrology. Edward III, for example, paid little attention to the advice he received from the scholarly John Ashenden of Merton College, Oxford. This was not because the astrologer was wrong, but because the King had a reputation for piety and was heavily influenced by his chaplain, Thomas Bradwardine, who bitterly denounced astrology on the grounds that it was offensive to God. Many churchmen were opposed to astrology, mainly because they couldn't control the astrologers' advice. Yet most used it, believing that the movements of the stars revealed the word of God.

Others, like Richard II, were enthusiastic supporters of all forms of divination, prophecy and forecasting. In France, Richard's contemporary, Charles V, founded a special college to guarantee the education of future generations of astrologers.

Often, it was considered foolhardy, even dangerous, to cast a monarch's horoscope without permission. The King's horoscope was sometimes difficult to obtain, for reasons of security, and only certain astrologers were permitted to see it. During the protracted negotiations prior to the marriage between Henry V and Catherine de Valois, daughter of the French King, astrologers were consulted at various stages. When the Bishop of Norwich sought advice from Jean Fusoris, he put the astrologer through a number of tests before allowing him to see the King's horoscope. Even then, Fusoris refused to make any forecasts for fear of the possible consequences.

William Parron, who advised Henry VII, fell from grace after forecasting a long and happy life for the Queen, Elizabeth of York, just before she died. Jerome Cardan made a similar mistake, forecasting a long life for the young Edward VI shortly before his death. In this case, though, it is thought that Cardan was attempting to stay out of trouble; to forecast the King's death could be a capital offence on account of its treasonable implications. Robert Allen, who successfully forecast Edward's death, was taken to task by Parliament and escaped punishment only when his forecast came true. Even a successful prediction was no defence, and when William Lilly forecast the Great Fire of London of 1666 fourteen years before it actually took place, he was accused of having started it!

Under Henry VIII (1509–47), all the major figures at court used astrology. Cardinal Wolsey, Henry's first Chancellor, is said to have had the King's horoscope cast so that his moves could be forecast, but also so that he could plan his own machinations at court. Unfortunately for him, he failed to survive the royal marriage crisis and was sent into disgrace after failing to arrange Henry's divorce from Catherine of Aragon. Thomas Cromwell, Henry's third Chancellor and the architect of the English Reformation, used one of the King's own astrologers as an ambassador, sending him abroad to ascertain continental attitudes to Henry. It was thought that an astrologer would possess special insights denied to ordinary people. Both royal servants were no doubt deeply interested in astrology as a result of Henry's enthusiasm for it, and during his reign the bishops were ordered not to criticise astrology. Henry employed two astrologers at court: the German Nicholas Kratzer and the English John Robins, and by all accounts they served him well. At least, they survived! Robins went on to serve Henry's daughter, Mary I, and no doubt she used him for advice on the plans of her sister and rival, Princess Elizabeth. At the same time Elizabeth was consulting John Dee concerning Mary's intentions. The situation becomes more complex when we realise that Mary was also consulting John Dee, and we can only imagine the scenes which must have taken place as the astrologers made their discreet visits to court and their even more secret visits to Elizabeth, who was held under house arrest. It's not inconceivable that Dee and Robins put their heads together to try and work out the best solution to the sisters' rivalry.

After Mary's death Elizabeth came to the throne, and her faith in John Dee was shown in her decision to have him choose the most auspicious time for her coronation. Dee achieved a larger-than-life reputation because of his experiments with alchemy (the pursuit of making gold from base metals) and spiritualism, and on one occasion a mob attacked his house, fearing that he was a sorcerer. But at court Dee was highly respected for his intellect, and he was considered one of the greatest mathematicians in Europe.

John Dee's counterpart in France was the celebrated Nostradamus. Nostradamus is famous for his hundreds of four-line prophecies, most of which are indecipherable riddles probably meant to make sense only to his contemporaries. Most of Nostradamus' prophecies were produced through clairvoyant means rather than through astrology. However, he made a name for himself by publishing annual almanacs of astrological predictions and it is as an astrologer that he is known to posterity, rather than as a psychic. Realising the dangers of becoming enmeshed in court politics, he preferred to stay at home in the south of France. On at least one occasion the Queen, Catherine de Medici, was so keen to consult him that she travelled all the way to his house in St Rémy to seek his advice.

Today Nostradamus is famous for his supposed forecasts of Hitler and Napoleon (which are open to doubt); however, in the sixteenth century his best-known forecast related to the sudden death of the French King Henry II in a jousting accident. Although he wrote in a form of medieval French rendered almost incomprehensible through his use of puns and metaphors, we can translate Nostradamus' relevant quatrain as follows:

'The young lion will overcome the old,
on the tournament ground in single combat,
Through the cage of gold his eyes will be pierced,
Two wounds become one, then a cruel death.'

The prophecy was published in 1555 and the King was instantly recognisable by his gold jousting helmet and the lion which formed its crest. It seemed clear that the King would be killed in a tournament as a result of a lance piercing his eyes. The whole of France was made aware of the forecast because it was independently supported by another French astrologer, Lucus Gauricus. He had already acquired a reputation as a skilled forecaster, successfully predicting the defeat of Henry's father King Francis I at the Battle of Pavia earlier in the century. Gauricus warned King Henry to beware of death during single combat in an enclosed space, due to an injury to the head in the summer of his forty-second year. Astrologers are often accused of being deliberately vague, but it's difficult to be more specific than that!

The King himself was made aware of the forecasts, but appears to have taken a robust response, typical of the Arien that he was. His only reply was that if he was going to die, he would rather that it was a noble death in open combat. In fact, Gauricus was slightly out in his calculations, and it was in his forty-first year – 1559 – that Henry was killed. The accident happened on the tournament ground during the celebrations honouring his daughter Elizabeth's marriage to Philip II of Spain. During the joust, Henry forgot to fasten the visor of his helmet and his opponent's lance unexpectedly splintered. The splinters passed through the helmet's visor, pierced both eyes and entered the King's brain. After prolonged and painful agony, as forecast, the King died. Amidst the mourning everyone praised the accuracy and skill displayed by the astrologers, Gauricus and Nostradamus, and their fame spread throughout Europe.

It was because of successes such as these that astrology was considered indispensable at all European courts. The greatest astronomers of the day were all employed as royal astrologers. Tycho Brahe, who revolutionised astronomical mathematics, cast horoscopes first for the kings of Denmark and then for the Holy Roman Emperors. There he was succeeded by Johann Kepler, the first man to work out the laws of planetary motion. Galileo, the first astronomer to use a telescope, became astrologer to the Medici family who ruled Florence. The Court Astrologers were some of the most respected people in royal circles, although never formally in the government. Morin de Vellefranche, Louis XIII's astrologer, did make a bid to become a member of the government, but was disappointed. He was, however, summoned to the Queen's bedside, where he recorded to the second the birth time of the future Louis XIV.

Louis XIV inherited his father's concern with astrology, at least in the early part of his reign, and sent astrologer the Abbé Pregnon as his ambassador to the court of Charles II of England. Louis' hope was that the Abbé would put his astrological skills to use in analysing and forecasting Charles' intentions. However, never one to miss an opportunity, Charles took the Abbé to the races with him, giving him instructions to pick the winning horses. Charles, apparently, was disappointed with the Abbé's lack of success; but then Charles had more serious uses for astrology. He was determined not to make the same mistake as his father, who was executed, and devoted a great deal of effort to the skilful manipulation of the potentially rebellious House of Commons. Whenever Charles had to give a speech to Parliament he asked Elias Ashmole to work out the most auspicious time for the speech to begin. By the end of his reign, the King had won every important step of his struggle with Parliament, and we can only assume that he was happy with Ashmole's work.

James II, Charles II's younger brother and successor, was tutored by the astrologer Anthony Ascham, but it is probable that his daughter Anne (1702–14) was the last English monarch to consult an astrologer until modern times. George I, who followed her to the throne would have had his horoscope cast at his birth in 1660, but because he was born in Hanover in northern Germany, all records have been lost. By the time he came to the throne it was no longer acceptable to have astrologers at court.

An interest in the occult and the paranormal in general continued, for such things are perennial human interests. Frederick, Prince of Wales, George I's grandson, was said to be superstitious and reportedly made frequent visits to fortune-tellers in Norwood Forest near London. Frederick's love of the occult is produced as evidence for his unsuitability to become king. In the event he died in 1751, leaving his son to ascend the throne as George III.

In France it was rumoured that Napoleon himself was a frequent visitor to the parlour of Mme Le Normand, a top society fortune-teller. She would probably have forecast the Emperor's future using a combination of simple astrology, perhaps based on little more than the date of birth, with tarot cards and clairvoyance.

Queen Victoria is also said to have been deeply superstitious and, according to the occultist Cheiro, who lived at the end of the nineteenth century, she 'often incurred the displeasure of her consort by bemoaning a broken mirror or the spilling of salt'. Victoria is also rumoured to have developed an interest in spiritualism, and the persistent rumours that she used the Scottish gillie, John Brown, to make contact with her beloved Albert are totally credible. Albert had died in 1861, plunging Victoria into over a quarter of a century of mourning. Some accounts suggest that she had been holding séances in the 1840s, others that she was driven to contact the dead only after Albert's death. We have one account of a séance held in 1853, recorded in the biography of Victoria by Elizabeth Longford. According to this version, 'One spring evening at Osborne in 1853 when the nightingales were singing and all the windows were open, she (Victoria) and Prince Albert decided to have a go. The table consented to spin round quite nicely for the royal pair but when Lady Ely applied her hands it fairly pushed along'. We have no knowledge of what messages Victoria may have received from the beyond.

The persistent rumours that John Brown had mediumistic powers can be traced back to 1861. On hearing of King Pedro of Portugal's death from typhoid on 13 November 1861, Victoria is reported to have recalled to the Princess Royal certain of Brown's utterances which suddenly seemed prophetic. On leaving Balmoral four weeks earlier, Brown had said to the Queen that he hoped she would be well through the winter and, 'above all that you may have no deaths in the family'. In her biography of Victoria, Elizabeth Longford comments, 'How much more striking must Brown's premonition have seemed when applied a month later to the death of Prince Albert. Who doubts that Queen Victoria repeated the story to her intimates and they in turn to a wider circle?'

If Victoria had indeed discovered that John Brown was a natural medium, she could hardly fail to have exploited his gifts to peer into the beyond and make contact with her lost love. Especially as she knew that Albert's untimely death at the age of forty-two had been forecast some time earlier by the top society astrologer known as Zadkiel. Zadkiel's aristocratic clients included Admiral FitzClarence, one of William IV's illegitimate children and Victoria's first cousin. Zadkiel's relationships with the court were kept at one remove, and his go-between with Prince Albert was Lord Robert Grosvenor, another client. Grosvenor transmitted Zadkiel's predictions direct to the Prince and, on the astrologer's behalf, requested Albert's exact birth time, essential information if a precise horoscope were to be cast. On 21 November 1840 the Queen gave birth to her eldest child, Princess Victoria. Grosvenor passed her horoscope, calculated by Zadkiel, on to the Prince and in return transmitted Albert's appreciation: 'His Royal Highness has been pleased to accept the horoscope of the Princess Royal, and has ordered me to thank you for it'.

Eventually Zadkiel's accuracy got him into trouble, and he ended up in court. In his almanac for 1861, compiled in the summer of 1860, he examined Albert's horoscope for 1861. Albert had been born with the Sun at 2° of Virgo, and in May Saturn was due to pass over this exact degree and, as seen from the earth, 'station', or temporarily stop moving. According to the ancient astrological texts which Zadkiel was using, this was a dire indication of great danger. He considered that Saturn's movement would prove 'very evil for all persons born on or near the 26 August (Albert's birthday); among the sufferers I regret to see the worthy Prince Consort of these realms. Let such persons pay scrupulous attention to health . . .' Looking at Prince Edward the Prince of Wales' horoscope, he confirmed his diagnosis: 'The lunation at the end of November 1860 gives warning of some suffering at hand, but let us hope it will not be violent; 1861 is evil for the father of the native (i.e. for Edward's father, Albert)'. This forecast caused a public row when Albert died, struck down by typhoid, on 14 December 1861.

Edward VII, Victoria's successor, was extremely interested in any means by which the future could be forecast, and on a number of occasions consulted the enigmatic occultist, Cheiro. The King was very superstitious, paid great attention to lucky numbers and believed that certain periods were fortunate, others unfortunate. Cheiro specialised in a combination of astrology, palmistry and numerology, and worked out favourable and unfavourable periods by assessing the numerical significance of Edward's birth date and name. On their first meeting he had been called to read the King's hands. Apparently, Edward sat on one side of a curtain, inserting his hands through holes so that his identity would remain unknown, and it was only after Cheiro had duly impressed his audience that the identity of his subject was revealed. According to Cheiro, it was on this occasion that, relying on numerology, he forecast that the Prince would die in his sixty-ninth year, a prediction which the King seemed to take in his stride.

On another occasion Cheiro was summoned to give astrological advice. For two hours the seer calculated simple horoscopes for a series of birth dates supplied by Edward. These included those of the Kaiser and the Czar of Russia, as well as various members of the royal family. Cheiro also explained to Edward the system by which countries are signified by signs of the zodiac, and Edward made notes for use in his future diplomatic negotiations. When Victoria died, Edward asked Cheiro to choose the most auspicious date for his coronation. Cheiro chose 9 August, and Edward's coronation therefore became the first to be fixed by an astrologer since the seventeenth century.

Cheiro achieved a celebrated reputation in top society circles, and advised a number of British politicians as well as royalty in other countries. In his autobiography he relates his encounters with King Léopold II of Belgium, King Umberto I of Italy, Louis Philippe the Orléanist pretender to the French throne and son of Louis Philippe, the last French monarch, the Infanta Eulalie of Spain, aunt of Alfonso XIII, Prince Alexia, cousin of the Serbian King Peter, the Shah of Persia and, in the USA, President Grover Cleveland.

The current Queen, Elizabeth II, is reputedly not keen on astrology, having been persuaded by Michael Ramsey, the former Archbishop of Canterbury, that it is forbidden in the Bible. However, even the Queen uses medical treatments which rely on a simple form of medical astrology. She, like most members of the royal family, is an enthusiastic supporter of the science of homoeopathy. The royal use of homoeopathy was established by Queen Adelaide, the wife of William IV, and has been a major factor in Prince Charles' support of complementary medicine and unorthodox healing methods. One of homoeopathy's central assumptions is that the quality of any disease varies with changes in bodily cycles. These cycles in turn are linked to the time of day, the orientation of the earth to the Sun and the phases of the Moon. Certain remedies are prescribed for conditions which, for example, are exacerbated before dawn or at the full Moon. What is important here though is not necessarily that human health is affected by lunar cycles, but that since the early nineteenth century the royal family has been patronising a system of healing closely related to ancient medical astrology.

Seen in the context of a thousand years of royal history, Prince Charles' esoteric interests and Princess Diana's use of astrology hold few surprises. Charles is perhaps unusual only in that he has looked beyond the fortune-telling and spiritualism which have preoccupied so many members of the royal family, and has developed an interest in their ancient underlying philosophies. We know that he is sympathetic to astrology for, on at least one occasion, it was on his suggestion that Diana went for a consultation with her astrologer, Penny Thornton. However, he is concerned less with the prediction of the future than with the development of self-understanding through those various teachings, which regard humanity's relationship with the cosmos as essential to a balanced lifestyle. With his keen interests in the works of Carl Gustav Jung, he is also aware of the significance of the collective unconscious and the mysteries surrounding the connection between unconscious archetypal forces and the cosmos. He is certainly aware that one of the best ways for understanding the nature of royalty is through its relationship to the heavens.

Planets and Patterns

Our popular images of kings and queens have always been subject to mythological overtones. The illusion that the marriage of Prince Charles and Lady Diana Spencer in 1981 was a fairy-tale wedding was but the latest in a series of fantasies which can be traced back to the twelfth century, when the myth of King Arthur was written. In former times the King was thought to be divine, a special being who formed a bridge between heaven and earth, drawing humanity closer to God. He was even believed capable of effecting miraculous cures for the sick; he was also thought to be represented by the Sun, the most splendid body in the sky. From this flowed a number of important ideas. One was that the King was the most glorious person on earth; he was crowned with gold, the metal sacred to the Sun, and seated on a raised throne, designed to move him closer to heaven. However, it was also thought that, just as the Sun sets at night or grows faint in the winter, so the power of kings waxes and wanes. All kings, it was believed, experienced life-cycles in which their power rose and fell. Frequently a divine sacrifice took place, in which the King was ceremonially replaced and even humiliated. There may also have been traditions in which the King was executed. Many of our monarchical myths are based around such cycles – chiefly, of course, the epic of King Arthur. Like the Sun, Arthur rises, reaches his full power in the glorious midday Sun of Camelot and then sets. The legend concludes with Arthur sailing off to the west, to the setting Sun, from where he will one day return.

Recent experience has shown only too clearly that the monarchy still has the power to inspire awe bordering on religious devotion, yet that we also have a desire to humiliate members of the royal family. It's as if we have some compulsive desire to drag down those whom we have first raised up. Is there a pattern in such events? Is there a cycle in the life of the monarchy? The first kings of the ancient Middle East believed that there was. They believed that because earth and stars were part of a single cosmos they must obey the same laws. As the Sun rose and set every day, the Moon passed through its cycle and the stars moved around the earth, so, they reasoned, governments and peoples had their own life cycles. Modern astrological analysis reveals that the patterns are more complex than was once thought, and that all the planets play their own role.

It is fascinating that many monarchs' horoscopes describe not only their own characters and lives, but also those of their times, and the changes which take place while they occupy the throne. A prime example was Victoria, whose birth, succession and coronation took place under astrological alignments which were successively more and more revolutionary in nature. The planetary patterns found on the day she was crowned were, intriguingly, remarkably similar to those for 27 March 1649, the day on which the monarchy was formally abolished and England set on its brief experiment with republicanism. Yet, in spite of the wave of republicanism which shook the country in the 1870s – and an assassination attempt – Victoria's reign substantially reinforced the monarchy's position. The revolutionary potential of her horoscope was instead felt through the sweeping social, economic and political changes which transformed the British landscape. Reform of the voting system, social reform, the spread of the railways and factories, the advent of electric light, the motor car and moving film, all represented the most radical changes ever experienced in a single reign. Even the status of the monarchy was transformed; when Victoria succeeded to the throne she was thought, as a woman, to be unfit to inherit the crown of Hanover. Yet when she died she was Empress of India and Queen of the largest empire ever seen.

The existence of patterns and cycles is precisely what causes the astrological connections between different monarchs. For example, Edward III's striking soldierly appearance has been compared to that of his great-great-great-uncle Richard Coeur de Lion. Edward was a greater general and a far more responsible monarch than Richard, but mythology is what matters, and Edward was cast in the noble mould established by Richard. Intriguingly, each was crowned during a very similar astrological relationship between the Moon and Uranus, an indication of flair and independence.

The horscopes of the Tudor monarchs also showed close astrological relationships, indicating that time cycles were repeating themselves at their births and succession to the throne. For example, if we check the positions of the three most important positions in any horoscope, the Sun, Moon and Ascendant, a very narrow band between 6° and 8° becomes important. The following pattern emerges:

* Henry VII, succession: Sun at 8° in Virgo.
* Henry VIII, birth: Ascendant in 6° in Virgo.
* Edward VI, birth: Ascendant in 8° in Virgo.
* Mary I, birth: Moon at 7° in Virgo.

The Ascendant, Sun and Moon each have their individual astrological meanings, but they all overlap as the three points which describe the overall character and have the greatest significance in the development of the personality. If we take the passage of the Moon, the rotation of the Earth and the Sun's annual cycle as separate measures of time, each had reached exactly the same point of the zodiac at the moment the Tudor dynasty was founded and at the birth of three of its five monarchs. Only Elizabeth I is excluded from this pattern, but she is connected to the rest of her family by other means. For example, only a few degrees of the zodiac separated her Ascendant from that of her sister Mary.

The history of the Stuart kings also demonstrates some remarkable patterns. Of the fourteen Stuart monarchs who sat on the thrones of England and Scotland, eleven were born with very close alignments between Mars and Pluto, nine of which indicated very difficult consequences. These patterns indicate extraordinary violence, so it is not surprising to find Scotland under Stuart rule in an almost perpetual state of anarchy, while in England it was the Stuart Charles I who provoked the civil war and the country's one experiment with republican government. The two most dangerous Mars–Pluto alignments are the 'square', which places the two planets 90° apart, and the 'opposition', which places them in exactly opposite degrees of the zodiac. Two Stuart monarchs were beheaded, Mary, Queen of Scots and Charles I. By an uncanny coincidence, when Mary was executed Mars and Pluto were 4° away from a square aspect, and when Charles' head was cut off the same two planets were but 4° away from an opposition. The pattern was repeated exactly!

Another striking Pluto pattern concerns this planet's connections to the Sun in the horoscopes for the deaths of English kings. There are variations on this cycle, taking into account horoscopes for succession and coronation as well as birth, but in this century both George V and George VI died while the Sun was in opposition to Pluto.

There are also remarkable planetary connections linking the different members of the Windsor family. For example, if we take the Queen's Midheaven at 25° in Scorpio, we see that it forms extremely powerful links with the following planets:

* Charles' Sun at 22° in Scorpio.
* Peter Phillips' Sun at 23° in Scorpio.
* Andrew's Moon at 25° in Scorpio.
* Henry's Moon at 21° in Taurus.
* Zara Phillips' Sun at 25° in Taurus.
* Philip's Moon at 22° in Leo.
* Anne's Moon at 22° in Leo.
* Eugenie's Moon at 22° in Aquarius.
* Diana's Moon at 25° in Aquarius.

All these planets are linked to the Queen's Midheaven by being either in almost the same degree of the zodiac, or by occupying the opposite degree of the zodiac, or by being 90° away. There are other planetary links which have been unfolding in very strange ways over recent years. It was fascinating, for example, that Charles and Diana's separation was announced on 9 December 1992, just one day before the anniversary of the announcement of Edward VIII's abdication, 10 December 1936. The two royal crises were therefore connected in the zodiac through the Sun's position, in each event at 18° of Sagittarius.

When we compare Charles and Diana's separation to the divorce crisis of 1821, when George IV attempted unsuccessfully to separate from Queen Caroline, the patterns become still more intriguing. One little-known astrological technique requires that we work out the 'midpoint' between two planets. Literally, this is the point on the zodiac exactly halfway between the two planets, and current evidence suggests that it embodies their combined potential. When midpoints from different sets of planets fall on the same degree of the zodiac then we know we have a very strong connection between the two events.

Let's take the two most important events in the marriage crisis of 1821 and compare them to Charles and Diana's birth dates. We arrive at the following pattern:

* 5 July 1820: divorce bill introduced into Parliament. Sun at 14° of Cancer.
* 10 November 1820: divorce bill fails. Sun at 18° of Scorpio.
* Midpoint: 16° of Virgo.
* 1 July 1961: Diana born. Sun at 10° of Cancer.
* 14 November 1948: Charles born. Sun at 10° of Scorpio.
* Midpoint: 16° of Virgo.

In the first instance we take the event, an attempted royal divorce, and in the second the birth dates of the first royal couple since Henry VIII to legally separate, and we find repeating patterns. We can of course go into much greater detail, but these are the first indications that there are patterns unfolding.

Looking at long-term planetary cycles and the British monarchy, there is one cycle in particular which seems to bring crises. In particular, it links three of the greatest royal humiliations. We could say that it's the cycle of sacrifice. This is the cycle of Uranus and Neptune which lasts a total of one hundred and seventy-two years; this is the period which separates 'conjunctions', when they occupy exactly the same degree of the zodiac. Each conjunction lasts for one or two years, with up to five years on either side, during which the planets are moving closer together and then separating. The latest conjunction reached its most exact point from February 1993 to January 1994. The last two conjunctions were in 1821, the year of George IV's marriage crisis, and 1650, the year after Charles I's execution. All three royal disasters are thus connected by a single repeating time cycle.

This was pointed out in 1977 by Roger Elliot in his book *Astrology and the Royal Family*. Writing about 1992, fifteen years before Charles and Diana's separation caused many people to question the monarchy's survival, Elliot wrote that, 'In the Queen's case, she has the three major outerspace planets locked in a firm embrace in her horoscope. Uranus and Neptune form a conjunction with her Ascendant. (They last formed a conjunction over a century ago, in the

1820s. The fact that it is taking place exactly on the Queen's Ascendant cannot be a coincidence.) . . . Something dramatic and perhaps violent will happen to the royal family itself and to the House of Windsor . . . It is perfectly credible that a revolution will sweep through Britain and obliterate the royal family . . . I must warn Her Majesty, just as a final word, that the previous Uranus–Neptune conjunction, before the 1820s one, was back in the seventeenth century. In the middle, actually. Well, to be absolutely honest it was in – er, 1649, the year that Charles I was beheaded'.

The Foundations of the Kingdom

Early Kings and Queens of Britain

The Kingdom of England came into being in a very gradual process, one step at a time, over about five hundred years. There were memories of great leaders from ancient times, such as the Celts Caractacus and Boudicea, who led resistance to the Romans. But until the Romans welded England, Wales and southern Scotland into a single province, there was no tradition of unity. The ancient British leaders relied on celestial divination to help them govern, and the Druids were employed to interpret strange or unusual events seen in the sky. It was the Romans who brought Babylonian astrology to the British Isles, and their leaders always turned to their astrologers in times of uncertainty. Britain began to flex its muscles when a succession of Emperors were proclaimed here. Perhaps the greatest was Constantine, who was proclaimed Emperor at York in 306. From Britain Constantine set out to conquer the rest of the Empire, establishing Christianity as the state religion. Yet he never abandoned his faith in astrology and, before every important state event, the stars were consulted.

The Romans left Britain in 410, leaving the citizens, the 'civitates', to defend themselves against the invaders from the sea, the Angles and Saxons. This was a year of powerful astrological alignments, and two planets in particular were in a very close connection. These were Uranus and Neptune, a combination which can bring wonderful dreams, but often also brings difficulties in dealing with practical affairs. Ever since, when these planets reach critical phases on their one hundred and seventy-two year long cycle, the English monarchy runs into confusion and uncertainty.

Even though England disintegrated into smaller kingdoms after the Romans left, a tradition of unity was maintained, and usually one of the Anglo-Saxon kings was recognised as Bretwalda, or Overlord. One by one, a succession of kingdoms – Sussex, East Anglia, Northumbria and Mercia – held the Bretwaldaship. Eventually, in the early ninth century, Wessex, under King Egbert, achieved a position of dominance in England. After many tribulations, including the Viking invasions which were repelled by Alfred the Great, the kings of Wessex fused the English kingdoms into one and founded the English royal house. Finally, in 973, under another crucial phase in the Uranus–Neptune cycle, Edgar, the King of Wessex, was crowned King of a united England.

The study of astrology went into decline when the Romans left, as did most of the other literary arts. It was important to follow the cycles of the New and Full Moons, and some astrological omens, like comets, were noted by scribes such as the Venerable Bede, who wrote one of the first histories of Britain. Yet Roman astrology, which had used all the planets, was forgotten, and kings no longer had their horoscopes cast.

The long centuries between the Romans and the Normans therefore leave us with few astrological clues. We know the names of some of the greatest kings – the British Arthur, the Saxon Alfred and the Danish Canute – but in most cases we have no idea of their year of birth, let alone the date. Without this information it is impossible to cast their horoscopes. However, we do know that the kings retained a high regard for the movements of the heavens and the significance they held for affairs of state.

The most famous celestial omen of Anglo-Saxon England appeared in the night sky early in 1066. At the time it was known as a 'long-haired star', although we now know that this mysterious creature was Halley's comet. The comet was regarded as a portent of great change, and from the chronicles of the Venerable Bede it was known that it might indicate war and invasion. Harold, the Saxon King, saw the comet at Easter 1066, and we can only guess at what thoughts must have run through his mind. He knew that his throne was claimed by the King of Norway and the Duke of Normandy, and that his position was dire. A lesser man might have decided that fate was stacked against him, but Harold resolved to fight. He defeated the Norwegians but, his strength sapped, the Normans eventually proved too much for him. He met William of Normandy at Hastings in October 1066, was defeated and killed. Had the Venerable Bede been writing his chronicle at the time, he would have nodded sagely and pondered on the comet's role as a message from God that it was time for English destiny to take a new course.

The
Houses
of
Normandy
and
Plantagenet

HOUSES OF NORMANDY
AND PLANTAGENET

William I   Henry II

William II

Henry I   Richard I

Stephen

John

Henry III

Edward I

Edward II

Edward III

Richard II

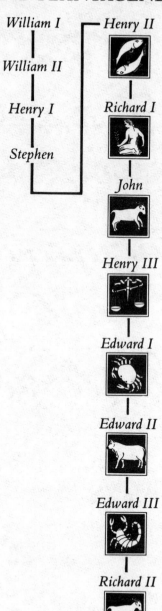

From the Normans to the Tudors

The Houses of Normandy and Plantagenet

WILLIAM I, THE CONQUEROR
1066–1087

Born at Falaise in Normandy in 1027. Succeeded as Duke of Normandy in 1035 at the age of eight, and crowned King of England on Christmas Day 1066, with the Sun in Capricorn and the Moon in Pisces. Died at Rouen on 6 September 1087 and buried at St Stephen's, Caen, Normandy.

William the Conqueror was the last overseas invader to rule in England, and any ancient astrologer would have associated him closely with Mars, which was believed to be the planet of war. Unfortunately we don't know what time William was born, so it is impossible to calculate his horoscope. We don't even know his date of birth, for in the eleventh century there were no clocks and such information was only recorded if there happened to be a particularly conscientious chronicler at hand.

Lacking a horoscope for his birth, it would have been the custom of the time for astrologers to cast horoscopes for important events in William's life. These would have included his victory at Hastings, after which his power in England was irresistible, and his coronation. The Battle of Hastings concluded at dusk when King Harold died, hit in the eye by the famous arrow. The Moon, appropriately, was in the royal sign of Leo and the Sun was very close to Venus which, according to the ancient astrologers, indicated victory in war.

At noon on the day of William's coronation, the Sun was in the conservative sign of Capricorn and assertive, energetic Aries was rising. Later astrologers found this most intriguing for, almost a thousand years earlier, the Greek astrologer Claudius Ptolemy had claimed that England was ruled by Aries. In the following centuries the astrologers who advised the English kings and queens made much of this, and if a planet was found in Aries, 'England's rising sign', they paid extra attention to it.

It is the modern custom to look back to 1066 as the foundation of modern English history; the previous Saxon kings belong to a period which seems much more remote. It is for this reason that modern astrologers use the horoscope for William's coronation as a horoscope for the entire country. Indeed, the Sun in conservative Capricorn on the day of the coronation seems a remarkably appropriate symbol for the famous English reserve and well-known stiff upper lip.

WILLIAM II
1087–1100

Known as William Rufus on account of his red hair. Born in 1056. Succeeded as King of England on 6 September 1087, with the Sun in Virgo and the Moon in Sagittarius. Crowned on 26 September, with the Sun in Libra and the Moon in Virgo. Never married. Died in mysterious circumstances on 2 August 1100 and buried in Winchester Cathedral.

William II was ten years old when his father rose from being mere Duke of Normandy to King of England. For astrologers it is frustrating not to know his exact date of birth, but we do know that he was born while Saturn and Jupiter were facing each other from opposite degrees of the zodiac, indicating someone who has problems exercising authority – not a good start for a future king!

It was never intended that William should succeed the Conqueror, and he was thrust into the succession when his elder brother Richard was killed by a stag while hunting in the New Forest. His eldest brother, Robert, inherited the Duchy of Normandy, leaving William to reign uneasily in England. William succeeded to the throne with the Sun in Virgo and was crowned with the Moon in the same sign, so it is not surprising to find him following the good housekeeping qualities typical of this sign. For example, when posts in the church fell vacant, William was in the habit of leaving them unoccupied and taking the revenue for the government. He even failed to fill the see of Canterbury until a bout of illness made him concerned that God was punishing him. Such behaviour was savagely denounced by the monks who saw their coffers emptying, and their bitterness is largely responsible for William's evil reputation. However, such practices were excellent government – and classically Virgoan.

A brave and capable warrior, he fought successfully in France, received homage from Malcolm III of Scotland, and built a chain of forts along the Welsh marches, securing the new Norman kingdom's western border. To any medieval astrologer such prowess was the preserve of Mars, the ancient planet of war, and this planet was indeed powerfully placed at both the King's coronation and succession. However, on 2 August 1100 Mars took on a very dangerous aspect to the Sun, one which indicated a serious risk of accident. This was the day which William chose to go hunting in the New Forest and on which he died, pierced through the breast by an arrow apparently fired by one of his companions, Walter Tyrell. Whether William's death was murder or accident, we will probably never know. However, the theory that he was ritually sacrificed finds strong support in the strange repetition of astrological patterns on the day he was killed.

HENRY I
1100–1135

Known as Beauclerk because he was the first king since Alfred the Great who could read fluently. Born in 1068. Succeeded as King on 2 August 1100 and crowned on 6 August, with the Sun and Moon in Leo. Died at Lyons-la-Forêt on 1 December 1135 and buried in Reading Abbey.

Henry I was William the Conqueror's fourth son, born two years after the Battle of Hastings. Like the rest of the Norman kings, his birth date was never recorded, and all we know is that he was born some time in 1068. However, in that time the three crucial outer planets (Uranus, Neptune and Pluto) had moved only a short distance. If the horoscope for William's conquest of England is a horoscope for the entire English nation, it is therefore fitting that Henry, whose horoscope was very similar, is remembered as a great king. He was indeed the monarch who placed William's achievements on a permanent and solid footing. Although as ruthless as his father and brother, he has come down to us as a wise statesman and a noble warrior. He also linked the Norman dynasty to both the Saxon and Scottish kings by marrying Matilda, daughter of Malcolm III of Scotland, great granddaughter of the Saxon King Edmund Ironside and a descendant of Alfred the Great. This was a deliberate act, designed to unite the blood royal of the Saxon kings with the new dynasty.

On the day after Henry's coronation there was a New Moon in Leo, the royal sign, the significance of which would have been plain to his rivals. It may also have something to do with his second nickname, 'The Lion of Justice', the lion being the animal connected to Leo. Certainly, his love of pleasure was Leonine. He had many mistresses, of whom the most notable was Nesta, daughter of Rhys ap Twdr (Tudor), the Prince of South Wales, and he acknowledged twenty illegitimate children – and that may only represent a small selection! Also prominent in his coronation horoscope were the planets Mercury and Venus in practical Virgo, a strong indication of careful government. However, Mars was in a dangerous alignment with the Sun, indicating the threat of violence. This pattern was to be tragically expressed in 1120 when William, his only legitimate son and heir to the throne, drowned in the White Ship. The same alignment was also connected to Uranus, a planet now associated strongly with unusual characters and revolutionary ideas. This indicates that Henry's success was partially based on his willingness to take risks.

Henry's radical tendencies came to the fore when his plans for the succession were upset. After his son's death he resolved to make a woman sit on the throne in England for the first time since Boudicea reigned as Queen of the Iceni, one thousand years earlier. He decided that when he died he should be succeeded by his daughter Matilda, and he forced all his barons, led by his nephew Stephen, to swear to support her succession. However, as soon as Henry died, Stephen broke his word and proclaimed himself King. Another four hundred years were to pass before the English people were prepared to submit to another woman on the throne, Mary I.

STEPHEN
1135–1154

Born at Blois in 1097, succeeded as King of England on 1 December 1135 and crowned on 25 December, with the Sun in Capricorn and the Moon in Leo. Died on 25 October 1154 and buried at Faversham Abbey.

King Stephen was the son of Adela, William the Conqueror's third daughter. We don't know when he was born, beyond the fact that it was some time in the year 1097, but we do know that Pluto, planet of the underworld, had reached a powerful aspect to the degree of the zodiac occupied by the Sun at William the Conqueror's coronation. This is a complicated way of saying that he was likely to damage William's royal legacy, and this is precisely what he did.

Stephen had been his uncle Henry I's favourite, yet he came to the throne through his betrayal of Matilda, the rightful heir. That treachery was to haunt him, for it plunged England into a civil war in which he was pitted against Matilda and her son, the future Henry II. Eventually, in 1141, Stephen was humiliated and captured by Matilda, who briefly ruled as Queen in her own right, although she was never crowned.

Turning to Stephen's coronation horoscope, we see that the Sun was in Capricorn – which would have been considered good for business – and the Moon was in Leo, considered fitting for such a royal event. However, no astrologer would have selected such a date, for the Moon was very badly aligned with two other planets, Venus and Mars, indicating a reign in which rational conduct was likely to be in short supply. Like William the Conqueror, Stephen tried to sanctify his rule by arranging his coronation for Christmas Day, but unlike his three Norman predecessors he found it difficult to control the barons. He was more interested in endowing churches than punishing his rivals, and the result was a damaging power vacuum.

No astrologer of the time could have known it, but Stephen was crowned under a conjunction of two planets, Uranus and Neptune, which have an uncanny habit of meeting in the sky whenever the English royal house is plunged into chaos. First, there was his capture and imprisonment by Matilda. Then, from 1147 onwards, he was forced to face continued invasions from France, led by the young Henry. Stephen is also the first king who, we believe, faced opponents using astrology; for the great scholar Adelard of Bath seems to have advised Henry, alerting him to the best moments to attack the English King.

Eventually, in 1153, Stephen's son and heir Eustace died, and the bishops persuaded the King to recognise Henry as his rightful successor. Stephen agreed and for the last year of his reign peace was restored. It was, however, too late for his reign to be considered anything other than a blot on the memory of the English royal house. It was said of him that he reigned, but never truly ruled.

HENRY II
1154–1189

Born at Le Mans on 25 March 1133, with the Sun in Pisces and the Moon in Aquarius. Succeeded on 25 October 1154 and crowned on 19 December, with the Sun in Capricorn and the Moon in Gemini. Died at Chinon on 6 July 1189.

Henry was the first of the long line of Plantagenet kings, although he and his descendants knew themselves as Angevins, after Anjou – his father Geoffrey was Count of Anjou. The name Plantagenet was derived later from the family's emblem, a sprig of broom or *planta genista*. There is some dispute over the date of Henry's birth. Some books claim he was born on 5 March; however, contemporary records point to 25 March, and the horoscope for this date is certainly very fitting. Henry was a tough king and a great soldier, and every medieval astrologer recognised this in his Sun in fiery Aries and Moon in uncompromising Scorpio. Both these signs of the zodiac were said to be ruled by Mars, and Henry was therefore given a double dose of military might.

Henry was also known as a man of passion, and any modern astrologer would recognise his powerful nature in the very strong Taurean influences in his horoscope. The close alignment of Mars and Pluto in this sign reveals a character which is liable to explode without warning. This is precisely what Henry did when his own friend

Thomas Becket the Archbishop of Canterbury defied him. The remorse Henry felt after he had encouraged Becket's murder was also typical of this same alignment.

At Henry's coronation the Sun was in the businesslike sign of Capricorn and the Moon was in the intellectual sign of Gemini. Sure enough, the King was known as an able administrator and a man of letters. However, the Moon was close to Pluto, confirming the uncompromising, intense and confrontational features in his birth horoscope. We therefore remember Henry primarily as the emperor who united most of the British Isles and France under his personal rule. Henry was also the first English king we know to have consulted astrologers, chiefly in his long war with King Stephen.

RICHARD I, COEUR DE LION
1189–1199

Born at Oxford on 8 September 1157, with the Sun in Virgo and the Moon in Libra. Succeeded to the throne of England on 6 July 1189 and crowned at Westminster on 3 September 1189, with the Sun in Virgo and the Moon in Gemini. Died at Châlus in Limousin on 6 April 1199.

Richard Coeur de Lion – 'the Lion Heart' – is one of the best-known of English kings and the very image of medieval chivalry. His prowess as a soldier was responsible for his nickname, and we would expect to find Leo occupying a powerful position at his birth. It's possible he had this sign rising. Unfortunately, we just don't know; his time of birth went unrecorded.

We do know that the horoscopes for both Richard's birth and coronation, dominated by the Sun in Virgo, are those befitting a competent administrator rather than a military adventurer. Richard's careful Virgoan and diplomatic Libran qualities are well-attested in the many examples of his shrewdness and spontaneous generosity, and in war he was a great tactician. However, at his coronation Jupiter was in a position indicating recklessness and irresponsibility. This became the strongest feature of his life and, as soon as he was crowned, he effectively abandoned the government, leaving Hubert Walter, the Archbishop of Canterbury, to implement the Virgoan aspects of his master's character. Fortunately, Walter was an extremely capable administrator, and he oversaw a move towards the involvement of the middle-classes in local government which still finds its consequences in, for example, the system by which amateur justice is dispensed by local magistrates.

A fascinating tale is told of a visit Richard paid to the great mystic and prophet Joachim of Fiore. Fiore was in the very south of Italy, a convenient journey from Richard's winter headquarters in Sicily. Joachim had acquired great fame as a result of his prophecy that the world was about to come to an end, and that all current states and governments were to be replaced by the kingdom of God. He believed that there were three great ages in history. The first, that of the Old Testament, was compared to the light of the stars; the second, which began with the New Testament, embodied the light of the Moon; the last age, which was due to begin in 1260, represented the light of the Sun, and was to see the final triumph of good over evil. This prophecy, it is thought, encouraged Richard to believe that his campaign to reconquer the Holy Land would be successful.

Modern historians have revised Richard's reputation, and he is now seen as incompetent and irresponsible, even one of the worst kings England has ever had. Most of his ten-year reign was spent fighting in the Holy Land or France, and the ransom which was raised to free him from captivity in Germany drove the country to the edge of bankruptcy. This becomes clear when we look at what the ancient astrologers said of the position of Jupiter at Richard's coronation: 'He will lose his paternal inheritance and be persecuted by crowds of strong and evil enemies'! Eventually Richard's reck-lessness resulted in his death in battle in France. Yet even on his death-bed he retained his Jupiterian generosity and, according to one story, when he was hit by the bolt which killed him, he congratu-lated the archer on his accuracy.

JOHN
1199–1216

Known as 'Lackland'. Born on 24 December 1167 in Oxford, with the sun in Capricorn and the Moon in Taurus. Succeeded to the throne of England on 7 April 1199 and crowned on 27 May

1199, with the Sun and the Moon in Gemini. Died on 18 October 1216 and buried at Worcester Cathedral.

John, Richard I's younger brother, was Henry II's eighth child. His birth was therefore a relatively unimportant event and the chroniclers of the time paid little attention to it. However, his birthday, Christmas Eve 1167, was noted for some splendid celestial patterns. At Mont St Michel, the monk Robert of Torigni observed 'two fiery stars in the west, one big and the other small, almost conjoined'. We know now that Robert had sighted a conjunction of Venus and Jupiter in Aquarius. To any medieval astrologer this was an indication of great good fortune, but the planets were overshadowed by an evil aspect from Mars. This revealed that the King would squander his fortune and arouse opposition by complacency and carelessness. This is exactly what happened when, in 1215, under similar astrological patterns, John lost control, the barons revolted and forced him to sign Magna Carta.

John did what he could to ensure the blessing of heaven on his reign. The day he picked for his coronation was both Ascension Day and a New Moon, and by his choice he would therefore have pleased both devout Christians and the followers of surviving pagan traditions. Modern historians recognise John as an exceptional administrator who ruled the country in a very businesslike manner, replenishing the royal coffers after the disaster of Richard I's ransom.

He was born with the Sun in Capricorn and the Moon in Taurus, one of the most practical combinations possible, and was crowned with both the Sun and the Moon in Gemini, indicating a reign marked by careful analysis and attention to detail. Although he had conspired against his elder brother (it was commonplace for Norman princes to plot against each other), Richard acknowledged John's good qualities and, before he died, recognised him as his heir.

Although John was a competent king, his performance was erratic, perhaps because he was crowned under a New Moon in changeable Gemini. Abroad, he lost most of the English lands in France, and at home was eventually out-manoeuvred by the barons, although not until after some very smart (and typically Geminian) moves of his own. However, when he died in 1216, he was humiliated and powerless.

HENRY III
1216–1272

Born at Winchester on 1 October 1207, with the Sun in Libra. Succeeded to the throne of England on 19 October 1216 and crowned at Gloucester on 28 October 1216 and at Westminster on 17 May 1220. Died on 16 November 1272 and buried at Westminster Abbey.

Henry III was born with the Sun in Libra and the Moon passing into Aquarius, and he seems to have expressed the weaker side of these two intellectual signs; he had many good ideas but was unable either to assess the practical consequences or even put them into effect. He was born without a single planet in the three practical 'earth' signs (Taurus, Virgo and Capricorn), which further undermined his ability to deal with matters of state. However, he appears to have had a more pleasant personality than many of his contemporaries, no doubt a manifestation of the well-recognised Libran desire for peace and harmony. Like many Librans, he loved beauty and was a patron of the arts; he gave us Westminster Abbey, largely in the form we know it today.

Henry is not one of the most well-known of English kings and never acquired the mythical characteristics attached to his father, John, and his uncle Richard. Yet his reign saw some of the most important developments to take place in English government, chiefly the foundation of the House of Commons.

Henry succeeded to the throne under an exact conjunction of Mars and Saturn. This is an alignment connected with practical difficulties, and, indeed, Henry was unable to cope with the realities of power. One old Roman astrological text which was available in England at the time said of these two planets that they 'produce a balanced character and soften fierce aggression with milder traits'. This is why Henry was defeated, like his father, abroad by the French and at home by the barons. When he died, old, humiliated and drifting into senility, the same alignment had recurred. To medieval astrologers this would have been the celestial pattern which first brought him to power and then laid him low.

He succeeded to the throne in 1216 at the age of nine, but it was not until 1227, when he was twenty years old, that his personal rule began. Interestingly, he was crowned twice, once in Gloucester two weeks after his succession and then at greater leisure in Westminster Abbey, four years later. Suspicion of astrological involvement in the two coronations is offered by the fact that each took place the day before a Full Moon. When we find patterns such as this it often indicates the unseen hand of a secret astrologer. However, we have no direct evidence of astrological manipulation, so it may merely reflect some superstition on the part of Henry's advisers.

EDWARD I
1272–1307

Known as 'Longshanks' on account of his outstanding height. Born at Westminster Palace on the night of 17–18 June 1239, with the Sun in Cancer and the Moon in Capricorn. Succeeded to the throne of England on 16 November 1272 and crowned at Westminster on 19 August 1274, with the Sun in Virgo and Moon in Pisces. Died at Burgh by Sands near Carlisle on 6 July 1307 and buried at Westminster Abbey.

Edward I was born with the Sun in emotional Cancer and the Moon in practical Capricorn. Being born with the Sun and Moon in exactly opposite signs of the zodiac can produce sharp internal contradictions, and no doubt Edward often felt pulled in two directions. There must have been times when he was not sure whether to react as a Cancer, in line with his feelings, or as a Capricorn, in view of what was best for business. Yet Cancer and Capricorn can also be a very powerful combination, and Edward was to bring these differing forces together. When, at the birth of his son and heir Edward, he presented the infant to the defeated Welsh princes, proclaiming him the first Prince of Wales, he combined the proud emotions of a father with the business of running the country in a manner which has rarely been bettered. As a Cancerian he produced one of the largest families of any English monarch, and in all he had twenty children.

Edward was not the first King of England to bear that name, for he had been preceded by three Saxons: Edward the Elder, Edward the

Martyr and Edward the Confessor. In fact, Edward was named after this last king, who had been one of his father's idols. Henry hoped that his son would inherit the Confessor's piety.

He was born under one powerful Full Moon and crowned under another, which would have been an indication to any thirteenth-century baron that here was a force to be reckoned with. When his father died, he was on crusade in the Holy Land, and it took him two years to return to England for his own coronation. On the evening of the day on which he processed to Westminster Abbey to take his solemn oaths, the Full Moon would have risen in Pisces at dusk, providing a fitting backdrop to the night's festivities. Edward was crowned with the Sun in practical Virgo but the Moon in visionary Pisces, and it is probably this last which gave him a sense of what was right, not just for the crown, but for the whole country; his summons to the representatives of England to appear at parliament was accompanied by the famous clarion call of democracy, 'Let that which toucheth all be approved by all'. His main task was to drag England kicking and screaming into the thirteenth century! This he accomplished through his powerful alignment of Mars, planet of war, with Jupiter, planet of growth and expansion; he secured English control of the remaining French lands, completing the conquest of Wales by 1282–3 and invading Scotland, of which he became King in 1296.

Edward succeeded to the throne under an alignment between Mars and Saturn, which in medieval astrology indicates that great effort will achieve great results, but is unlikely to find ultimate success. However he was born under a Saturn–Uranus–Pluto alignment which has been found to be utterly ruthless, and indicates that whatever Edward did, he always made the maximum effort. He therefore never managed to assert his undisputed control over Scotland, although the magnificence of his failure is reflected in one of his nicknames: the 'Hammer of the Scots'. It was while on campaign near Carlisle, on 6 July 1307, that Edward died, in the thirty-fifth year of his reign. Uranus and Neptune had returned to the same difficult alignment they held at Stephen's coronation, and it was time for the monarchy to go into another decline.

EDWARD II
1307–1327

Born at Caernarvon on 25 April 1284, with the Sun in Taurus and Moon in Leo. Succeeded to the throne of England on 7 July 1307 and crowned at Westminster on 23 February 1308, with the Sun in Pisces and the Moon in Pisces. Abdicated on 20 January 1327, murdered on 22 September 1327 and buried in Gloucester Cathedral.

Edward II is the first king for whom we have a surviving horoscope. According to his astrologer, whose identity is unknown, he was born at 8.28 a.m., giving him an Ascendant in the sensitive sign of Cancer. His Sun was in the practical sign of Taurus, and his Moon in the courageous sign of Leo; the combination of these two signs confers a character which is extremely obstinate and inordinately fond of pleasure. This simple description sums up both Edward's character and the reasons for his alienation of the nobles and people of England. However, no astrologer at the time could have been aware of the fateful conjunction of Uranus and Neptune which took place when he succeeded to the throne. It is this pattern which had last occurred during the civil war under Stephen, and has a reputation for weakening the monarchy. Edward's coronation took place on the day after a New Moon in Pisces, a highly imaginative sign. It is this which, more than anything, indicates a king who was driven by his fantasies rather than a sense of the best way to survive and administer his country. It seems that England was incapable of producing two competent kings in succession and, after the great Edward I, Edward II, his father's fourteenth child, was weak, vacillating and incompetent. He had no interest in government, and the rebellion which eventually overthrew him was brought about by a complete failure to learn from his own mistakes. All this smacks of a king following the negative aspects of a Piscean New Moon.

Edward's poor military leadership and favouritism consistently alienated the barons, and eventually his wife Isabella led a rebellion with the aim of replacing the King with his son, also called Edward. The King was captured and taken to Kenilworth, where he was forced to abdicate. From there he was taken to Berkeley Castle near Bristol, and on 22 September 1327 he was brutally murdered.

Edward had been born under a particularly dangerous alignment between the Sun and Mars, and to an astrologer of the time this would have indicated a serious danger of injury. It so happened that the same alignment was repeated within days of his abdication and, in a slightly different form, on the day of his murder. It was almost as if Edward had wilfully exacerbated all that was most difficult in his birth horoscope, and that the heavens had passed judgment on him accordingly.

EDWARD III
1327–1377

Born at Windsor on 13 November 1312, with the Sun in Scorpio and the Moon in Taurus. Succeeded to the throne of England on 20 January 1327 and crowned on 1 February 1328 at Westminster, with the Sun in Aquarius and the Moon in Libra. Died at Sheen on 21 June 1377 and buried at Westminster Abbey.

According to a horoscope which survives from the fifteenth century, Edward III was born at forty-three minutes and twenty-three seconds past five in the morning, although such a precise time is an indication that the astrologer had refined the reported time of birth using various mathematical techniques. It was believed that by fine-tuning the horoscope in this way, the royal forecasts would be more accurate. Edward's was possibly also the first royal horoscope to be widely circulated, and was reportedly set in glass in a window in the Royal Closet at St George's Chapel, Windsor. Another version of his horoscope, set for the slightly earlier time of 5.39 a.m., is known to us in a copy made by Elias Ashmole, Charles II's astrologer.

Edward was born at a Full Moon with the Sun in Scorpio, indicating an intense, determined and secretive character, and the Moon in Taurus, adding a practical streak. In its own way this combination is as obstinate as that of his father, but Edward III was by temperament more suited to the art of government. A third version of his horoscope was deliberately miscalculated to place the Moon in Aries, perhaps because the astrologer wanted to show that this fiery sign had made the King a great warrior. Warlike qualities were added by the presence of the Ascendant, the Sun and Venus in Scorpio, the sign of Mars. In addition, Mars itself was in Scorpio, adding further to his military prowess.

Three hundred years later, the astrologer William Lilly, who advised both Charles I and Oliver Cromwell, wrote that Edward's horoscope 'giues a strong able body, capable of labour, or hardship in any employment providence shall cast vppon . . . very valiant . . . violent, impetuous, furious subject vnto choller and passion . . . generous and princely spirits, high thoughts, majesticall, ayming at high matters, yet ever with a kind of nobleness and generous resolution, scorning baseness or treacherous actions'. This is a reasonable estimate of Edward's horoscope, for we must remember that he became King through violence, when his father was deposed and murdered. Eventually he avenged his father, and in 1330 he imprisoned his mother and hanged her lover, Mortimer, at Tyburn. In France he proclaimed himself King, began the Hundred Years War and triumphed at Sluys, Crécy and Poitiers.

The planet Mars, which governed Edward's warlike disposition, has a reputation for burning itself out, and the last part of Edward's reign lacked the glories which characterised his early years. Abroad, the French counterattacked and recaptured all his territorial gains; at home social tension increased, religious discontent grew and the barons, sensing that the government was drifting, grew restless. The King had succeeded to the throne at a revolutionary moment, the deposition and execution of his father, Edward II. The heavens reflected this disorder in the horoscope for his succession and, although he ruled wisely, the threat of disruption remained throughout his life. Eventually, towards the end of his reign, the planet Pluto moved over this alignment. In ancient mythology Pluto was the god of the underworld, and psychologically it often induces a desire to withdraw into privacy and seclusion, away from the pressures of the world. And so it was with Edward.

In 1369 the Queen, Philippa of Hainault, died, having given Edward thirteen children. The King retreated to Windsor with his mistress Alice Perrers (by whom he had three children), while matters in the country went from bad to worse. Eventually, in 1376, the heir to the throne, Edward the Black Prince, died and the old King lost the will to live. He died on 21 June 1377, having reigned for fifty years.

RICHARD II
1377–1399

Born at Bordeaux on 6 January 1367, with the Sun in Capricorn and the Moon in Pisces. Succeeded as King of England, Wales and Ireland on 21 June 1377, and crowned at Westminster on 15 July 1377. Abdicated and deposed on 29 September 1399 and died in 1400, probably murdered, on 14 February. Buried first at Langley, then at Westminster Abbey.

Richard II was the grandson of Edward III and the only surviving son of Edward, the Black Prince. He was born in Bordeaux while his father was governing the Duchy of Aquitaine and, unusually, his birth was recorded accurately by the chronicler Froissart, who was present at many of the major events of the time. Much later, Froissart recalled the scene: 'I remember I was in Bordeaux, sitting at table, when King Richard was born. He came into the world on a Wednesday, on the stroke of ten. At that hour Sir Richard de Pontchardon, who was Marshal of Aquitaine at the time, entered and said to me: "Froissart, write down and place on record that her Highness the Princess has been delivered of a fine boy, who has come into the world on Twelfth Day. The child comes of royal stock and by right he will yet be a king." '

De Pontchardon clearly believed that to be born twelve days after Christmas was highly auspicious. To people of the time it was significant that Christ had twelve disciples, the Hebrews had twelve tribes and that there were twelve months of the year and signs of the zodiac. To be born on the Twelfth Day therefore implied completion and perfection. The young prince was also born with the Sun in Capricorn, and the Moon and Ascendant in Pisces, indicating a relatively kindly disposition and an attraction for beauty and the arts rather than affairs of state. His astrologers, though, would have been unaware that Uranus and Neptune, the two planets which repeatedly undermine the British monarchy, had reached another important phase in their cycle. The long-term prognostication was therefore very poor.

The horoscope for his coronation was cast for 8.18 a.m. on 15 July, although this time may be derived not so much from actual events as from what the astrologer believed should have happened. We know that astrologers were active in political intrigue, and it may have been that the astrologer who picked this moment was trying to portray Richard's reign in a particular light, encouraging his enemies in their opposition. Certainly, the horoscope for this moment is an intriguing one. Venus was rising in Virgo, indicating a reasonably businesslike and amiable reign. However, to a medieval astrologer, Mercury, the 'chart ruler', was 'combust', and this indicated very poor judgement on Richard's part. And so it proved when in 1399 Henry, Duke of Lancaster exploited the King's many mistakes, rebelled and forced Richard to abdicate.

If Richard's enemies were using his horoscope to pick the best moments to pursue their conspiracy against him, it is interesting that Mars and Saturn, which together indicate military might, were in a very tense aspect to the coronation chart when they imprisoned Richard in the Tower and forced him from the throne, ending the unbroken rule of Plantagenet kings from Henry II. Intriguingly, when Richard was forced to abdicate in September 1399, his horoscope indicated to every astrologer of the time that his enemies would be at their most powerful. There is therefore excellent circumstantial evidence that the plotters were relying heavily on astrological advice.

The House of Lancaster

HOUSE OF LANCASTER

Henry IV

Henry V

Henry VI

The House of Lancaster

HENRY IV
1399–1413

Born at Bolingbroke, Lincolnshire, on 3 April 1367, with the Sun in Aries. Succeeded as King of England and Lord of Ireland on 30 September 1399 and crowned at Westminster Abbey on 13 October 1399, with the Sun in Libra and Moon in Aries. Died on 20 March 1413 and buried at Canterbury.

Henry IV, Duke of Lancaster, Edward III's grandson and Richard II's cousin, was a Plantagenet, but his rebellion against Richard represented a break in historical continuity and he is usually seen as the first of the three kings of the House of Lancaster. He was born with the Sun in Aries, one of the most powerful signs, and was not one to see what he considered his birthright snatched away. So when it looked as if Richard might produce an heir, depriving him of the succession, he led the barons in revolt and on 30 September he had himself proclaimed King. This was the opening shot in the Wars of the Roses.

At Henry's birth the Moon was in Gemini, and he was to display all the best Geminian traits, being able to analyse events shrewdly and outmanoeuvre his rivals before they even realised what was happening. However, he overthrew Richard under a violent conjunction of Mars and Saturn, and he himself was never free from the threat of rebellion. He arranged his coronation for 13 October, St Edward's Day, in an attempt to invoke King Edward the Confessor's blessing and manipulate popular superstition. Yet the Mars–Saturn conjunction was still in force and, if anything, had become stronger. He was preoccupied with continuous rebellion for the first six years of his reign, and at the end he had lapsed into ill health. When he became King, Henry was deeply affected by a powerful conjunction of

Uranus and Pluto. Both planets are known to unleash powerful unconscious forces, provoke confrontation and often also drive people into seclusion. Eventually the planets had their way and, like Edward III, he withdrew from affairs of state, leaving the running of the country to his son, Henry, who succeeded him in 1413.

HENRY V
1413–1422

Born at Monmouth on 16 September 1387, with the Sun in Libra and the Moon in Cancer. Succeeded as King of England and Lord of Ireland on 20 March 1413 and crowned on 9 April 1413, with the Sun in Aries and Moon in Leo. Died at Vincennes on 31 August 1422 and buried at Westminster.

Confusion surrounds Henry V's birth. He was the second English king (after Edward II) to be born in Wales, but for some reason the date was not accurately recorded. Perhaps this was because, although of noble birth, he was Richard II's cousin once removed, and so not in the first rank of royalty. Some books claim he was born on 9 August, and due to muddles in the medieval calendar there is even dispute as to the year. Our only surviving horoscope for Henry states clearly that he was born at 11.22 a.m. on 16 September 1387. This information is probably reliable, for it may have come from astrologers close to the reigning King, who himself seems to have been keenly interested in astrology.

Henry was born with the Sun in Libra (excellent for diplomacy), the Moon in Cancer (enabling him to sense the concerns of his followers) and an Ascendant in Scorpio (which gave him a deep sense of purpose). The astrologers of the time were impressed by Scorpio because its ruling planet was Mars, the planet of war. Therefore, they reasoned, Henry was destined to be a great soldier – and when he vanquished the French at Agincourt, he proved them right.

One astrologer of the time, Tito Livio, wrote that until the death of his father, Henry 'exercised equally the feats of Venus and Mars', but changed radically on his succession. Venus was the ruler of love and beauty, and the implication was that, on becoming King, Henry renounced a life of pleasure and was overwhelmed by the cares of government and the demands of war. Henry's coronation took place with the Sun conjunct Mars in Aries, a further indication that he was to be successful in war, while the Moon in Leo added exactly the right touch of regal majesty.

In 1420 Henry finally married, for dynastic reasons, Catherine de Valois, daughter of Charles VI of France, and was recognised as heir to the French throne. As part of the preliminaries to the marriage, Richard Courtenay, Bishop of Norwich and Chancellor of Oxford University, had consulted the astrologer Jean Fusoris. Fusoris had concluded that although the marriage would not be celebrated that year (1415), it would take place eventually. His cautious optimism encouraged Courtenay to continue pressing for a successful outcome to the marriage negotiations between Henry and the French king over the following five years. Courtenay and Henry may also have consulted other astrologers over the marriage question, such as Edmund Lacy, the Dean of the King's Chapel and future Bishop of Hereford.

In due course, the dynastic union took place and the thrones of England and France were set for a peaceful union which would probably have changed the course of history. However, Henry died in 1422, two months before the French king Charles, and never lived to inherit the French throne. That honour was to be left to his son, Henry VI.

HENRY VI
1422–1461, 1470–1471

Born at Windsor on 6 December 1421, with the Sun in Sagittarius and Moon in Taurus. Succeeded as King of England and Lord of Ireland on 31 August 1422 and as King of France in October 1422. Crowned on 6 November 1429, with the Sun in Scorpio and the Moon in Pisces. Murdered in the Tower of London on 21 May 1471 and buried first at Chertsey, then at Windsor.

Henry VI was an enthusiastic supporter of the use of astrology by kings. He believed devoutly that, unless the monarch understood changes in the cosmos he had little chance of understanding developments in his realm. This is perhaps why we have six different horoscopes for the King, and we can imagine his astrologers fine-tuning their calculations in order to perfect their forecasts. Two horoscopes are set for between 3.18 a.m. and 4.24 a.m., giving Henry an Ascendant in Gemini. Another, set for 1.31 a.m. with an Ascendant in Taurus, may have been calculated under Charles I by a royalist astrologer out to prove that the saintly King Charles was Henry's spiritual descendant. At least one surviving horoscope was cast by the astrologer Thomas Southwell, not for the King but for Eleanor Cobham, Duchess of Gloucester. Apparently, this version was for use by Henry's enemies, who hoped to use it to pick the best times to attack him.

Henry was born with the Sun in philosophical Sagittarius. Those born under this sign are often unhappy with fixed responsibilities, not an ideal attitude for the heir to the throne. Sagittarians often prefer the realms of imagination to worldly action, and Henry's love of religion provided a substitute for the exercise of power. His intellectual Geminian Ascendant added to his bookish interests and only his Taurean Moon provided him with staying power and a belief that, having been born to reign, he had to stick with the job.

He was crowned with the Sun in Scorpio, and it is his coronation horoscope which reveals the most intense pressures. The Sun in Scorpio and the Moon in Pisces, two emotional signs, reinforced his irrational attitude to government, and a close conjunction between Mars and Saturn brought military threat. Eventually Pluto, planet of the under-world, joined the fray and Henry was overthrown. In 1461 Edward, Duke of York proclaimed himself King as Edward IV. Henry was imprisoned and, after a brief restoration in 1470–1, murdered.

Although all kings were believed to be representatives of God on earth, few lived up to the spiritual side of their calling. However, Henry's piety became legendary and after his death he joined that select band of kings, including the Anglo-Saxons Edmund and Edward the Confessor, who were recognised not just as great kings, but as holy men. Indeed, so powerful were the relics and shrines connected with Henry's life that very soon they were thought to be responsible for miraculous cures. Henry's cult continued until the Reformation in the 1530s, when, although the monarch was still thought to be the embodiment of the stars and heavens, king-worship was abandoned.

The House of York

HOUSE OF YORK

Edward IV

Edward V

Richard III

The House of York

EDWARD IV
1461–1470, 1471–1483

Born at Rouen on 28 April 1442, with the Sun in Taurus and the Moon in Sagittarius. Proclaimed King of England and Ireland on 5 March 1461 and crowned on 28 June 1461, with the Sun in Cancer and Moon in Pisces. Died on 9 April 1483 and buried at Windsor.

Edward IV was Henry VI's third cousin, and his rebellion in 1459 set in train the second phase of the Wars of the Roses. Edward triumphed in 1461 and became King, but Henry made a comeback in 1470, before being murdered in 1471. It is curious to find that the two were astrological opposites, Henry with a Sagittarian Sun and Taurean Moon and Edward with a Taurean Sun and Sagittarian Moon. This is an alignment of the type we often find in the horoscopes of married couples whose relationship thrives on disagreement, even conflict. Intriguingly, both men were also crowned under a very auspicious 'trine' aspect between the Sun and the Moon in Pisces. At Henry's coronation the Sun was in Scorpio, and at Edward's it was in Cancer, but the astrological effects would have been regarded as almost identical. This helpful alignment worked for Edward, if not for Henry, but the main question is whether this was pure coincidence or, more mysteriously, were the astrologers operating according to the same rules in each case?

The first king formally to bear the name Plantagenet, Edward was born in Rouen on 28 April 1442. His horoscope, cast by Dr John Argentine, was set for twenty-two minutes and thirty-two seconds past two in the morning. It's highly unlikely that the King's birth was recorded so precisely, and we can see here the astrologer's attempt to calculate a horoscope so accurate that his forecasts would be faultless. Whether he was successful or not, we have no record.

Edward was crowned under an alignment of Mars and Saturn, which is one of the most practical and down-to-earth possible; it also signified the military force he used to seize power. He was crowned under a similar relationship between the Sun and the Moon, which was one of the most auspicious possible. He therefore came to power under relatively helpful astrological indications. Edward was as ruthless and greedy as any medieval monarch, as much as William Rufus and John, but he was an extremely efficient administrator, and history has been relatively kind to him.

EDWARD V
1483

Born at Westminster on 2 November 1470, with the Sun in Scorpio and Moon in Pisces. Succeeded as King of England and Lord of Ireland on 9 April 1483, deposed on 25 June 1483 and murdered in the Tower of London, probably in late August 1483.

Edward V was Edward IV's eldest son and, like his father, his horoscope was cast by Dr John Argentine. He was born with the Sun in Scorpio and the Moon in Pisces, a delicate and sensitive combination which suggests that had he lived he might have been devoted to religion or the arts, but not able to exercise power with the consistent ruthlessness required of a king. His Ascendant fell in Taurus, helping to stabilise his character and, like Henry VI, whom he resembled, he would have combined weak rule with a sense of duty. However, he was never given the chance to prove his worth, for after ten weeks on the throne he was deposed, imprisoned in the Tower of London and, together with his younger brother, the Duke of York, mysteriously murdered.

Interestingly, John Argentine's horoscope for Edward indicated a threat to his life. At 4.06 p.m., the time Argentine set for the young King's birth, the Sun and Mars were exactly setting over the western horizon. It was dusk, and to have two such planets so placed at this time was a warning of personal violence. When in late August Edward was murdered, the Sun and Mars had once again come together, and the cycle was complete. His murderer would have been informed of this fact and so once again we encounter powerful circumstantial evidence of astrology being used to influence the murky plots and conspiracies of the medieval court.

RICHARD III
1483–1485

Born at Fotheringay Castle, Northamptonshire, 2 October 1452, with the Sun in Libra. Succeeded as King of England and Lord of Ireland on 25 June 1483 and crowned at Westminster on 6 July 1483, with the Sun in Cancer and Moon in Leo. Died in battle at Bosworth on 22 August 1485 and buried at Leicester.

Richard III is one of the trio of English kings condemned by popular mythology as being evil and unfit to have reigned; the other two members of this unholy alliance were of course William Rufus and John. Richard's behaviour, it is believed, sank way below the minimum required of a king anointed by God. Yet his poor reputation is due largely to the prejudice of the Tudor chroniclers. Richard was overthrown by the first Tudor king, Henry VII, in 1485; after which, criticising Richard was a convenient means of demonstrating loyalty to the new régime. The chroniclers' words, in turn, were reflected in Shakespeare's play, which effectively demonised the king for ever.

We have no accurate record of Richard's time of birth, only of the date, 2 October 1452. We do know that a horoscope was cast for him after his death which included an Ascendant in the middle of Scorpio. This, however, may have been an attempt to blacken his reputation, for many astrologers regarded Scorpio as a 'bad' sign. These suspicions are supported by the fact that the horoscope was included in a history of the Kings of England dedicated to Richard's rival and successor, Henry VII.

He was born with the Sun in Libra, a sign noted for its diplomatic skills and excellent public presentation. A conjunction between the Sun and Saturn would have brought out certain negative Libran qualities, making him punctilious, authoritarian, but also fair and impartial. He would have taken a long time to make up his mind and then, having reached a decision, would have been unable to change it for fear of creating more uncertainty. All things considered, Richard earned a reputation as a good administrator and able soldier while Duke of Gloucester. Interestingly, he was proclaimed King under an exact relationship between the Sun in Cancer and Moon in Pisces, which in a strange way repeated the pattern at the coronations of his predecessors, Henry VI and Edward IV.

When Richard came to the throne he was already suspected of collusion in the murders of Henry VI and his brother the Duke of Clarence (perhaps in collusion with his other brother, Edward IV). The murder of the Princes in the Tower, for which he was held responsible, together with the ruthless extinction of anyone who stood in his way, encouraged aristocratic opposition. In 1485, when Richard had come under the sway of Pluto, planet of the underworld, rebellion broke out and Henry Tudor invaded. At last, on Bosworth Field on 22 August 1485 Richard was killed, becoming the last English king to die in battle. A new era had begun.

The House of Tudor

HOUSE OF TUDOR

Henry VII

Henry VIII

Edward VI

Jane

Mary I

Elizabeth I

The House of Tudor

HENRY VII
1485–1509

Born at Pembroke, 28 January 1457, with the Sun in Aquarius and the Moon in Pisces. Proclaimed himself King of England and of France, Prince of Wales and Lord of Ireland after the Battle of Bosworth on 22 August 1485. Crowned at Westminster on 30 October 1485, with the Sun in Scorpio and Moon in Leo. Died on 5 April 1509 and buried at Westminster.

Henry VII's horoscope is known to us from both his mother's Book of Hours and the work of the prolific Dr John Argentine. This records his birth as 3.00 a.m. on 28 January 1457. Henry was born shortly after a New Moon in Aquarius, although by the time he came into the world the Moon had moved from this sign into Pisces. The result, when taken with his Ascendant in philosophical and adventurous Sagittarius, was to make him a highly independent thinker, capable of carving out his own path in the world. These qualities were seen in Henry's brilliant reorganisation of English government. He curbed the barons, elevated commoners to positions of state, avoided war and restored lost revenue to the royal coffers. He concentrated on creating trade links with other countries, laid the foundations for the navy and began the English exploration of North America. He showed the best side of his sensitive Piscean Moon, winning supporters through his compassionate treatment of his enemies.

The combination of Sagittarius, Aquarius and Pisces, while marvellous for lateral thinking, lacks the ruthlessness necessary for firm government. Tougher qualities were provided by Uranus and Pluto, which were exactly opposite the Sun at his birth. If Henry's Piscean Moon was the velvet glove, these planets represent the iron fist. They indicate a man for whom victory was everything, a true revolutionary, someone prepared to do anything to win, including overhauling the entire system of government. While Henry laid the foundations for modern government, Uranus and Pluto gave him the absolute determination to get his own way, and the system he established has been called the 'Tudor Despotism'. Intriguingly, the despotic alignment between the Sun, Uranus and Pluto was strongly featured first at midday on 22 August 1485, when he picked up the crown at the Battle of Bosworth, and then on 30 October the same year, when he was formally crowned.

One of Henry's treasured possessions was a gilt-edged de luxe copy of the *Liber Astronomicus*, a great astrological classic from the thirteenth century, written by Guido Bonatti, one of Italy's foremost political astrologers. When considering matters of state, however, he took outside advice and consulted another Italian astrologer, William Parron. With his knowledge of myth and feel for popular superstition, Henry named his eldest son and heir Arthur, after King Arthur. Like the Arthur of Brittany who had been murdered by John, it was hoped that the young Arthur Tudor would unite the British people and restore the glories of the lost kingdom of Camelot. Yet it was not to be. Arthur died, leaving the succession to his younger brother, Henry.

HENRY VIII
1509–1547

Born at Greenwich on 28 June 1491, with the Sun in Cancer and Moon in Aries. Succeeded as King of England and Lord of Ireland on 5 April 1509 and crowned at Westminster on 24 June 1509, with the Sun in Cancer. Died on 28 June 1547 and buried at Windsor.

Henry VIII is perhaps the most famous of all English kings. A larger than life character in all ways, he is renowned for his six tumultuous marriages, and in public affairs he changed the course of English history by instituting the Reformation and breaking with the Roman Catholic Church. Perhaps it was his combination of womanising and wisdom which sets Henry apart from the other English monarchs (except perhaps Charles II). His role in popular memory is truly Olympian, and if we were to find a mythological origin for the images and impressions we all have of him, it would probably be Zeus, the king of the Greek gods.

Henry was born between 8.30 and 9.00 a.m. on 28 June 1491, although some astrologers cast his horoscope, setting it for various times later in the morning. Jerome Cardan, who was one of the greatest astrologers of the time and worked for the Pope, claimed that Henry was born at 10.40 a.m. The discrepancy was probably necessary to make Cardan's forecasts fit with what he knew of the King's life!

The Sun in sensitive Cancer and Moon in fiery Aries were responsible for Henry's petulant character. Both these signs are quite emotional – Cancer more so than Aries – and both like to be obeyed – Aries more so than Cancer. It is no surprise that Henry elevated his favourites to positions of great power, only to humiliate or execute them when they failed to do his bidding. Sir Thomas More, Thomas Cromwell and Cardinal Wolsey all felt the warm breath of Henry's favour, only to be destroyed when they outlived their usefulness.

Henry was a keen supporter of astrology's use in matters of state and consulted two astrologers, John Robins and the German Nicholas Kratzer. He succeeded to the throne under a Full Moon, which would not have been considered auspicious, but he had no control over this. However, there is some evidence that his coronation date may have been chosen with astrological considerations in mind. For example, there was a curious relationship known as a 'mutual reception' between two important planets, Mercury and the Moon. This means that each was in a sign 'ruled' by the other, and was a very important factor for any astrologer of the time. At the time it would have been considered that this pattern was destined to deepen the King's wisdom and judgment.

If we want to know about Henry's greed, his cruelty and impatience, the answers are revealed in a powerful alignment of Mars (ruling anger) and Jupiter (indicating excess) at his birth. In this sense, his sacking of the monasteries and execution of two of his wives become mere manifestations of his deeper all-consuming passion for indulgence. If we want to know why he pitched church and state into a confrontation which changed the face of England for ever, the answer lies in the Full Moon which shone as his father died and he ascended the throne. It was this Full Moon which tore Henry's private life apart and drove his quest for an heir. Without this, the course of English history would have been very different.

Henry's family trials were reinforced by a similarly difficult Moon in his birth horoscope, but his attack on the church itself is indicated by another planetary alignment. Jupiter and Neptune, two planets ruling religious belief, were in a very difficult relationship both with each other and with Mars, planet of conflict and confrontation. This is a combination which combines warlike tendencies with religious conviction, and in different circumstances Henry could have been a crusader. In the event, politics and the need to produce a male heir pushed him into divorce, for which it was necessary to break with the Roman Church. For purely secular reasons Henry therefore became a somewhat unwilling crusader on behalf of the new Protestant cause.

Four of Henry's queens – Anne Boleyn, Jane Seymour, Katherine Howard and Catherine Parr – were commoners, albeit aristocratic ones. This meant that their birth dates were not officially recorded, so we have no idea of their horoscopes. We only know that Anne Boleyn, his second wife, was born at the end of May or early June, which would have given her the Sun in Gemini. However, two of his wives were born to ruling dynasties and so their birth dates were set down in the official chronicles. Anne of Cleves, whom Henry rudely called the 'Flanders Mare' and resolved to divorce as soon as he had married her, was born, like Henry, with the Moon in fiery Aries. This alone would have made her more than a match for him, had the marriage got off to a better start. However, the Sun in Libra gave her a distaste for confrontation and a willingness to accept her fate as the second of Henry's divorced wives – not that she had any choice in the matter.

Catherine of Aragon, Henry's first wife, was born on 16 December 1485, the daughter of the Spanish monarchs, Ferdinand and Isabella. This also gave her the Moon in Aries, and under different circumstances she might have responded to Henry's divorce proposal more vigorously. However, as a foreign princess she had few supporters in England, and had to endure her humiliation without complaint. No doubt her Sun in businesslike Capricorn helped her see that, although she had been replaced as Queen and her beloved Catholic Church had been destroyed, life had to go on.

Curiously, Catherine was born under the strong conjunction between Uranus and Neptune which repeatedly causes chaos in the monarchy. Her birth horoscope has powerful connections to the horoscopes for the murder of the Princes in the Tower and the Battle of Bosworth, which took place a few months before she was born. It is as if a cosmic script had been written into her horoscope, as if she was to involuntarily serve a vital purpose on behalf of the English monarchy, almost to be sacrificed. Her first husband, Arthur, Prince of Wales, died, and she was married to Henry, his younger brother. She was then unable to bear a male heir and was publicly humiliated and cast aside. Had Arthur lived and had she given birth to a son, Henry VIII might never have ascended the throne; England would have remained a Catholic country, and the monarch would never have become head of the Church.

Margaret Murray, in her book, *The Divine King in England*, speculated on the possible deliberate ritual sacrifice of kings in the middle ages. Yet there are different ways to be sacrificed, and Catherine had to be ritually humiliated on the altar of political necessity in order for history to move one step forward. The strongest connection between her horoscope and Henry's linked her to his crusading, reforming alignment of Mars, Jupiter and Neptune; when heaven called for change, she became its vehicle. Henry was the executioner, symbolically in Catherine's case, but in the future, literally.

EDWARD VI
1547–1553

Born at Hampton Court on 12 October 1537, with the Sun in Libra and the Moon in Capricorn. Succeeded as King of England and Ireland on 28 June 1547 and crowned at Westminster on 20 February 1547. Died at Greenwich on 6 July 1553 and buried at Westminster.

Edward VI was the son of Henry VIII and Jane Seymour, of all his wives the one he loved most. Tragically, she died of complications after the birth, leaving Henry at last with the male heir he needed to secure his dynasty and England's future. Edward was born at about

1.50 a.m. on 12 October 1537, and the close relationship between his horoscope and his father's was quite remarkable. The Moon at his birth was in Capricorn, opposite Henry's Sun in Cancer, indicating that in many ways they were very different; he was a quiet and retiring boy with none of his father's dramatic flair. Yet both men were born with the Ascendant in exactly the same degree of Virgo, indicating an identical attention to detail and a shared capacity to take life extremely seriously. While it is widely known that Edward took his religion very seriously and was a devout Calvinist, it is less well appreciated that Henry VIII, as a young man, acquired a reputation as something of an expert in matters of theology.

The most astonishing connection between the two kings, however, lies in the exact degree of the zodiac occupied by the Sun at Edward's birth. This was exactly the same position as the fateful Full Moon which lit the night sky on the evening of Henry's accession, and which was the omen which presaged his traumatic personal life and assault on the Church. The curious astrological patterns unfolding in Edward's life became deeper and more intense when Henry VIII died, and he ascended the throne, on 28 June, his father's birthday. Such coincidences would have been remarked upon by the leading astrologers of the time, including John Cheke, his tutor, and Jerome Cardan, the papal astrologer invited to England specifically in order to read the King's horoscope. The fact that Edward was crowned under a New Moon strongly suggests the secret hand of an astrologer at work on the selection of the date.

However, no astrologer of the time could have known that the Sun in Pisces was exactly opposed by Uranus, a planet now known to bring revolutionary shocks and sudden surprises. After coming to the throne at the age of ten, Edward gave the greatest possible encouragement to the Calvinist reformers, the revolutionaries of their day. His death at the age of fifteen denied England the king for whom Henry VIII had divorced Catherine and started the Reformation. England was once again plunged into uncertainty.

JANE
1553

Born at Bradgate, Leicestershire in 1537. Proclaimed Queen of

England and Ireland secretly on 6 July 1553 and publicly on 10 July 1553. Imprisoned in the Tower of London on 19 July 1553 and beheaded on 12 February 1554.

Lady Jane Grey, the Nine Days' Queen, is one of the tragic figures of English royal history. A great-granddaughter of Henry VII, she was manipulated by her powerful father, the Duke of Suffolk, and Protestant nobles, and proclaimed Queen on Edward VI's death. The public proclamation on 10 July 1553 took place under a New Moon in Cancer, and in other circumstances this would have indicated that astrological advice had been taken. However, in this case, the plotters would have been under too much pressure to proceed to wait for astrologers to pick the most auspicious moment. Jane was therefore proclaimed immediately after Edward's demise. So obscure was Jane that we are unsure even of her birth date, let alone her birth planets. When on 19 July she was overthrown by Mary, the rightful heir, the Moon had reached one of the degrees of the zodiac which connected Edward VI, Henry VII and Henry VIII. It was time for the main branch of the Tudor dynasty to reassert itself, and Jane was propelled into historical obscurity.

MARY I
1553–1558

Born at Greenwich on 18 February 1516, with the Sun in Pisces and the Moon in Virgo. Succeeded as Queen of England and Ireland on 19 July 1553 and crowned at Westminster on 1 October 1553. Died at St James's Palace on 17 November 1558 and buried at Westminster.

Mary Tudor, Queen Mary I of England was the only child of Henry VIII and his first wife, Catherine of Aragon. According to a chronicle compiled in the time of Queen Elizabeth: 'In the year of our Lord 1516, and the seventh year of our Sovereigne Lord Kinge Henry the eighth, the eighteenth day of February beinge Monday about four of the clock in the morninge was borne the Princesse at Greenwich'.

Mary was born with the Sun in sensitive Pisces, the Moon in practical Virgo and the Ascendant in businesslike, conservative

Capricorn; so far, so good. There is a great deal of positive potential in this combination. Pisces is infinitely flexible, although sometimes over-attached to beliefs which have little to do with real circumstances. The Moon in Virgo is superb at coping with detail and, together with a Capricorn Ascendant, makes for a superb administrator. For the first few years of her reign Mary was a reasonably sensible monarch, and her desire to turn the clock back and restore the Roman Catholic Church was tempered by her husband, Philip II of Spain. However, eventually she lost the capacity for compromise and began the executions which earned her the name 'Bloody Mary'. In all, six hundred Protestants were burnt at the stake, including Archbishop Cranmer.

Philip himself was proclaimed King of England but never crowned. The marriage was doomed from the outset for the English could never accept a Spanish king, and even if Mary had lived it is doubtful whether the match would have survived. Philip was born on 21 May 1527 in Vallodolid, and according to a horoscope which survives from the seventeenth century, he came into the world at 4.15 p.m. This placed his planets in an alignment with Mary's that is commonly found in relationships which are intense but short-lived.

We find the origin of Mary's family difficulties and bad reputation in two negative factors in her horoscope. First of all, she was born at a Full Moon, a factor which, considered along with the rest of her horoscope, indicated her personal problems; Henry divorced her mother, Parliament proclaimed her illegitimate, her marriage was a failure and she never managed to conceive, in spite of her longing for a child. Secondly, she was born with Pluto exactly on her Ascendant, indicating an almost compulsive urge towards emotional confrontation. During the entire span of her reign this obsessive planet occupied an extremely powerful position in her horoscope. Eventually, when it reached the peak of its power, she died, and for ever after has been vilified by the triumphant English Protestants.

ELIZABETH I
1558–1603

Born at Greenwich on 7 September 1533, with the Sun in Virgo and the Moon in Taurus. Succeeded as Queen of England and

Ireland on 17 November 1558 and crowned at Westminster on 15 January 1559. Died on 24 March 1603 and buried at Westminster.

Few English reigns have been subject to the same degree of myth-making as Elizabeth I's. Hers was the age of the English Renaissance, the plays of Shakespeare and Marlowe, the buccaneers and explorers Sir Francis Drake and Sir Walter Raleigh. At home, political stability deepened and Parliament grew in confidence. Abroad, Spain was humiliated and, with the defeat of the Armada, England was free from any serious threat of invasion for two hundred and fifty years. Ever since, Elizabeth's reign has been remembered as a Golden Age. Even poets of the time looked back to the ancient Greek myths in order to explain England's contemporary glories. In particular, they looked back to the prophecy that a new Golden Age would appear when the world was ruled by a virgin. This is why, knowing that Elizabeth was born with the Sun in Virgo, the sign of the Virgin, the royal propagandists of the day developed the myth of the Virgin Queen. They understood that to be a virgin was not merely to be pure, but to be venerated as the Great Mother of ancient religion, that is, a true Universal Monarch.

It was Eustace Chapuys, the Ambassador of the Holy Roman Emperor, who recorded the moment of Elizabeth's birth: 'On Sunday last, the eve of our lady, about 3.00 p.m., the King's mistress was delivered of a daughter, to the great reproach of the physicians, astrologers, sorcerers and sorceresses, who affirmed that it would be a male child'. Henry needed a son, and all the forecasters of the time were consulting the stars to establish the baby's sex. Even William Cecil, one of the King's chief ministers, made his own astrological investigations into the question. Evidently, wishful thinking shaped Cecil's forecasts and he was wrong.

Elizabeth's mother was Anne Boleyn, Henry VIII's second wife. When Anne then consistently failed to produce a male heir, she fell out of favour and was beheaded when Elizabeth was barely three years old.

Elizabeth was in many ways similar to her sister Mary. Both were born with the same conservative Capricorn Ascendant in an exact harmonious relationship with the Moon. Whereas Mary's Moon was

69

in practical Virgo, Elizabeth's was in the equally practical sign Taurus. The similarities between their horoscopes and their brother Edward's and their father Henry's are truly remarkable, demonstrating the close astrological relationships we often find between members of the same family. However, in one important sense, Elizabeth was Mary's opposite; Elizabeth was born with the Sun in Virgo, contrasting with Mary, the sensitive Piscean, making Elizabeth the most calculating, businesslike and efficient of all the Tudors. In any circumstances she would have become a superb administrator and would have excelled in business. It was her shrewdness and the very effectiveness of her government that persuaded most of the leading nobles to support her, making her the first successful queen in English history, and the first woman since Boudicea to exercise real power. Elizabeth survived partly through her intelligent manipulation of her most powerful courtiers, maintaining their personal loyalty to her and forestalling the development of serious conspiracies. She was fortunate to have two planets, Mercury and Venus, in diplomatic Libra, enabling her to sense and play on her rivals' weaknesses.

Elizabeth's astrologer, the scholar and philosopher John Dee, was one of the most foremost thinkers of the century. At great risk to himself, he advised Elizabeth when she was held under house arrest by Mary (for whom he was also making forecasts) and when Elizabeth ascended the throne she asked Dee to arrange the most auspicious moment for the crown to be placed on her head. This he clearly did with great success. We don't know exactly what time Dee selected, but we do know the date – 15 January 1559. First of all, he looked at her horoscope. Then he picked a day when the Sun, the Moon and the two most auspicious planets, Venus and Jupiter, were in the best alignment to the positions occupied by the planets at her birth. After the coronation Dee became one of Elizabeth's faithful servants, offering her detailed astrological advice on the character and prospects of her marriage suitors, as well as other matters of state; she even used him for espionage, and for a while he worked as a secret agent.

The Virgin Queen died between 1.00 and 2.00 a.m. on 24 March 1603. At that moment the Tudor dynasty, founded by Henry VII at noon on 22 August 1485, came to an end. The Moon had reached the degree occupied by the Sun at the coronation of William the

Conqueror. For astrologers, at least, their grief would have been coloured by the knowledge that this was, at the very least, a suitable day to welcome a new monarch. That monarch was to come from Scotland.

The
Kingdom
of
Scotland

KINGDOM OF SCOTLAND

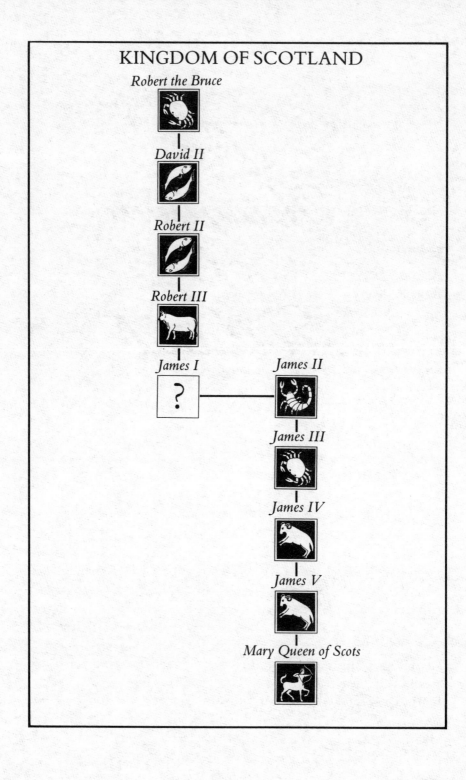

Robert the Bruce

David II

Robert II

Robert III

James I

James II

James III

James IV

James V

Mary Queen of Scots

From Robert the Bruce to Union with England

The Kingdom of Scotland

Although the modern royal family traces its descent – and thus its right to reign – from the kings of Wessex, it should also look to Scotland. The Kingdom of Scotland was formed in 842 when Alpin, ruler of the small western Scottish kingdom of Dalriada, created the first unified kingdom. Like the early kings of England, the horoscopes of the first kings of Scotland have long been lost. Their birth times, and in many cases even their year of birth, went unrecorded. It is not until the fourteenth century that we find any reliable recording of dates, and even then there are instances of kings whose year of birth is unknown. Our astrological investigation therefore begins with one of Scotland's most famous kings, Robert the Bruce.

ROBERT THE BRUCE
1306–1329

Born at Writtle, near Chelmsford, Essex on 11 July 1274, with the Sun in Cancer and the Moon in Libra. Assumed the crown of Scotland at Scone on 27 March 1306, with the Sun in Aries and Moon in Virgo. Died on 7 June 1329 at Cardcross, Dumbartonshire and buried at Dunfermline.

Robert the Bruce may have been born with the Sun in Cancer, but anyone who mistook him for a sweet-tempered and sensitive man would have been making a major mistake. He was also born with the Sun in a powerful conjunction with Venus and Mars, a combination of planets which is highly skilled in the art of human manipulation.

Venus enabled Robert to persuade sufficient Scottish nobles to support him, while Mars, the planet of war, gave him the sheer force of personality necessary to scare them into submission.

After years of weak government, English interference and ten years without a king, Robert restored Scottish independence and unity, founding the dynasty which was to rule Scotland until its unification with England in 1603. He was helped in this venture by another very important planetary feature, the Moon in Libra. Like anyone born with the Moon in this position, Robert had the ability to charm other people, but always with the knowledge that if they failed to succumb to peaceful persuasion, he would use stronger methods.

When he seized the crown on 27 March 1306 the Sun was in Aries, a splendid position for anyone asserting their control. Aries is known as a cardinal sign, which means that it encourages people to take command of their environment. Fortunately for Robert, Cancer and Libra, which contained the Sun and Moon at his birth, are also cardinal signs. He was therefore ideally placed to assert his rule over the entire country. When he died on 7 June 1329, the Moon had returned to its place in Libra. This was not in itself unusual, for it happens once a month. More important was Pluto's position in relation to the Sun, pushing the King towards seclusion and isolation. As it was he died, bequeathing the crown to his son, David.

DAVID II
1329–1371

Born in Dunfermline on 5 March 1324, with the Sun in Pisces and the Moon in Cancer. Succeeded to the throne on 7 June 1329, with the Sun in Gemini and the Moon in Libra. Died at Edinburgh on 22 February 1371 and buried at Holyrood Palace, Edinburgh.

David II was one of many Scottish monarchs who ascended the throne at a tender age. He was only five when his father Robert the Bruce died and the crown was placed on his head. He was born with the Sun in sensitive Pisces and the Moon in emotional Cancer, a wonderful combination for an artist, less good for a king. David might have succeeded in more peaceful times, but he lacked his father's ability to hold back the forces of chaos. When the English supported his rival, Edward Balliol, David was forced to flee first to England and then to France.

He was born with the Sun in a very close aspect to Venus, indicating a generally good nature. He would have been better off had he been born in some civilised corner of the world with little to do except indulge his private fantasies. However, at his birth the Sun was also perilously close to Pluto, and this represented his tragic flaw – he was motivated by revenge. The simple fact was that he couldn't forget the past, and when Edward Balliol was finally defeated David decided to take his revenge on the English, in spite of the English King Edward III's untarnished reputation as a war leader. We may see here the impractical hand of Pisces at work, for many people born under this sign are unable to see the consequences of their actions. Eventually Pluto, planet of the underworld, expressed itself in its most negative manner. David was imprisoned, and, for the last eleven years of his reign until his death on 22 February 1371, he languished in an English dungeon.

ROBERT II
1371–1390

Born on 2 March 1316, with the Sun in Pisces and Moon in Gemini. Succeeded to the throne of Scotland on 22 February 1371, with the Sun in Pisces and Moon in Gemini. Died at Dundonald, Ayrshire on 19 April 1390 and buried at Scone.

Robert II was grandson of Robert the Bruce and the first king of the Stuart dynasty. The Stewarts, as they were then known, were formerly the High Stewards of Scotland. From 1603 to 1714, they sat on the throne of England, and the dynasty died out in 1807 when their last representative, who claimed to be King Henry IX, died in exile in Rome.

The dynasty founded in 1371 may have had a long future, but nobody could have guessed this at the time. By a strange coincidence Robert was born and succeeded to the throne while the Sun was in Pisces and the Moon in Gemini. This is a delightful combination, but better suited to a writer or radio presenter than to a medieval king. We can imagine Robert being far more interested in the philosophical nature of monarchy than in doing the job. He was no doubt charming company, but his ability to see all sides of every question made him indecisive and easily swayed. He was, in short, an ineffectual ruler. So strong were the basic planetary patterns in his horoscope that he also died with the Moon in Gemini, as if this planet and this sign had to be joined at all important events in his life.

ROBERT III
1390–1406

Born about 1337 and succeeded to the throne of Scotland on 19 April 1390, with the Sun in Taurus and Moon in Gemini. Died at Dundonald on 4 April 1406.

Robert III had the misfortune to be born with a name considered very ill-omened for a king – John. When he succeeded his father, Robert II, he therefore took on the name Robert III, which he thought would make him more fitted to reign. He was wrong; he proved as unable as his father to control the ambitious nobles and anarchic Highlanders.

It is impossible to cast a horoscope for Robert's birth, for we have no idea what year he was born, let alone the date or time. However, we do know that he ascended the throne with a horoscope which can only be described as rather charming, practical and inventive. His personable qualities derived from a poetic combination of the Moon and Venus in Gemini, a sign which often confers skills in communication. His practical qualities can be attributed to a sound relationship between the Sun and Saturn, a planet of self-discipline and control. His original approach to government was related to the powerful position held by Uranus in relation to the Sun.

Like his predecessors, Robert ascended the throne under planetary patterns suited to the ruler of a peaceful land, not the monarch of a warring medieval state. Mars, which indicates military prowess, was in a very weak and erratic position: it was in Pisces, wonderfully useful for artists, less so for generals. But there was worse: a double alignment to Jupiter and Saturn provided his tragic flaw, which was that, having once decided on a course of action, he changed his mind. First Robert relied on his brother as Guardian (Regent). Then he was dismissed in favour of Robert's son David, who was made Lord Lieutenant. When David fell from grace, he died under suspicious circumstances.

The key to Robert's troubled reign lay in planetary alignments not on the day of his succession, but a few days earlier. Seventy-two hours before he became King the Moon had eclipsed the Sun. This was one of the worst omens possible, indicating symbolically that the King himself (the Sun) was eclipsed. The old King, Robert II, had died but, due to a series of additional planetary factors, what was in medieval eyes a very evil omen gave its character to the new King's reign. Ultimately though, it was not his stars which trapped Robert, but his circumstances. He would have made an intelligent administrator, but Scotland required a strong warlord.

JAMES I
1406–1437

Born at Dunfermline in December 1394. Succeeded to the throne of Scotland on 4 April 1406, with the Sun in Aries and the Moon in Scorpio. Died on 21 February 1437 and buried at Perth.

Even though James I was the son of a king, his birth was unrecorded, and we are not even certain of his date of birth. All we know is that he came into the world some time in December 1394. He may have had his Sun in adventurous Sagittarius – or it might have been in cautious Capricorn. What we do know is that he was born under an extraordinarily powerful alignment between Neptune and Pluto in Taurus, and Uranus, which was in the exactly opposite position in Scorpio. This was an alignment of historical significance. Abroad, it signified the great revival of learning in the Italian Renaissance. In England, it was to be the catalyst for the Wars of the Roses. True to this historic alignment, James found himself caught up in circumstances beyond his control, and spent the first eighteen years of his reign as a prisoner in the Tower of London.

It is the horoscope for James' succession on 4 April 1406 which indicates the nature of his rule. The Sun was in Aries, giving him a tough and commanding edge. Mars, planet of war, was powerfully aligned with Neptune, Pluto and Saturn. This is an indication of violence, but it is impossible to see whether the King who comes to power under this combination will be the perpetrator, victim or, as is more usual, a mixture of both. It is therefore far from surprising to discover that, on his release from captivity, James executed his father-in-law, uncle and two cousins, who had controlled Scotland while he was in the Tower. Then he imposed an uneasy discipline on the Highlands and for twelve years maintained his grip with ruthless determination.

Even the manner of James' passing was in line with the astrology of his reign: on 21 February 1437 he was murdered by Sir Robert Graham, just one of many who had suffered under James' iron hand.

JAMES II
1437–1460

Born at Holyrood Monastery, Edinburgh, on 16 October 1430, with the Sun in Scorpio and the Moon in Libra. Succeeded to the throne of Scotland on 21 February 1437, with the Sun in Pisces and the Moon in Virgo. Died in Roxburgh on 3 August 1460 and buried at Holyrood.

James II was born at a New Moon, became King of Scotland under a Full Moon, and died at another Full Moon, as if this planet had taken a special role in guiding his affairs. At his birth the Sun was in Scorpio, and at his succession it was in Pisces. Both signs indicated a personality dominated by emotion and unsuited to the hard decisions and determined action required to control the unruly Scottish barons. James was effectively a titular king who failed to exert any more than a minimal degree of authority. Interestingly, there was just one planetary alignment at James' succession which indicated a potential war leader. This was the exact opposition between Mars, which was in Capricorn, and Pluto, which was in Cancer. This is one of those planetary alignments we find in the horoscopes of people who are brought into contact with sudden and unexpected violence. At the beginning of August 1460, Mars had returned to activate this alignment and was joined by Saturn. When linked to Mars, Saturn often indicates the risk of accidents. It so happened that on 3 August James was present at the siege of Roxburgh, an English-held castle, when a cannon exploded, an event exactly in line with the dangerous indications of his horoscope. James was killed in the blast, leaving his divided kingdom to his son.

JAMES III
1460–1488

Born at Stirling on 10 July 1451, with the Sun in Cancer and the Moon in Sagittarius. Succeeded to the throne of Scotland on 3 August 1460, with the Sun in Leo and the Moon in Pisces. Died on 11 June 1488 and buried at Cambuskenneth, Stirlingshire.

James III was not the first Scottish king born to reign but unable to rule, and neither was he the last. This was a shame, though, for his horoscope reveals a character of quite extraordinary generosity. He was born with the Sun in powerful alignments to Uranus (indicating an original manner), Jupiter (the planet of generosity itself) and Neptune (revealing a vivid imagination). His Sagittarian Moon provided an adventurous streak. Yet James came to the throne under an alignment between the Sun and Pluto which threatened confrontation and conflict. Mars, which we would look to for signs that he might assert his will over the rebellious barons, was muddled and weak, and indicated the threat of deception. For much of his reign he was the prisoner of one aristocratic faction or another, and when he was killed it was at the hands of a man masquerading as a priest.

JAMES IV
1488–1513

Born on 17 March 1473, with the Sun in Aries and the Moon in Scorpio. Succeeded to the throne of Scotland on 11 June 1488, with the Sun in Gemini and the Moon in Cancer. Died on 9 September 1513.

Born with the Sun in fiery, energetic Aries and the Moon in intense, emotional Scorpio, James IV was a force to be reckoned with. His Sun sign provided energy and his Moon sign confirmed determination. After succeeding to the throne at the age of fifteen, he gradually managed to assert his will over that of the rebellious Scottish nobles, he even managed to impose order on the Highlands and the Western Isles. He was also, as a matter of interest, the last king of Scotland to speak Gaelic.

He was born with the Moon in a very close alignment with Neptune, planet of the imagination – so close that he was perilously open to deception. In fact he was so gullible that when Perkin Warbeck, the pretender who claimed to be one of the murdered Princes in the Tower, arrived in Scotland, James backed him to the hilt, supporting his claim to the throne of England, giving him money, marrying him to a kinswoman and invading England at his side. Warbeck later proved to have been one of the great confidence tricksters of English history.

Mars, planet of war, indicated both James' military prowess and the threat of violence to his own person. This planet was aligned with Pluto at his birth, and it is this pattern which indicated danger to the King's life. At the beginning of September 1513 two celestial events took place: one was that Mars moved to occupy the degree held by Pluto at the King's birth; the other was an eclipse of the Sun which was simultaneously aligned with both planets. In August James marched into England, determined to win a glorious victory while the King, Henry VIII, was in France. Instead, on 9 September the army was annihilated at Flodden Field, and James himself was killed.

JAMES V
1513–1542

Born at Linlithgow on 10 April 1512, with the Sun in Aries and the Moon in Aquarius. Succeeded to the throne of Scotland on 9 September 1513, with the Sun in Virgo and the Moon in Capricorn. Died on 14 December 1452.

James V was born with the Sun exactly on the cusp, or dividing line, between energetic, assertive Aries and stubborn, cautious Taurus. The inevitable question arises as to which was the strongest sign in his character; fortunately, the answer lies elsewhere in his horoscope. At the time of his birth the Sun was on exactly the opposite degree of the zodiac to Saturn, the planet of limitation and control, and this serious alignment brought out all the Taurean elements in James' horoscope.

Yet, like almost all the Stuart kings, his character contained a fatal flaw, in this case represented by the exact alignment between Mars and Pluto which indicated violence, oppression, passion and danger.

James inherited the throne when he was seventeen months old and never managed to control the divisive forces which repeatedly tore his country apart. After he asserted his personal authority, at the tender age of fourteen, he sought alliances with the baronial armies and ordered the extermination of rebellious Highland clans. Such ruthlessness is just what we would expect from the King born under such a close relationship between Mars and Pluto.

Eventually, on the night of 13 December 1542 a New Moon fell exactly on the King's Mars–Pluto alignment. It was as if the power of the Sun and the Moon combined with the intensity of his birth horoscope was more than James could bear. The next day, worn out at the age of just thirty, he died, leaving his infant daughter Mary to reign as Queen.

MARY, QUEEN OF SCOTS
1542–1567

Born at Linlithgow on 7 or 8 December 1542, with the Sun in Sagittarius. Succeeded to the throne of Scotland on 14 December 1542, with the Sun in Sagittarius and the Moon in Capricorn. Died on 8 February 1587.

Mary, Queen of Scots is one of the most romantic figures in Scottish – and British – royal history. She came to the throne at the age of six or seven days old, after her father's premature death, and had no more chance than her predecessors of overcoming the barons and unifying the country. If anything, she had even less chance for, as a woman, she was treated as no more than a marriageable property by the aristocratic warring factions. She was born with the Sun in adventurous Sagittarius in a harmonious alignment with expansive Jupiter. This was an ideal indication of great generosity, but also of poor judgment. Just as she was very giving, she could not understand the limitations to which she was subjected by her position. After the Protestant faction betrothed her to Edward, son of Henry VIII of England, the Catholics kidnapped her and sent her to France where they married her to the dauphin Francis.

Yet Mary had a powerful will of her own. She was born under the same close Mars–Pluto alignment which had brought such danger to so many of her predecessors, and which gave an intense and passionate streak to her character. It was almost as if as soon as she sensed opposition she was determined to fight all the harder. Her downfall was precipitated by her passionate marriages to Lord Darnley and the Earl of Bothwell. Darnley was murdered by Bothwell, Mary's lover, after only two and a half years of marriage. This was too much for the other nobles and Protestant reformers to accept, and Mary was forced to abdicate on 24 July 1567.

It was Mary's Mars–Pluto alignment which brought about her downfall. At her birth these two planets were in almost the same degree of the zodiac. At her abdication they had reached another crucial alignment, and were 90° apart. Yet still Mary continued on her stubborn way, refusing to compromise with her cousin Elizabeth I, whose throne she claimed. Eventually, in February 1587 Mars and Pluto reached their third alignment and Elizabeth decided that she had had enough. On 8 February 1587 Mary was led into the courtyard of Fortheringay Castle, where she had been imprisoned and, true to the power of Mars and Pluto, was beheaded.

The House of Stuart

HOUSE OF STUART

James I of England (VI of Scotland)

Charles I

Charles II

James II

William III —— *Mary II*

Anne

James III

Charles III

Henry IX

The United Crown of England and Scotland

The House of Stuart

JAMES I OF ENGLAND AND VI OF SCOTLAND
1603–1625

Born at Edinburgh on 19 June 1566, with the Sun in Cancer and the Moon in Leo. Succeeded to the throne of Scotland on 24 July 1567, with the Sun in Leo and the Moon in Pisces. Succeeded as King of England and Ireland on 24 March 1603 and crowned at Westminster on 29 July 1603, with the Sun in Leo and the Moon in Virgo. Died on 27 March 1625 and buried at Westminster.

James I was the first king to rule as King of Great Britain. He had succeeded as King of Scotland in 1567 and, although England and Scotland remained separate nations under his rule, he was strongly in favour of union. James was born with the Sun in Cancer and the Moon in Leo, a combination frequently found in the horoscopes of actors; Leo theatricality has the effect of exaggerating Cancerian sensitivity and producing a powerful performance. However, it is not a good indication in the horoscope of politicians, being too inclined to provoke emotional reactions and favouritism. James was born between 10.00 and 11.00 a.m. and had a Virgo Ascendant. This endowed him with an analytical and bookish quality, and he relished intellectual argument. Yet he channelled his powerful mind into discussing issues such as how to deal with witches – on which he was considered something of an expert – rather than concentrating on good government. The historian Macaulay said of him that 'He was made up of two men – a witty, well-read scholar who wrote, disputed and harangued, and a nervous, drivelling idiot who acted'. More famously, he was called the 'wisest fool in Christendom'.

James was born under the same Mars–Saturn alignment which occurs in the horoscopes of many of the kings who suffered violence. His father, Lord Darnley was murdered when the young Prince was only eight months old; his entire childhood was spent in an atmosphere of danger and intrigue. Perhaps the most famous incident of his reign was the Gunpowder Plot of 1605 when, allegedly, Guy Fawkes was caught attempting to blow up the Houses of Parliament.

James lived at a time when Copernicus' discovery that the Sun was the centre of the solar system was beginning to affect the way men thought about politics. Those who supported the divine right of kings to rule as they pleased argued that, like the Sun in the solar system, the King was the focal point of the country. Everybody, it was maintained, should bow before the King, their cosmic master. Astrologers of the time found it highly significant that James was born with the Moon in Leo, the sign they believed was 'ruled' by the Sun, succeeded to the throne of Scotland with the Sun in Leo – and was crowned King of England with the Sun in the same sign. In his supporters' eyes he was therefore completely Leonine and solar, which meant that he was thoroughly and completely regal. However, by his feeble government and uncontrolled extravagance, James did his best to discredit the monarchy, and not even the new political cosmology could dent his reputation as a bungler. He died on 27 March 1625, under the influence of Pluto, leaving an unstable and impoverished inheritance to his son, Charles.

CHARLES I
1625–1649

Born at Dunfermline on 19 November 1600, with the Sun in Sagittarius and the Moon in Virgo. Succeeded as King of England, Scotland and Ireland on 27 March 1625 and crowned at Westminster on 2 February 1626, with the Sun in Aquarius and Moon in Virgo. Beheaded at Whitehall on 30 January 1649 and buried at Windsor.

Charles I was born shortly after midday on Wednesday 19 November 1600. Like his father James he has two reputations. He was remembered as a devout, even saintly, man by his supporters, but as an arrogant and incompetent fool by those who say that the civil war and his own execution were disasters entirely of his own making. His Moon in Virgo gave him an attention to detail admirable in a politician, but he was so attached to minutiae that he was incapable of distinguishing the important issues of the day from irrelevant trivia. His Sun was in Sagittarius, a sign of high ideals, and his Ascendant was in Aquarius, which often places ideas above practical experience. This is an excellent horoscope for a philosopher, but not for a monarch grappling with the realities of power. Charles' commitment to the theory of the divine right of kings was deeper than his father's, and his refusal to compromise on this single point led directly to the rebellion which broke out in 1642. Finally, in 1649, he became the only English king to be beheaded. Previous monarchs had been murdered in secret, but Charles was the only one to be put on trial and suffer the humiliation of a public execution.

William Lilly, the most famous astrologer of the time, was consulted by many of the leading participants in the civil war. Both Oliver Cromwell, the leader of the rebel Parliamentary forces, and Charles sought advice from him through intermediaries. However, Charles does not appear to have taken astrological advice on a routine basis, believing that, since he had a hot-line to God, no mere mortal could have anything useful to say to him. Lilly himself made a detailed study of Charles' horoscope which he published under the title, *The Nativity of King Charles*. According to Lilly, Charles 'died in the middle of his climacterial year, fatal many times where killing Directions in the Nativity threaten'. Astrologers like Lilly believed that every seventh year brought important changes (the origin of the famous 'seven-year itch'), and the forty-ninth year – seven times seven – was therefore extremely important. Other astrologers agreed, and those who remained true to the royalist cause considered that, had the King taken astrological advice, he would have survived.

However, Lilly and his contemporaries would have been unaware of two patterns which were very unfortunate for the monarchy. One was the difficult alignment of Pluto, which brought trouble for many of Charles' predecessors. The other was the conjunction of Uranus and Neptune in the same degree of the zodiac. These two planets have a strange effect on the English monarchy and, when they come together in the sky, bring it to a low ebb.

Charles was beheaded on the afternoon of 30 January 1649. The astrologers who recorded the moment set their horoscopes for 2.00 p.m. Like so many other kings, Charles died under the influence of Pluto, which had then reached a very difficult alignment with his birth horoscope. A few days later, on 7 February, the House of Commons resolved to abolish the monarchy itself and on 17 March they took this final step. For eleven long years England was a republic.

CHARLES II
1660–1685

Born at St James's Palace, London on 29 May 1630, with the Sun in Gemini and Moon in Taurus. Succeeded to the throne of England on 30 January 1649, a few days before the monarchy was abolished. Crowned King of Scotland at Scone on 1 January 1651. Proclaimed King of England on 8 May 1660 and crowned at Westminster on 23 April 1661, with the Sun in Capricorn and Moon in Virgo. Died on 6 February 1685 and buried at Westminster.

Charles II is best remembered as one of the great fun-loving English monarchs, much like Henry VIII. If Henry was 'Bluff King Hal', Charles became the 'Merrie Monarch'. His reputation is partly due to the fact that he acknowledged fourteen illegitimate children by ten of his mistresses, but also because the entire country felt immense relief at the collapse of the dour, puritanical Republic.

In fact the horoscopes for his birth and coronation are those of an exceptionally gifted administrator, combining analytical ability with practical skill. His coronation horoscope shows striking similarities with Elizabeth I's birth chart, and he too spent much time out-manoeuvring his enemies in Parliament. Also like Elizabeth, he usually proved the smarter and came out on top.

Charles was born around noon on 29 May 1630 with the Sun in Gemini culminating at its highest point in the sky. This would have been enough to enthuse any optimistic poet and one chronicler thanked God and the stars: 'This year Heaven was liberal to His Majesty in giving him a son to inherit his dominions'. Others were intrigued by the location of the Moon and Venus in Taurus. Both planets were thought to exert a very strong influence when found in this sign, and as Venus was the ruler of love and Taurus indicated great fertility, here lay the foundations of his womanising. These planets were also believed to confer immense good fortune. The poet Robert Herrick penned the 'Pastoral', which was set to music by Nicholas Lanier for presentation to the King:

> 'And that his birth should be more singular,
> At noon of day, was seen a silver star,
> Bright as the wise men's torch, which guided them
> To God's sweet babe, where born at Bethlehem . . .'

The astrologers were confused when, at the age of nineteen, Charles saw his father executed and the monarchy abolished. Yet, with Mars in Leo indicating immense physical courage, Charles never accepted the Republic and always fought against it. He was crowned King of Scotland at Scone on New Year's Day 1651, before fleeing to France. His patience and fortitude were rewarded and when in 1660 Parliament abolished the Republic, he returned in triumph. He entered London on his thirtieth birthday, 29 May 1660. According to John Evelyn, the diarist, the time was 2.00 p.m., and the splendid procession of retainers, soldiers and supporters took seven hours to pass through the city gates.

It seems likely that the time of Charles' entry into London was selected on the basis of astrological advice. The twenty-ninth of May was, of course, his birthday, and that alone was reason enough to celebrate. In addition, every astrologer (indeed every person with the faintest knowledge of the stars) would have known that there was a New Moon and that, falling on the King's birthday, this was extraordinarily auspicious. The suspicion of astrological involvement in the timing of Charles' entry is reinforced by the fact that every important feature of the horoscope was positively helpful.

Unlike his father, Charles II relied on astrological advice at crucial moments, using Elias Ashmole, the founder of the Ashmolean

Museum in Oxford, to help select the most auspicious time for addressing the troublesome House of Commons. On one occasion though, when the French despatched an astrologer to spy on Charles, the King used him instead to pick winners at the horseraces!

Eventually, Charles lived up to the astrologers' expectations and died peacefully in his bed. We can only guess what part their advice played in his success, but it is noticeable that he succeeded where his father, who had rejected astrology, failed.

JAMES II OF ENGLAND AND VII OF SCOTLAND
1685–1689

Born at St James's Palace, London on 15 October 1633, with the Sun in Scorpio and Moon in Leo. Succeeded as King of England, Ireland and Scotland on 6 February 1685 and crowned at Westminster on 23 April 1685, with the Sun and Moon in Taurus. Left England on 23 December 1688 and was deposed on 28 January 1689. Died at St Germain on 6 September 1701.

James II ascended to the throne through one of those accidents which change the course of history. Charles II's Queen, Catherine of Braganza, was unable to bear children, so even though the King had at least fourteen bastards, none was legally entitled to succeed him.

James was born at midnight as the day began with the Sun in Scorpio and both the Moon and Ascendant in Leo, a combination which indicates extraordinary stubbornness. Both signs are known to astrologers as 'fixed', which means that they find it difficult to adapt to changing circumstances. Leo succumbs too often to pride and Scorpio is intensely committed to its chosen beliefs. James' problem was his devout Catholicism and his unshakeable belief that it was his duty to restore England to the Roman Church.

Anthony Ascham, James' old tutor, was an astrologer, so it is likely that he took at least some astrological advice during his political career. His coronation, on 23 April 1685, was arranged to take place on the New Moon, and it seems probable that an astrologer picked the date. However, like his father, Charles I, James believed that kings had a direct line to God and therefore could dispense with ordinary human advice.

Within four years James had offended and alarmed so many of his most important subjects that his daughter Mary and her husband William were invited to take over the throne. They accepted and in December 1688 James fled to France, where he died in 1701. On the night of his death the Full Moon shone close to Saturn, the ancient planet of death. Curiously this alignment was to be repeated two hundred and seventy years and eight months later when another English king, Edward VIII, died in exile in France.

MARY II
1689–1694

Born at St James's Palace, London on 30 April 1662, with the Sun in Taurus and the Moon in Aquarius. Succeeded as Queen of England and Ireland on 23 February 1689 and of Scotland on 11 May 1689. Crowned at Westminster on 11 April 1689, with the Sun and Moon in Taurus. Died on 28 December 1694 and buried at Westminster.

Mary was the eldest surviving child of James II and his first wife, Anne Hyde. She was born at 1.00 a.m. on 30 April 1662 to general disappointment for, inevitably, James, then Duke of York, wanted a son to succeed him. The diarist Samuel Pepys summed up the general mood of anticlimax with the simple words: 'I find nobody pleased'. Mary was born with the Sun in Taurus, indicating a loyal, practical and businesslike disposition. However, this was heavily qualified by the position occupied by the Moon. This powerful planet was in Aquarius and rising over the eastern horizon at the exact moment when Mary came into the world. The Moon was also in a very close alignment with Uranus, a planet strongly connected to revolutionary movements. The entire picture is of a popular and strong-willed character, not afraid to defy convention. Mary was certainly very popular and was widely mourned when she died of smallpox in 1694. She also became the willing vehicle for the Glorious Revolution, the movement which swept James II from power and established parliamentary government in England.

WILLIAM III
1689–1702

Born at The Hague on 4 November 1650, with the Sun in Scorpio and the Moon in Pisces. Succeeded as King of England and Ireland on 23 February 1689 and of Scotland on 11 May 1689. Crowned at Westminster on 11 April 1689, with the Sun and Moon in Taurus. Died on 8 March 1702 and buried at Westminster.

William III was the son of William II, Prince of Orange and Ruler of the Netherlands and Princess Mary of England, daughter of Charles I. This made him the nephew of both Charles II and James II, and the first cousin of his wife Mary II. He was born just one week after his father's death from smallpox, and came into the world at 8.30 p.m. on 4 November 1650 – but whatever joy there might have been at his birth was buried beneath the grief and mourning for his father. In some strange way, William's character reflected the circumstances of his birth, and he was known as a cold and aloof person, unable to show his feelings and on occasion given to cruelty.

William was born with the Sun in Scorpio, and he exhibited the secretive and introverted qualities of this deep sign. Modern astrologers understand that Scorpios often need to be helped to show their feelings. The infant William had no such assistance and withdrew behind a defensive barrier, a mask which belied his inner feelings. His Cancer Ascendant compounded his inhibited emotions; as modern astrologers put it, the sensitive Cancerian Crab retreats inside its hard shell, concealing its depth of feeling.

Born as he was, ten months after the death of Charles I, William's horoscope included the same close alignment of Uranus and Neptune which had brought the monarchy to its lowest ebb. It is interesting that William then came to the throne when another king, James II, was overthrown. Before his coronation he, together with his wife Mary, had to accept the end of the divine rights of kings and the subordination of the monarchy to parliament. But in so doing he removed the crown from the rough and tumble of everyday politics, protecting it against revolution and ensuring its survival to the present day.

The aristocratic conspirators who, in early 1688 resolved to depose James II, invited William to England later that year. He landed on English soil at 9.00 a.m. on 5 November 1688. Interestingly, this was the day after William's birthday, reminding us that Charles II had chosen to return to London on his birthday. Other factors suggest that astrological advice had been taken. We know, for example, that important politicians such as Sir John Trenchard, William's future Secretary of State, were using astrology. It is likely that some consideration was given to the timing of such an important event. Astrologers of the time would have been unaware that the Full Moon a few days earlier was in a very powerful alignment with the revolutionary planet Uranus, suggesting that a great cosmic drama was indeed being played out.

William made his way to London, arriving at 3.00 p.m. on 28 December. He then waited while Parliament went through the complicated procedure of disinheriting James and his heirs, until finally, he and Mary were proclaimed and crowned. Interestingly, they were crowned with revolutionary Uranus strong and exactly aligned with the Moon. The coronation was arranged for the day after the New Moon, one of the most auspicious times of the lunar cycle, again pointing to secret astrological advice.

It is fascinating that at the exact moment that William died, 8.00 a.m. on 18 March 1702, the Ascendant was aligned with the important moments for William's landing and coronation. It's as if British history, at this revolutionary period, was unfolding according to some deep rhythm of growth and decay in the collective psyche. After the trauma of the civil war, which opened as many wounds as it healed, the revolution led by William set Britain on a course towards peaceful political evolution.

ANNE
1702–1714

Born at St James's Palace on 5 February 1665, with the Sun in Aquarius and the Moon in Pisces. Succeeded as Queen of England, Scotland and Ireland on 8 March 1702 and crowned at Westminster on 23 April 1702, with the Sun in Taurus and the Moon in Leo. Died on 1 August 1714 and buried at Westminster.

Queen Anne was the last of the Stuarts, and her twelve-year reign failed to make an impact on the historical imagination. It's as if she provided a mere footnote to the great dramas of the Stuart dynasty. Anne's half-brother, James the 'Old Pretender' and her two nephews Bonnie Prince Charlie, the 'Young Pretender', and Henry Stuart claimed the throne, but never reigned.

She was born at 11.39 a.m. on 5 February 1665, the younger daughter of James, then Duke of York, and his first wife, Anne Hyde. She was then the younger daughter of the King's younger brother, and nobody would have thought that she would ever have become Queen. Her horoscope is an interesting one, though a little impractical. Her Sun was in Aquarius, revealing an independent disposition; her Moon was in Pisces, revealing a sensitive and vulnerable character, and her Ascendant was in Scorpio, indicating intense and secretive emotions. Were Anne to have received modern careers advice she might have been pointed towards the arts or the caring and healing professions. Yet she was not the first junior member of the royal family to be thrust into the limelight, and neither, as it turns out, was she to be the last.

Anne was married to the notoriously dull Prince George of Denmark, of whom Charles II said that he had tried him drunk and tried him sober – and couldn't tell the difference! She had many children, but only one, William, Duke of Gloucester, survived for more than a few years. He died in 1700 at the age of eleven, and the Stuart dynasty was left with no legal heir.

Anne's coronation took place under an extraordinarily powerful alignment involving Mars, which since ancient times had been associated with war. And, appropriately, her reign is remembered not so much for what she did at home, as for what her greatest general accomplished abroad. It was John Churchill, the first Duke of Marlborough, who fulfilled what contemporary astrologers would have called the 'promise' of Anne's coronation horoscope, in his series of brilliant victories over the French, of which the most dramatic was the Battle of Blenheim in 1704. The Stuarts may have been dying out, but the Duke of Marlborough established two great dynasties of commoners, the Churchills and, importantly for the recent history of the royal family, the Spencers.

The Stuart Pretenders

JAMES III OF ENGLAND AND VIII OF SCOTLAND, THE OLD PRETENDER

Born on 10 June 1688 at St James's Palace, London, with the Sun in Gemini and the Moon in Pisces.

James, the 'Old Pretender', spent much of his life claiming to be the true ruler of Britain. Yet it was his birth at about 9.45 a.m. on 10 June 1688, and the prospect of the heir to the throne being brought up a Roman Catholic, that prompted the nobles of England to expel his father, James II. James III, as he called himself, was born with the Sun on the exact dividing line between Gemini and Cancer, and the Moon in sensitive Pisces; not good for a prospective ruler. It is more surprising, though, that he was born with a powerful Mars–Pluto alignment, exactly like a series of Scottish Stuarts who were unable to rule: James II, James IV, James V and Mary, Queen of Scots. The same two planets were also linked at the execution of Mary, Queen of Scots and Charles I, and at the birth of James' father, James II of England and VII of Scotland. Unfortunately for James, the planets were linked yet again at the moment chosen for his proclamation in Scotland, 19 August 1745. James was recognised as King in Scotland until the disaster of the Battle of Culloden in 1746. After that the Stuart cause was effectively dead.

CHARLES III, BONNIE PRINCE CHARLIE

Born in Rome on 31 December 1720, with the Sun in Capricorn and the Moon in Aquarius.

Bonnie Prince Charlie, the 'Young Pretender', is one of the most romantic figures from British royal history, perhaps because everyone loves a loser! Certainly, there is nothing to suggest that Charlie would have made a competent king, even if he was no worse than the Hanoverians. Capricorn and Aquarius, his Sun and Moon signs, have many strengths, but in combination they often undermine one another; Capricorn is practical and businesslike but Aquarius follows its ideals and independent course. In part, this contradiction explains the Prince's erratic behaviour during the rebellion of 1745–6, when he attempted to seize the throne for his father, the 'Old Pretender'. After a very determined start to the campaign, during which he advanced as far south as Derby, he unexpectedly retreated to Scotland, losing the initiative and costing his father the crown. Perhaps fitting for such a romantic figure, the Prince was born with Cancer in the Ascendant, one of the most romantic of signs.

HENRY IX

Born in Paris at 11.00 am on 6 March 1725, with the Sun in Pisces and the Moon in Sagittarius.

Henry IX, as he called himself, was the last of the Stuarts. He inherited the claim to the throne after the death of his elder brother, Bonnie Prince Charlie, but had little genuine interest in recovering the throne. When George III offered him a pension for life in return for an agreement not to press his claim, Henry readily agreed. This was a wise move, for his Sun in mystical Pisces and Moon in Sagittarius, the sign of philosophy, made him more fitted for a life in the church than in politics. When the Pope made him a cardinal he found a role more suited to him than potential leader of Scottish rebellion. When Henry died on 31 July 1801 the Stuart dynasty, which had known such drama and such tragedy, finally came to an end.

The
Houses
of
Hanover
and
Saxe-Coburg-Gotha

HOUSES OF HANOVER
AND SAXE-COBURG-GOTHA

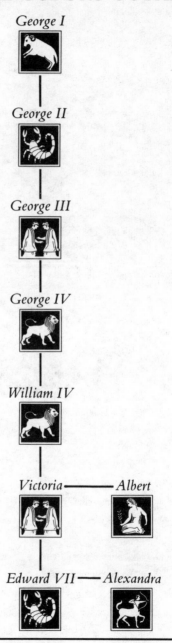

The Houses of Hanover
and Saxe-Coburg-Gotha

GEORGE I
1714–1727

Born at Hanover on 28 March 1660, with the Sun in Aries and the Moon in Libra. Succeeded as King of Great Britain and Ireland on 1 August 1714 and crowned at Westminster on 20 October 1714. Died on 12 June 1727 and buried at Hanover.

George I was a great-grandson of James I and was Queen Anne's second cousin. Like William III, he was brought over to England to do the bidding of the English aristocracy, and was therefore a hostage to fortune. His lack of real power was exacerbated by the fact that he spoke only a few words of English and was more interested in developments in Hanover, which he ruled as Elector, than in England.

George was born with the Sun in Aries, normally an indication of considerable self-will. On this basis alone we might have expected him to interfere in English affairs and attempt to overcome the constitutional hurdles placed in his path. However, two very important factors in his horoscope indicated that he was prepared to do anything for a quiet life: his Sun was in a powerful aspect with Neptune, planet of dreams, and his Moon was in diplomatic, beauty-loving Libra. In general, he was content to let his ministers do whatever they wanted, and it was during his reign that Sir Robert Walpole became the first Prime Minister, virtually ruling the country on the King's behalf. George's militant Arien character found expression only in trivial matters, such as the long feud he initiated with his son, the future George II. Arguments between Hanoverian kings and their sons were henceforth to be something of an eighteenth-century tradition.

When the time came for George's coronation the Sun was in Scorpio. Yet what was more important was that it was once again in a difficult alignment with Neptune, this time indicating the potential for corruption and intrigue. It is therefore appropriate that his reign was marked by the South Sea Bubble, one of the worst financial scandals until modern times, and the constant conspiracies centred around the household of George, the King's son.

George I was born under a close Venus–Saturn alignment, indicating a rather restricted romantic life; he was the opposite, we might say, of the debauched Charles II. His marriage to his cousin Sophia was dissolved in 1694 after twelve years, and from then until her death in 1726 she was confined to house arrest in the castle of Ahlden. George was also renowned for his two mistresses, who were mocked in London for being extraordinarily ugly, one being small and round, the other tall and thin.

Although George can be regarded as the first king of the new constitutional age, in which monarchs served their ministers rather than the other way round, he died under very similar patterns to many of his medieval predecessors. In 1727 Pluto, planet of the underworld, had reached a difficult relationship with the Sun, and George's uninspired reign finally drew to a close.

GEORGE II
1727–1760

Born at Herrenhausern, Hanover, on 10 November 1683, with the Sun in Scorpio. Succeeded as King of Great Britain and Ireland on 12 June 1727 and crowned on 11 October 1727 at Westminster. Died on 25 October 1760 and buried at Westminster.

George II was born with the Sun in Scorpio, a sign with a reputation for great secrecy. His tendency to keep his feelings to himself may be one reason why his reign is so easily forgotten. But then, his interest in government was minimal and his political skills thoroughly un–distinguished. This is not to say that his horoscope was a weak one, for he was born with Mars, planet of war, and Pluto, planet of the underworld, in a very difficult relationship. This is an alignment associated with impulsive violence, and in the King's personal life it produced a deep desire for conflict which found expression in his prolonged and bitter feud with his son, Frederick, Prince of Wales. He also, at the Battle of Dettingen in 1743, achieved the distinction of being the last reigning British monarch to lead his subjects in the field. The same violent Mars–Pluto alignment was again strong in 1745 when Bonnie Prince Charlie (James II's grandson) claimed the throne on behalf of the Stuarts. The rebellion was crushed in 1746 with all the savagery associated with Mars and Pluto at their worst, and Scottish culture was ruthlessly destroyed.

The most significant developments of George's reign took place overseas. Notably, Clive's victory at Plassey in 1757 and Wolfe's at Quebec in 1759 paved the way for British rule in India and Canada. These triumphs took place as part of the Seven Years War, in effect a general European war, and were therefore indicated by planetary patterns which went beyond George's horoscope. In particular, Uranus and Pluto, whose one hundred and twenty-seven-year cycle had reached a critical phase, indicated a shift in the historical balance of power and an important move towards the supremacy achieved by Britain in the nineteenth century.

George's emotional life was dominated by Venus, planet of love, in secretive Scorpio in a very close relationship with the Sun. This alignment was partially responsible for his irrational approach to government and his unpredictable nature. However, it was the Mars–Pluto pattern which summed up the major events of his reign. People born under this planetary feature can be both the perpetrators and victims of confrontation, and while George could be irascible and impatient, he was also bullied by his Queen, Caroline of Ansbach, who supported her own political favourites. In 1751, also under the influence of Mars and Pluto, Frederick, Prince of Wales, died. When the King himself died on 25 October 1760, he left his grandson to ascend the throne as George III.

GEORGE III
1760–1820

Born at Norfolk House, St James's Square, on 4 June 1738, with the Sun in Gemini and Moon in Gemini. Succeeded as King of Great Britain and Ireland on 25 October 1760 and crowned at Westminster on 22 September 1761. Died on 29 January 1820 and buried at Westminster.

George William Frederick, the eldest son of Frederick Lewis, Prince of Wales and his Princess, Augusta of Saxe–Gotha, was born at 7.30 a.m. on 4 June 1738. As George III, he ascended the throne on 25 October 1760 and was crowned just over one year later, on 22 September 1761.

History has not been kind to George, and he is remembered as a dull, domesticated and plodding figure who lost the thirteen American colonies and then went mad. His nickname, 'Farmer George', and his reputation as a boring family man is strangely evoked in the lunar positions at his succession and coronation, Taurus and Cancer. However, George's birth horoscope gives a very different picture. At the moment he was born, Sagittarius was in the Ascendant and the Sun and Moon were in Gemini. It is difficult to come into the world with astrological indicators which are more lively than this. We can imagine the young George bursting with ideas, asking perpetual questions and experimenting with new theories and lifestyles. He became a patron of the arts and sciences and his collection of books laid the foundation for the future British Library.

It was inevitable that Geminian George would take a keen interest in government. As soon as he succeeded to the throne he reacted against the pattern set since the Glorious Revolution and the overthrow of James II in 1689, and attempted to restore the monarch's personal rule. He had too many policies and proposals of his own and was completely unable to stand aside while his ministers ran the country. However, although the combination of Gemini and Sagittarius is excellent when dealing with ideas, it is less so when faced with practical realities. When the American colonists began to complain about excessive taxation, which to George seemed like a good way of raising revenue, he failed to see their point of view. Under a powerful relationship from visionary Neptune to the Sun, he was driven by a dream of the future, rather than an understanding of the present, and his treatment of the Americans was characterised by incompetence. The American rebellion in 1776, and the British recognition of their victory in 1783, put paid to George's personal rule and his influence began to wane. After 1811 he lapsed into bouts of madness, and from then until 1820 his son, George, ruled as Prince Regent.

On 1 January 1801 George became the first monarch of the new United Kingdom of Great Britain and Ireland. The Union came into legal effect at midnight, and at 3.15 p.m. that afternoon George was proclaimed King of the new realm with due ceremony. Interestingly, the new state came into existence hours after a Full Moon. This might not have been of significance had George not been born under a New Moon, and succeeded to the throne of Britain under a Full Moon. Finally on 29 January 1820, he died under a Full Moon.

GEORGE IV
1820–1830

Born in St James's Palace on 12 August 1762, with the Sun in Leo and Moon in Taurus. Succeeded as King of Great Britain and Ireland on 29 January 1820 and crowned at Westminster on 19 July 1821. Died on 25 June 1830 and buried at Windsor.

George IV, the eldest son of George III, was born at about 7.30 a.m. on 12 August 1762. Like Charles II and Henry VIII, he is remembered as a pleasure-loving monarch, yet his unpleasant and decadent behaviour has deprived him of the fond memories bequeathed to royal history by Charles. George could be as unpleasant as Henry VIII, yet, unlike Henry, had no political skills, nor are there any reasons of state to excuse his treatment of his wives. Interestingly, all three kings were born with the Ascendant in Virgo and George also shared a Taurean Moon with Charles II. The common link between their horoscopes is a love of sensual pleasure typical of the 'Earth' signs, Taurus, Virgo and Capricorn. Virgos have a reputation for prudery which results from a misunderstanding of their basic character, which is to pick and choose and criticise. In George, no less than in Henry and Charles, Virgo in the Ascendant played a central role in reinforcing the discrimination which made him a leader of fashion.

George's Sun was in Leo, a sign famed for its theatrical aspirations. Due to the Sun's difficult connections with Mars and the Moon, his character veered towards the negative sides of the Leonine personality; vanity, pride, obstinacy and arrogance. This is not to say that he couldn't be likeable, or that his patronage of the arts has not left us with legacies such as the National Gallery and the Brighton Pavilion, but his political instincts were based on a typically Leonine refusal to compromise.

A fascinating feature of George's horoscope was the close connection between the Sun and Neptune, planet of dreams. These two planets were located on the edge of a sector known as the twelfth house, and psychologically this alignment drives people to one of two extremes. Either they become mystical visionaries or they veer towards total decadence; in some cases they combine the two. George's tutor had obviously spotted George's split personality when he predicted that the Prince, then aged fifteen, would become either the most accomplished gentleman or blackguard in Europe.

George's reputation as a blackguard is largely due to the way he treated his wives. His first marriage, in 1785, was an illegal union with Catholic widow Mrs Maria Fitzherbert. Although the relationship continued until 1805, in 1795 George was formally married to his cousin, Caroline of Brunswick. He hated his new Princess and confined his attention to his mistresses, of whom there were at least eighteen. Caroline was born on 17 May 1768 with the Sun in Taurus and the Ascendant in Libra. Both these signs are ruled by Venus, and when found together they often denote the desire to avoid unnecessary confrontation. Between 1814 and 1820 she lived abroad, but when George succeeded to the throne in 1820, she had come under the influence of Mars, an altogether more vigorous planet. She decided that she would, after all, like to be Queen and in 1821 returned to England with the intention of attending the coronation. George, however, had instituted divorce proceedings. The cabinet gave him permission to end the marriage but Parliament refused and the monarchy was reduced to its lowest ebb since its abolition in 1649. George was profoundly unpopular, due to his continued outrageous extravagance during the economic recession which followed the Napoleonic wars. Caroline, on the other hand, partly because of the Prince's treatment of her, had the nation's sympathy; she was cheered in the streets of London while her husband was booed and jeered.

George must obviously bear personal responsibility for dragging the monarchy down, but the crisis of 1820–1 offers the clearest evidence of a deeper cycle operating in the affairs of the English monarchy. Once again, Uranus and Neptune had come together in the zodiac, completing one cycle and initiating another. These planets were not to meet again until 1992–3.

WILLIAM IV
1830–1837

Born at Buckingham Palace on 21 August 1765, with the Sun in Leo and Moon in Libra. Succeeded as King of Great Britain and Ireland on 25 June 1830 and crowned at Westminster on 8 September 1831. Died on 20 June 1837 and buried at Windsor.

William IV, the third son of George III, was born at 3.00 a.m. on 21 August 1765. In some respects his horoscope resembled his elder brother's – like George IV, he was a Leo. He was also born with a Leo Ascendant, which all adds up to a thoroughly theatrical character. The Moon in Libra gave him a pleasant disposition, although as a royal Prince he was not above losing his temper to get his own way. Compared to George IV, though, William was a thoroughly likeable character and did much to improve the monarchy's image. Like George III, he was respected for his discretion and, after his marriage in 1818, his exemplary private life.

In other circumstances, William's horoscope would have taken him towards work in the theatre, perhaps as a showman or impresario. Yet he expressed his dramatic talents through his unofficial wife, Mrs Jordan, an actress. William lived with Mrs Jordan for twenty-one years, from 1790 to 1811, and the couple produced ten children, the FitzClarences.

Interestingly, William's horoscope also included a revolutionary alignment: the Moon and Uranus occupied opposite degrees of the zodiac. This combination of planets produces sudden twists of fate in private affairs, and often pushes people born under its sway towards radical politics. The twist of fate worked out when William un-expectedly became heir to the throne, his two elder brothers having failed to produce a surviving heir. In his politics William was as opposed to reform as was the Leonine George IV, but soon after his succession he realised that constitutional change was inevitable. When George died, on 25 June 1830, public opinion had swung firmly behind the view that the monarch might be permitted to reign, but never to rule. Eighteen-thirty was a revolutionary year in Europe, and across the channel in France Charles X was overthrown. William bowed to history and in 1832 agreed to the Great Reform Bill, a reform of the franchise which, although limited, acted as a safety valve, channelling the pressure for revolution into peaceful directions.

William was crowned on 8 September 1831 under a profoundly threatening alignment between the Moon and Pluto, from which we can deduce that when he came to the throne violent revolution was a near certainty. That he compromised and defused the coming disaster is a tribute to his wisdom. In the event, reform was accomplished with no more than a scattering of provincial riots.

The question of the personality differences between the Leonine brothers, George IV and William IV, can be answered in part by their contrasting circumstances. While George was heir to the throne, William lived in near poverty. It was even believed that Mrs Jordan probably supported him and their ten children on her wages as an actress. By the time William became King the potential revealed in his birth horoscope had been shaped and moulded by a lifetime spent living on a naval officer's income. On ascending the throne his financial prudence even led him to doubt whether a coronation was necessary. In the event he was crowned with the Sun in Virgo, a fitting position for such a careful man. When he died and bequeathed the throne to his niece, Victoria, he had saved the monarchy from extinction.

QUEEN VICTORIA AND PRINCE ALBERT

VICTORIA
1837–1901

Born in Kensington Palace at 4.15 a.m. on 24 May 1819, with the Sun and Moon in Gemini. Succeeded as Queen of Great Britain and Ireland on 20 June 1837 and crowned at Westminster on 28 June 1838. Died at Osborne, Isle of Wight on 22 January 1901 and buried at Frogmore, Windsor.

ALBERT

Born at Rosenau at 6.00 a.m. on 26 August 1819, with the Sun and Ascendant in Virgo and the Moon in Scorpio. Died in 1861.

Queen Victoria must be counted amongst the most remarkable individuals of the modern era. True, she was not the only ruler to have given her name to an age, for Elizabeth I had already given her name to her times – the Elizabethan Era. Yet Victoria is associated with an entire culture, a set of principles, a code of behaviour and an outlook on life, as well as the century of Britain's greatness. In many respects she was the mother of the modern age. It is therefore not surprising to discover that her horoscope was an extremely powerful one which, in almost any walk of life, would have obliged her to attract attention to herself.

Victoria was born at 4.15 a.m. on 25 May 1819 in Kensington Palace, with the Sun rising over the eastern horizon. This was enough to confer on her a powerful, commanding character. Symbolically, we may say that the child born at dawn comes into the world prepared to make a fresh start and challenge the existing order; experience shows that such people often have a need to take charge. But that was not all. She was born only hours after a New Moon, indicating that the Moon was also exactly placed on the eastern horizon. This is a powerful indication of deep maternal instincts. Indeed, people with the Moon born in this position often exert an almost universal motherly role, taking people under their wing at home, in the community and at work. This remarkable planetary alignment is an extremely potent symbol of Victoria's role, both as the founder of the modern concept of the royal family, and as the mother of almost every European dynasty.

The Sun and Moon were both in Gemini at the time of her birth, and the fact that they were rising over the eastern horizon means that her Ascendant was in Gemini as well. This is a remarkable configuration which occurs only for about thirty minutes every year. A configuration as exact as Victoria's would occur even less frequently. She was therefore the ultimate Geminian – lively, witty, humorous and full of ideas. In Victoria's case, Gemini's reputation as a writer is confirmed by the statistical research conducted in the 1950s by the French statistician Michel Gauquelin. He demonstrated that great writers tend to be born with the Moon in the position which it occupied at Victoria's birth. Was Victoria a great writer? In the 1980s an intriguing piece of computer research was done by an American academic, comparing Victoria's journals with Lewis Carroll's sentence structure. The results led him to conclude that Victoria was the secret author of *Alice in Wonderland* and *Alice Through the Looking Glass*! Whether or not we are inclined to take such a claim seriously, it can certainly be said that Victoria had a gift for communicating via the written word, as we would expect from a triple-Geminian. She was a copious and dramatic correspondent, and kept in touch with her royal relatives all over Europe by letter, often weekly, sometimes even daily.

Surviving archive film of Victoria shows her Geminian manner even more vividly than her surviving writings. Even in the 1890s, when she was in her seventies, she had the swift, decisive movements of the Mercurial individual. She was also quick to form attachments, and her sudden enthusiasm for Prince Albert, with whom she fell in love on their second meeting, was typical. Her effusive love for her first Prime Minister Lord Melbourne and her similar enthusiasm for Disraeli, as well as for her mysterious Scottish companion John Brown, were all revealed in the poetic manner of the true Geminian. Her writings to them reveal clearly her joy and love of those to whom she felt especially close.

Victoria's coronation horoscope was also extraordinarily lively. It is true that the Moon, which symbolised the Queen as the mother of the nation, was in Virgo, and this is precisely the position we would expect in the horoscope of someone who famously claimed, 'We are not amused.' Yet when we look at the Moon's relationship to the other planets, such as expansive Jupiter, revolutionary Uranus, energetic Mars and witty, intellectual Mercury, we see the potential for a truly inspiring reign. Any baby with such a horoscope would be destined to make a most unusual mark on the world. To an extent, the coronation horoscope describes Victoria's function as Queen rather than private individual. Such was her instinctive skill in forging dynastic alliances that, by the time of her death, through the marriages of her nine children, virtually every European crowned head or heir presumptive was one of her grandchildren. In the country as a whole she presided over the unprecedented spread of technology and industrialisation, as well as the most intense wave of social reform ever seen. Internationally, Britain became the leader of the world's largest ever empire. Yet the horoscope must also say something about Victoria as a person, and while she could be fussy, her true goal was the pursuit of only the highest standards.

So why do we have such a dour image of Victoria as the severe old woman in black who instigated an era of unremitting puritanism? Geminians have a reputation for sudden changes of mind, for blowing hot and cold. As a triple Geminian, Victoria went through a complete transformation, and it was Albert's death in 1861, when she was aged forty-two, that plunged her into the gloom and bouts of seclusion which were to dominate her life until her death, forty years later.

To understand why Victoria's dramatic change of life was so intense and unrelenting we have to look at other factors in her horoscope. As she was born shortly before George IV's marriage crisis, her horoscope contained the same Uranus–Neptune alignment which brought the monarchy to a low ebb in 1820–1. Victoria was the queen who rebuilt the monarchy, but she also contained within herself the capacity to damage that very institution. In addition, Uranus and Neptune were in a close relationship with Saturn and Pluto. When activated, these powerful planets bring confrontation with the deepest and most disturbing elements in life, including death. (It is as well to remember that Victoria was born at a turbulent moment in British history, and only three months after her birth the Peterloo massacre took place at a parliamentary reform meeting in Manchester.) When Albert died it was these planets, rather than her Geminian configuration, which were activated. From then on Victoria ceased to be a young vivacious queen and became an old woman shrouded in mourning. So thorough was her seclusion that her popularity slumped and the government began to fear the rise of republicanism. She emerged only in 1887. By then Pluto had moved into Gemini, exactly over her Sun and Moon. This time it pulled her back from the depths and returned her to the land of the living.

The romance between Victoria and Prince Albert has achieved legendary status as the ideal royal relationship. Although Albert was fond of the Queen, in reality it seems that she was the one who was deeply in love, while he was more inclined to play loyal husband and dutiful consort. Albert was born shortly after dawn on 26 August 1819, the son of Ernst, Duke of Saxe-Coburg-Saalfeld. Albert was a

Virgo; in fact he was a double-Virgo, for the Sun and Ascendant were both in this sign. From this it appears that his relationship with Victoria was one of intense mutual fascination, but, on occasion, equally intense irritation. Gemini and Virgo are both said to be 'ruled' by Mercury, the planet of the intellect, and Victoria and Albert shared an equally obsessive desire to analyse information and organise the world in line with their precise preconceptions. Each would have relied on the other, and Albert would have valued Victoria's greater flexibility of thought while she relied on his more developed practical sensibilities. Yet there would have been occasions when she might have found him a mite restricting, and he would have grown impatient with her occasionally poor grasp of the real world, as he saw it.

Albert has a reputation for being a strict puritan and moralist, yet his horoscope tells a slightly different story. He was born with the Moon in Scorpio, a sign renowned for its secretive instincts. Scorpio and Virgo together add up to great shyness and a tendency to protect deep vulnerability behind a still and often formal façade. Albert was neither a snob nor a prude; rather, he was a deeply private man whose public manner was widely misunderstood. He performed his public duties well, supporting the arts, sciences and social reform, and most notably organising the Great Exhibition in 1851. But he insisted on keeping his personal life to himself.

When Victoria died at 6.30 p.m. on 22 January 1901, the door was closed on the nineteenth century, and a new chapter opened. Death came peacefully, just a day after a New Moon, which formed an easy and harmonious relationship with her horoscope. Uranus and Neptune, the regulators of monarchy, were at the peak of their cycle. As if by some great celestial conspiracy the British crown, while its actual power had diminished, now reigned over the greatest empire in the history of the world.

KING EDWARD VII AND PRINCESS ALEXANDRA

EDWARD VII
1901–1910

Born at Buckingham Palace at 10.48 a.m. on 9 November 1841, with the Sun in Scorpio and the Moon in Virgo. Succeeded as King of Great Britain and Emperor of India on 22 January 1901, and crowned at Westminster on 9 August 1902. Died at Buckingham Palace on 6 May 1910 and buried at Windsor.

ALEXANDRA

Born in Copenhagen on 1 December 1844, with the Sun in Sagittarius and Moon in Leo.

With Edward VII, Britain once again acquired a decadent, pleasure-loving monarch. He was born with the Sun in Scorpio, and even in the 1860s astrologers had him marked out as a *bon viveur* and a sensualist. The belief that Scorpios are 'sexy' is a misunderstanding of Scorpio's close relationship with the reproductive organs in medieval medical astrology. Still, in Edward's case this contradiction seemed to fit, and nineteenth-century astrologers were content to give such a slant to his horoscope. We know that he had many mistresses, including the music-hall star Lillie Langtry and the actress Sarah Bernhardt, and rumours abound of illegitimate children, although none were acknowledged.

Edward was born on 9 November 1841. The official bulletin issued that day announced that 'The Queen was safely delivered of a Prince this morning at 48 minutes past 10 o'clock'. At that precise moment Sagittarius was in the Ascendant, rising over the eastern horizon. It is in the combination of this adventurous happy-go-lucky sign with the intense passions of Scorpio that we find the origin of his love of sensual pleasures. Edward was an enthusiast of sport and outdoor pursuits, which is a typically Sagittarian trait. But in Scorpio we find skill in the art of human manipulation, and each of his sexual conquests would have been treated as a personal triumph, much like an athlete crossing the finishing line.

Life was not all fun, however. He was born with Saturn exactly rising over the eastern horizon. Any planet in this position has a profound significance on an individual's life and character. In Edward's case, we may say that he took his pleasures seriously. Looking more closely at his horoscope, we see that Saturn was in an exact alignment with the Moon, which for him symbolised his mother, Victoria. For Edward, the major obstacle was therefore Victoria herself, who disapproved of his lifestyle, saw him as a potential rival (with the Sun and Moon on her Ascendant Victoria could brook no opposition), and stood between him and the throne.

As Saturn moves around the zodiac it presents many difficulties, but only after challenges have been met does it confer eventual rewards. In 1871 Saturn returned to the place which it occupied at Edward's birth and he was confronted by his first crisis. During the wave of republicanism which built up during Victoria's long mourning for her beloved Albert, Edward was first of all accused of adultery in a celebrated divorce case and then almost died of typhoid. At its second return to this same position in 1901, Edward finally ascended the throne, assuming the Saturnine role for which he had been born.

Aside from his personal life, Edward's reign contained little of wider significance. In international affairs it is probably chiefly remembered for the Entente Cordiale, the ceremonial ending of nine hundred years of enmity and war with France. For an astrological understanding of this peaceful event we should look back to Edward's succession horoscope and compare it to the horoscope for William the Conqueror's invasion, the event which drove the two countries into historic rivalry. Appropriately, we find Venus, ancient planet of peace, powerfully placed and in a strong relationship with the Sun at William's coronation. It is as if the time had finally come for the two nations to begin to cooperate rather than compete.

The date of Edward's coronation was apparently determined by the society astrologer Count Louis Hamon, otherwise known as Cheiro. The ninth of August was picked according to simple principles, but did in fact contain powerful portents of peace, and these Cheiro would have noticed on double-checking his calculations. The Moon and Venus, ruling peace, were in a simple astrological alignment known as a 'mutual reception', which had been a mainstay of the medieval astrologers' royal work. In Edward's case, this meant that Venus was in the sign of Cancer (ruled by the Moon), and the Moon was in the sign of Libra (ruled by Venus). The effect was to strengthen both planets and give the King his nickname, 'Edward the Peacemaker'.

Edward's Queen, Alexandra, was born on 1 December 1844, with the Sun in Sagittarius and the Moon in Leo. On this basis alone she is revealed as a competitive, fun-loving and adventurous soul and, in any circumstances, more than a match for her womanising husband! Although Edward is remembered as a *bon viveur* and chronic adulterer, Alexandra was not one to play the neglected wife. It was said that her youthful charm persuaded Victoria to accept her as a suitable daughter-in-law, and when she did withdraw from Edward's lively social life it was only because of illness. At the time the public felt sorry for the Queen, who retained enormous popularity. In private, however, she was more than capable of standing up for herself.

The major tragedy of Edward and Alexandra's life was the death, in 1892, of their son and heir, Prince Albert Victor Christian Edward. At the time, Eddie, as he was known, was regarded as anything but monarchical material. He was dreamy, dull and seemingly un-interested in anything except enjoying himself; a life of dissipation took its toll on his health. Rarely has there been a case of an heir to the throne being more grievously misunderstood. The Prince's horo-scope revealed two very important personality traits. Firstly, with the Sun and Moon in businesslike Capricorn and the Ascendant in practical Virgo he found it difficult to do anything which lacked a practical purpose. Secondly, with his Sun and Moon in the most creative part of his horoscope, he was an artist. In the 1990s a job in the theatre would have been ideal, but poor young Eddie had the misfortune to be born out of his time. As the heir to the throne he was never given a role of his own, but had he become King, he would have surprised everyone by performing his tasks with all the skill of an accomplished actor.

The House of Windsor

HOUSE OF WINDSOR

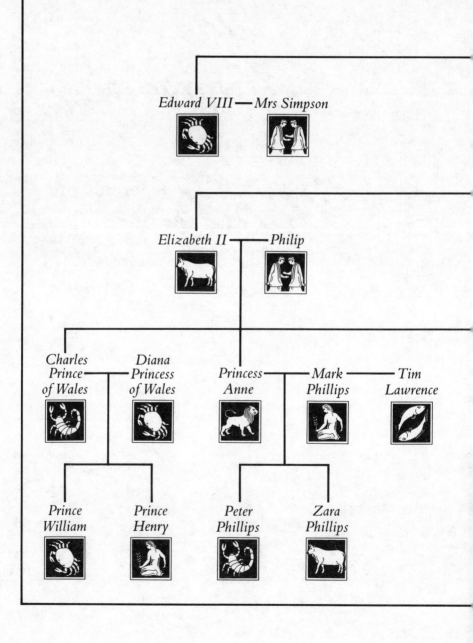

Edward VIII — Mrs Simpson

Elizabeth II — Philip

Charles Prince of Wales — Diana Princess of Wales

Princess Anne — Mark Phillips — Tim Lawrence

Prince William

Prince Henry

Peter Phillips

Zara Phillips

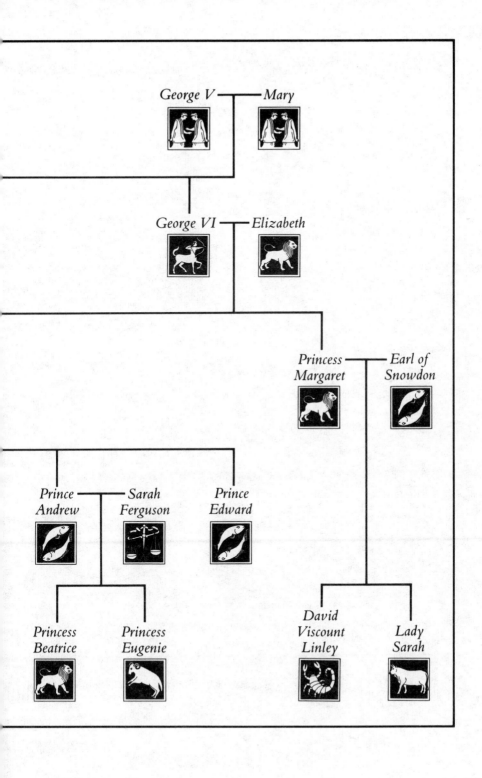

The House of Windsor

KING GEORGE V AND QUEEN MARY

GEORGE V
1910–1936

Born at Marlborough House, London at 1.18 a.m. on 3 June 1865, with the Sun in Gemini and Moon in Libra. Succeeded as King of Great Britain and Ireland and Emperor of India on 6 May 1910 and crowned at Westminster on 22 June 1911, with the Sun in Gemini and the Moon in Taurus. Died on 20 January 1936 and buried at Windsor.

MARY

Born in London at 11.59 p.m. on 26 May 1867, with the Sun in Gemini, Moon in Pisces and Ascendant in Aquarius.

George V is remembered more for the political and international upheavals which took place during his reign than for either his personality or private life. He steered the monarchy through the crisis over Irish home rule and the 1916 rising, the First World War, the revolutions of 1917–18, the Great Crash of 1929 and the rise of Hitler and Mussolini. George coped skilfully with the many pressures he encountered, including the Liberal reforms of the House of Lords and the first Labour government in the 1920s and, had he not been King, he might have made an excellent diplomat.

His horoscope was that of a genial, optimistic individual, easy to get on with and happy to talk to anyone, whether rich or poor, male or female, black or white. In the class-ridden context of the early twentieth century this made him somewhat unusual. In other circumstances, George would no doubt have been salesman of the year, and his reputation as a rather dull king is purely the result of his dutiful attempt to fulfil the role to which he was born.

He had the Sun of an exceptionally inquisitive and talkative Gemini, and his Moon in charming Libra, and Jupiter at the very summit of his chart. Such a combination endowed him with this strong genial streak. His rising sign, Aries, added a healthy dose of aggression, tempered by a delicate Neptune, enabling him to sense the right time to assert himself and, alternately, the correct moment to give way. If George might have made an excellent salesman, he nonetheless also had the horoscope of a potential bankrupt! In the event, it was the western world as a whole which plunged into the Great Depression of 1929, while George did much to lay the foundations for the royal family's current wealth.

George became heir to the throne after the untimely death of his elder brother Prince Albert, in 1892. He found himself in a similar position to Henry VIII, whose elder brother Arthur had also died before he had the chance to ascend the throne. Just as Henry had inherited Arthur's wife, Catherine of Aragon, so George inherited his brother's fiancée, his second cousin, Mary of Teck. Unlike Henry and Catherine, George and Mary formed an ideal partnership.

Mary was born just before midnight on 26 May 1867, with a horoscope which was broadly sensitive, thoughtful and with a stroke of originality. Her Moon was in Pisces in a very close relationship to Jupiter, indicating a soft and sensitive soul, capable of great generosity. Her Ascendant was in Aquarius, indicating just a touch of eccentricity and disregard for convention and, like George, she had the Sun in Gemini. Both George and Mary have a reputation for being cold with their children and are blamed for Edward VIII's short and disastrous reign and George VI's shyness and speech impediment. We have to remember, though, that then, as now, certain customs dictated the upbringing of the aristocracy, and Mary simply acted towards her children in the socially accepted manner. George was born with the Moon exactly setting over the western horizon. In a woman's horoscope this reveals profound maternal powers, but in a man's it usually reveals the search for a wife who will fulfil a motherly role. Mary was also born with a powerful Saturn, like her husband's father Edward, and George found in her a figure to be relied on. She had a deep sense of duty and for George she was a rock in an unstable world.

When George died on 20 January 1936 the planetary indications were highly contradictory. The Sun's alignment with Pluto and Uranus suggested, appropriately, confrontation and loss. Yet the Moon was in a position which can only be described as optimistic and outgoing. This was the legacy inherited by Edward VIII.

KING EDWARD VIII AND MRS SIMPSON

EDWARD VIII
1936

Born at White Lodge, Richmond Park, at 9.55 p.m. on 23 June 1894, with the Sun in Cancer and Moon in Pisces. Succeeded as King of Great Britain, Ireland and the British Dominions beyond the Seas, Emperor of India on 20 January 1936 and abdicated on 11 December 1936. Died in Paris on 28 May 1972 and buried at Windsor.

MRS SIMPSON

Born in Blue Ridge Summit, Pennsylvania, at 7.00 a.m. on 19 June 1896, with the Sun in Gemini, Moon in Libra and Ascendant in Cancer.

Edward VIII was not the first king to abdicate; Edward II and Richard II had both stepped down, as had Mary, Queen of Scots. However, he was the first monarch in British history to renounce the throne voluntarily. Curiously, he was born with Saturn, a planet which often brings promising careers to an untimely end, in the same degree of the zodiac as a number of other heirs who were never crowned – including Prince Albert who died in 1892, and Prince Charles, Charles I's eldest son, who died in infancy.

Like his mother, Edward was born with the Moon in sensitive Pisces and independent Aquarius in the Ascendant. In a horoscope such as this an astrologer would look for the signs of self-discipline which encouraged Mary (who had similar planetary alignments) to be diligent in performing her duty. Edward possessed no such sturdy astrological features. Instead his Sun was in Cancer and this, combined with his Piscean Moon, gave him one overriding priority – to follow his instincts. His sensitivity to the suffering of his fellow man, shown in his sympathy for the unemployed during the depression, accounted for much of his public popularity. It also resulted in his being regarded with suspicion by many members of the establishment. His love for Wallis Simpson, which sprang from exactly the same planetary alignments, eventually cost him his throne. Many have doubted Edward's love for Mrs Simpson, but from an astrological point of view, this question is irrelevant. Edward was born under planetary alignments which predisposed him to sacrifice all for love, and Wallis Simpson fitted the bill.

Mrs Simpson was born at 7.00 a.m. on 19 June 1896, in the small town of Blue Ridge Summit, Pennsylvania – at least that is the authorised version. It is quite possible that her birth details were later falsified, although her published horoscope is based on the time as given. Wallis was born with the Sun in talkative Gemini, the Ascendant in romantic Cancer and the Moon in charming Libra, not a bad combination for someone whose adult life was spent gracing one aristocratic salon after another. When we consider the nature of Wallis' relationship with Edward, it is particularly strange that they are completely lacking in the close astrological patterns which normally indicate marriage. The closest we come to any sort of compatibility is in their birthdays – she was born on 19 June, he on 23 June. But even this made her a Gemini and him a Cancerian, which indicates that they were not naturally drawn to each other. Instead, Wallis' horoscope related to the various important dynastic horoscopes. The following patterns are the strongest:

* When King George III was proclaimed the first King of the United Kingdom, at 3.15 p.m. on 1 January 1801, the Moon was at 27° in Cancer.
* When the royal family adopted the name Windsor on 17 July 1917 the Midheaven (the fourth most important degree in any horoscope after the Sun, Moon and Ascendant) was in exactly the opposite degree, 27° of Capricorn.
* When Wallis was born the Ascendant was at 27° in Cancer.

These are precisely the astrological patterns we find connecting the horoscopes of people who fall in love. This gives us a deep insight into the nature of Wallis' fascination for Edward: she had fallen in love with the idea of being Queen. This need not diminish the strength of her feelings for him, but unconsciously, what he represented for her was inextricably linked, in her eyes, with him as a man. The pattern was confirmed when Edward succeeded to the throne, for on 20 January 1936 the Sun was at 29° in Capricorn and in an exact opposition to Pluto at 26° of Cancer. This was an alignment indicating deep conflict. Connecting these planetary aspects with horoscopes for other members of the dynasty, it seems that the preordained issue was to be the succession to the throne. Wallis Simpson, the divorcee who was barred by the Church of England from marrying a king, was simply the catalyst of this historic upheaval. As a postscript, perhaps I should mention that when the unfortunate Charles I had his head cut off, the Moon was at 27° of Capricorn. Clearly, there is something about this degree of the zodiac which draws the monarchy into crisis.

One other astrological pattern should be mentioned here: that Wallis was born with the Sun at 29° of Gemini, the same degree occupied by the Moon when the House of Windsor was founded. One of the ideal marriage relationships places the man's Sun in the same degree as the woman's Moon. Once again, we see Wallis marrying not Edward the man, but the Windsor dynasty itself. She did, of course, become the first and only Duchess of Windsor, and that brought with it all the social charisma which comes from being married to a man who had once been Emperor of India. However, the patterns become stranger still when we look back to a former king who lost his throne. This was James II, who lost his crown not for a woman, but on the birth of his son, James the Old Pretender. It was the birth of a male heir to James II which raised fears that he would establish a Catholic dynasty and which ultimately led to his expulsion. So what did James and Wallis have in common? Both were born with the Sun in exactly the same degree of the zodiac, 29° in Gemini, and both cost a king his crown.

Wallis herself had her horoscope cast on several occasions. Like many society women, she visited spiritualists, and when she divorced Ernest Simpson she had a sitting with one of the most famous astrologers in America, Evangeline Adams. Wallis was warned of crises which lay ahead and was told that between the ages of forty and fifty she would exercise considerable emotional power and this power would be related to a man. Given that Edward's abdication took place when Wallis was forty, we can only assume that this forecast gave her the courage and determination to press on with her goal of marriage.

Edward abdicated at 1.52 p.m. on 11 December 1936, and went into exile. Yet, as a former king, he continued to live out the planetary cycles which brought monarchs high and then laid them low. As with so many medieval kings, Pluto had become the strongest planet in his horoscope, and on 28 May 1972 a Full Moon fell on exactly the same degree as Pluto at his birth. For Edward, it was time to move on. Astonishingly, the same pattern – a Full Moon aligned with Pluto – was repeated when Wallis died on 24 April 1986, bringing a traumatic episode in the modern monarchy to a close.

KING GEORGE VI AND QUEEN ELIZABETH

GEORGE VI
1936–1952

Born at Sandringham at 3.05 a.m. on 14 December 1895, with the Sun in Sagittarius and the Moon in Scorpio. Succeeded as King of Great Britain and Emperor of India on 11 December 1936 and crowned on 12 May 1937, with the Sun in Taurus and the Moon in Gemini. Died on 6 February 1952 and buried at Windsor.

ELIZABETH

Born in London at 11.31 a.m. on 4 August 1900, with the Sun in Leo, Moon in Scorpio and Ascendant in Libra.

There were few less likely monarchs than George VI. After his suave, debonair and popular elder brother Edward VIII, George was shy, relatively unknown and, due to a severe stammer, had great trouble speaking in public. However, if ever a horoscope revealed hidden talents, it is his. He was born with the Sun in Sagittarius, very close to

Mercury and strongly aligned with Neptune, planet of the imagination. Viewed in this way, George was an effortless communicator and a great conversationalist, always full of the latest ideas. The obvious question then is, what was the cause of the stammer which made it so difficult for him to talk to people?

The answer lies in the sheer intensity of George's Moon. This was in Scorpio, a sign of fierce passions; it was also in an extremely close alignment with Uranus, a planet which brings sudden changes, surprises, eccentricity and revolutionary change. As applied to George psychologically, we can only assume that he experienced an Uranian shock which, Scorpio being such an intense sign, affected him more deeply than anyone realised. There was an obvious gulf between the intensity of his Scorpionic feelings and the carefree spirit of Sagittarius. In ordinary circumstances this would have made George a difficult person to understand, yet his Libran Ascendant made him even more of a mystery. Librans need to be liked. They cannot bear to think that they have offended their friends, and to that end they often cover up ordinary human emotions such as anger. They have a tendency to conceal tensions and often give the impression of being well-balanced, while deep inside they are experiencing one emotional trauma after another. George was an unknown quantity when he came to the throne, a completely misunderstood, profoundly underestimated man.

Yet when the Second World War broke out in 1939, George came into his own. He discovered communicative skills which required a great deal more than fluency with the spoken word. By maintaining a highly visible profile in London during the Blitz, he created one of the most enduring images of the twentieth-century monarch, touring the ruins of the East End with his Queen, Elizabeth. After Edward had caused such offence by abandoning the country to its fate, George and Elizabeth restored the potent image of the King and Queen as mythical Mother and Father of the nation. In this he was helped by being born with Jupiter in a very strong position. At its best, this planet manifests itself in great nobility of character and is invariably an important ingredient in a successful reign. Intriguingly, the Jupiterian pattern in George's chart repeated that in the horoscope of William IV. Both men assumed the crown reluctantly, succeeding elder brothers who had done their best – albeit

127

inadvertently – to discredit the monarchy, and proceeded to restore much of its former reputation.

In ancient times it was believed that the monarch embodied the life and soul of the entire nation. This is an idea which is now regarded as an old-fashioned superstition, incompatible with modern democratic notions. Yet what happens if, for example, we compare George VI's horoscope to that for the outbreak of the Second World War? George was born at 3.05 a.m. on 14 December 1895 and Britain declared war on Germany at 11.00 a.m. on 3 September 1939. What did these two moments have in common?

* When George was born the Ascendant, the degree of the zodiac rising over the eastern horizon, was 27° of Libra.
* When war was declared, the Ascendant was 29° of Libra.
* When George was born the Midheaven, the culminating degree, was 6° of Leo.
* When war was declared the Midheaven was 9° of Leo.

George was also born with Jupiter on the Midheaven, and this was the single most fortunate alignment in his horoscope. Indeed, if we were to pick one astrological reason why he became King, this would be it. As war began, Jupiter was in Aries, 120° distant from its position at George's birth. This is the most harmonious relationship possible, and indicated that George was about to come into his own, to fulfil his destiny. The war was indeed ideal for him, personally speaking, in that it enabled him to create a powerful role for himself as leader of the nation during its darkest days. Interestingly enough, Winston Churchill shared the King's Sagittarian Sun and Libran Ascendant, and this was the influence by which George restored the monarchy's reputation and central role in national life.

However, there was more. Throughout the war, Pluto was passing over George's Midheaven degree, a factor which in the best of circumstances brings intense personal conflict. In George's case, his horoscope represented the burden and suffering of the entire British people during the war, as well as their eventual victory. The alignment was in operation for the entire war, but at its most exact on 10 July 1943. This was the day of the first allied seaborne landings in Sicily, at which point the liberation of Europe began. The astrological turning point coincided exactly with the turning point in the affairs of the nation. These astrological patterns actually support a concept of monarchy which is thousands of years old, namely that what happens to the King will also happen to his subjects. This, of course, is why the King's person was always regarded as sacred and why such pains were taken to protect him. When George remained in Buckingham Palace during the Blitz, rather than be evacuated, it was as if he had transformed himself into a lucky talisman, not dissimilar to the ravens in the Tower of London.

This does not mean that the war, in a metaphysical sense, sprang out of George's horoscope, for the patterns can be traced further back. In 1914 Britain had declared war on Germany with the Sun at 9° of Leo, exactly the same position which was occupied by the Midheaven in 1939. The two great conflicts between Britain and Germany were therefore linked by this single zodiacal degree.

When we consider Edward VIII's role in the unfolding pattern we notice that, at the exact moment of his abdication, the Midheaven was at 7° Aquarius, the degree of the zodiac opposing that which symbolised George's position as war leader. It was as if, in some unfathomable way, Edward was moving aside, allowing his brother to move in and take control during the coming holocaust. Was it, perhaps, impossible for Edward to lead Britain into war? Was this because of his misplaced admiration for Hitler? From all angles it looks as though Edward was being laid low in order to fulfil a greater design; that his abdication was necessary. This, at any rate, is the only conclusion we can draw from the remarkable astrological patterns linking George and Edward to the war with Germany.

George VI's close Moon–Uranus alignment is relevant to his succession in a rather curious way. This pattern is usually found in the horoscope of people who experience drastic and unexpected changes in their family circumstances. At the very minute that George succeeded his brother to the throne the Moon had returned to this position. The previous day would have been too early; the next day would have been too late. In fact, the Moon was only in the required position for a few hours, during the exact time that Edward was reading out his abdication speech!

On 14 December, three days after George became King, he

celebrated his forty-first birthday. On the day before this, 13 December, there was an eclipse of the Sun. This would not have been an auspicious time for George to ascend the throne. His finest hour came during the London Blitz, when the country was in its greatest peril. Yet if we consider George's personal health, independent of the events which took place during his reign, the eclipse supports the belief that when George became King he dramatically shortened his life. This is what his family believed, and was one reason why they never forgave Edward VIII and Wallis Simpson for the abdication.

It is often said that the most sensible move George ever made was to marry Lady Elizabeth Bowes-Lyon. Like her predecessor, Queen Mary, she provided an essential sense of stability for a King who required a solid contact with the real world. She encouraged George to develop confidence that he had been born to the job. The marriage was a love match without any trace of dynastic pressure. To the public eye George and Elizabeth were unalike: he, shy and withdrawn; she, bubbly and outgoing. Yet their horoscopes reveal two very similar characters, and the attraction between them was that of couples who see themselves mirrored in each others' eyes. He had charming, good-natured Libra in the Ascendant, as did she. They both shared a Moon in passionate Scorpio. He had the Sun in fiery, adventurous Sagittarius and she had the Sun harmoniously aligned to George's, although in fiery, extraverted Leo. Her horoscope lacked the intense planetary patterns which made it difficult for him to express himself and she, because of her great similarity to her husband, became the vehicle through which he spoke.

George and Elizabeth were also born with the Sun very close to Mercury, an indication of powerfully-held opinions. Yet both of them, with their charming Libran Ascendants, avoided any public display of ill-humour. Elizabeth's behaviour is perhaps the more remarkable, for at the time of writing she has outlived her husband by over forty years. Yet never once has her public conduct and demeanour been anything less than impeccable. Her Libran achievement becomes even more remarkable when we see that most of the royal family has slipped up on at least one occasion. It is noticeable that the only one of the current Queen's three children to have glided through the last few years without once embarrassing himself in public is Prince Edward, who was also born with Libra rising. People born under this sign frequently set such a high premium on polite behaviour and a pleasant outward manner that they instinctively avoid many of the public gaffes which afflict those born under other signs. George V, who also put a high value on impeccable public conduct, was born with the Moon in this sign.

The astrological source for Elizabeth's remarkable popularity as Queen Mother lies in the combination of her extraverted Leonine Sun and good-mannered Libran Ascendant. Librans are sometimes shy and Leos often brash, yet when these two signs are found in combination they confer a boundless charm. This is why the Queen Mother, it is said, is always ready with a kindly word, no matter how tedious the public engagement may be.

The connections between the horoscopes of all the members of the current royal family are extremely tight, and time and time again we find the same few degrees of the zodiac occupying the important positions. They therefore all tend to experience periods of difficulty or success at the same time. It is this simple process, in which astrological patterns are doubled up through a series of horoscopes, which enables the royal family to operate as a unit.

The Queen Mother experienced a series of extremely powerful planetary transits at the end of the 1980s and beginning of the 1990s. Uranus and Neptune, which from 1989 to 1993 formed their first conjunction since 1821, made a very stressful alignment with her Ascendant. This was the same alignment, remember, which occurred when Charles I was executed and when George IV brought the monarchy to its knees through his failed attempt to divorce his wife Queen Caroline. She has also experienced the passage of Pluto over her Moon. This is one of those patterns which often coincides with great emotional stress and which frequently drives people into long periods of seclusion. To cut oneself off from the world is sometimes the only defence against the seemingly endless whirl of emotional trauma. We can only assume that, behind that Libran façade, the Queen Mother was highly distressed by the break-up of two of her grandsons' marriages, with the attendant public hue and cry. From 1993 onwards her planetary pressures, in common with those of the rest of the family, begin to ease.

131

QUEEN ELIZABETH II AND PRINCE PHILIP

ELIZABETH II
1952–

Born in Bruton Street, London at 1.40 a.m. on 21 April 1926, with the Sun in Taurus and the Moon in Leo. Succeeded as Queen of Great Britain and Northern Ireland on 6 February 1952 and crowned on 2 June 1953, with the Sun in Gemini and Moon in Aquarius.

PHILIP

Born in Corfu on the evening of 10 June 1921, with the Sun in Gemini, Moon in Leo and Ascendant in Capricorn.

When Elizabeth was crowned in 1953 the press was, perhaps inevitably, full of speculation about the new Elizabethan Age. At the time, Sir Edmund Hillary's achievement in reaching the summit of Mount Everest reminded many people of the great adventurers of the sixteenth century, Sir Walter Raleigh and Sir Francis Drake. The Festival of Britain had already raised hopes of a cultural revival similar to the Renaissance which had flowered in England under Elizabeth I. Not surprisingly, there are strong astrological connections between the two Queens. Both were born with the practical 'Earth' signs in powerful positions; the first Elizabeth had the Sun in Virgo, Moon in Taurus and Ascendant in Capricorn, while the second has the Sun in Taurus and Ascendant in Capricorn. Like her namesake, the current Queen therefore possesses a sound and commonsense approach to the job.

When we look at the two Queens' succession and coronation horoscopes, the pictures change quite dramatically. Elizabeth I succeeded in 1558 with the Sun in adventurous Sagittarius and the Moon in independent Aquarius. Elizabeth II succeeded in 1952 with the Sun in independent Aquarius and the Moon in lively Gemini. Elizabeth I was crowned in 1559 with the Sun in independent Aquarius and the Moon in fiery Aries, Elizabeth II in 1953 with the

Sun in lively Gemini and the Moon in independent Aquarius. The significance is that, while each birth horoscope reveals a character which inclines towards the routine management of society and the practical pursuit of daily survival as the highest goal of monarchy, each presided over periods of great cultural upheaval. The reign of Elizabeth I brought a renaissance in the arts, of which Shakespeare's plays are a living testimony. Elizabeth II's reign has witnessed the sexual revolution of the sixties, radical innovation in the arts, including the abolition of theatre censorship, the spread of recreational drug use, the decline of the nuclear family, the transformation of Britain into a multi-cultural society and experimentation with alternative lifestyles. It was also early in her reign that the Queen opened the world's first civil nuclear power station, a sign of the technological revolution to come.

The optimistic mood of the times was enhanced by the date chosen for the coronation, 2 June 1953, when the moon was approaching its most harmonious possible relationship with the Sun. If we look at the coronation horoscope in greater detail, it becomes clear that the Moon was involved in a relationship with both the Sun and Jupiter, which would have been used by any medieval astrologer in selecting the best moment for a coronation. The Moon would have been said to be translating the light of Jupiter to the Sun. In plain English, this was a way of giving a massive boost to the energy and optimism already present in the sky. If anything in the Queen's astrology signified the extraordinary energy and optimism of the 1960s, it was this.

The Queen's birth horoscope, though, presents a very different picture. True, she was born with the Moon in Leo, a sign famous for its theatrical qualities. Indeed, Elizabeth's Moon occupies exactly the same degree of the zodiac as her mother's ebullient Sun. In part, this is the aspect which has ensured such a close, enduring bond between mother and daughter. For the Queen, it is the single factor in her chart which enables her to mix with people on anything like the relaxed level which comes so easily to her mother. Over and above the fact that her Sun and Ascendant are in two conservative signs, Taurus and Capricorn, Elizabeth was born with Saturn at the very summit of her horoscope. This is an indication of the saturnine individual *par excellence*. She can never escape her duty, never entirely let the public

133

mask slip. And she can never truly relax without wondering what other people are thinking, or whether she is doing the right thing. Far from escaping from formality, she takes refuge in it as the great bulwark against the encroaching chaos of an unstable world.

In many cases, such a strong Saturn occurs in the horoscopes of people who spend their lives trying desperately to prove something to themselves. We can assume that the Queen is no exception. But what might she be trying to prove? Perhaps that she can be a successful head of state in what was until recently very much a man's world. In this case, the comparison with Margaret Thatcher, her Prime Minister for eleven years, is most revealing. Thatcher was born with Saturn in a similar position, and in her it provoked her famous resistance to compromise. 'The lady's not for turning' and 'There's no alternative' were two of her great Saturnine slogans, and the nickname coined for her by the Soviet Union, the 'Iron Lady', embodied perfectly her unbending determination to succeed on her own terms. We saw these qualities more clearly in Mrs Thatcher because she faced a much tougher battle, conquering a bastion of male control through merit and strength of character. Elizabeth inherited her position, but is equally forthright in her dedication to the task in hand.

Elizabeth was ten when she became heir to the throne. Had the monarchy not been her destiny, no doubt she would have been perfectly happy to lead an uneventful domestic life, including such typical Taurean pursuits as grooming her horses, taking care of the dogs and, with her Leonine Moon, organising country house parties. However, when in 1936 Pluto moved to a powerful and harmonious aspect to Saturn in her horoscope, her destiny was irrevocably changed. At 1.52 p.m. on 11 December 1936 Elizabeth became heir to the throne, prospective leader of the British Empire. Later that afternoon the Moon glided across the Midheaven in her horoscope, the very degree of the zodiac ruling her public life. The heavens had spoken and life was never to be the same again. It was as if Sarah Armstrong-Jones or young Zara Phillips were suddenly thrust into the succession. Elizabeth's situation was not unique, although the laws of succession meant that women have never been expected to succeed. Mary I and Elizabeth I ascended the throne only because their brother Edward died young and childless. Mary II and Anne both became Queen only because their father and his infant son were sent into exile. Victoria succeeded William IV only because he and her uncles Frederick and George died without male heirs. Yet Elizabeth, with her all-embracing Saturn, feels the burdens of responsibility more than her predecessors. For her, being Queen is not an excuse to have a good time. Neither is it a reason to order other people about. Rather it is duty. It is not her divine duty, for the Queen is not impressed by archaic theories of the monarch as bridge between earth and heaven; but it is her duty.

Elizabeth's devotion to her responsibilities is such that it has always been very difficult ever to envisage her abdicating. The argument has been put forward that Edward VII, while he was Prince of Wales, wasted his time in the pursuit of pleasure while waiting to ascend the throne; the inference is that Elizabeth should move aside and make room for Charles. However, Elizabeth believes that if one is born to do a job one should jolly well get on and do it! Although she has passed through a number of planetary alignments which might have encouraged abdication in someone of a different mental persuasion, and it may well have crossed her mind that it would be pleasant indeed to lead the life of a private person, the possibility has never been seriously entertained. One such period occurred in 1981. Her private thoughts were borne out in an almost ritualistic manner by the young man who leapt out of the crowd at the Trooping of the Colour and fired a starting pistol at the Queen as she passed by. At this precise moment, 10.56 a.m. on 13 June 1981, the Midheaven was at 23° in Taurus – exactly opposite the degree occupied by both Saturn, the fount of the Queen's devotion to her responsibilities, and the Midheaven, her public destiny, at her birth. It was almost as she was being given a chance to look at life from a completely new direction, or perhaps to stand her normal preconceptions on their heads. The next period occurred around 1984–5 and the most recent from 1990–3. This last turbulent time was the most intense, but eventually at the end of 1992 the public debate focused on the fitness of her heirs to succeed her and there was a general feeling that she should not abdicate. Elizabeth, by remaining loyal to her Saturnine principles during the years when she was being advised to make way for Charles, had saved the country a major constitutional crisis. Thanks to her, in 1992 it

135

was not the King and Queen who separated, just the heir and his wife.

Yet, great as the Queen's devotion to her duties is, her horoscope contains one very unusual and original feature which is rarely seen by the public: Mars and Jupiter are in an extremely close alignment in Aquarius. This powerful pattern would normally be found in the horoscopes of social revolutionaries, or crusaders who devote their lives to fighting for causes. True, Elizabeth has devoted herself to the nation, but that is a cause imposed on her by other people. We would normally expect individuals born under such a crusading pattern to take up a mission contrary to their family interests or on the fringes of society. The question is, where has this planetary energy gone? We may say that it has been expressed not in Elizabeth's own life but through the lives of her subjects. In that case, the Queen's horoscope offers us another angle on the cultural upheavals of the 1960s. We may also see in this eccentric alignment the Queen's devoted support of homoeopathy. This unusual method of healing stands well outside accepted scientific practice and even now most regular medical doctors treat it with scorn. In employing a homoeopath as her personal physician, the Queen is maintaining a long-established royal tradition, but she is also placing herself on the fringes of society. She has also, for all her conservatism, provided a model for Prince Charles' vocal support for many other alternative beliefs and practices. By taking a public stand on these matters, Charles has been publicly mocked. The Queen, by remaining silent, has preserved an air of total conservatism while receiving medical treatment considered close to witchcraft by many orthodox scientists and evangelical Christians. Never mind the fact that she seems to do extremely well on it!

There is one last feature of the Queen's birth horoscope which often passes unnoticed, and that is Venus in Pisces. Venus reveals her capacity to express affection, and in Pisces it is placed in the most romantic and sensitive of all the signs of the zodiac. Here is someone who, when her heart is touched, will fall helplessly in love. Those who saw the young Princess Elizabeth with Prince Philip during their courtship and the early days of their marriage were struck by how in love she was with him. He seemed to fulfil the images of the romantic sailor and war hero which were bound to sweep Elizabeth off her feet.

It is often said that she seemed to be much more in love with him than he was with her. That is hardly surprising, for Philip has Venus in Taurus. If he was in love he'd hardly be likely to show it to complete strangers; for while Taurus can be passionate and devoted, it is a discreet sign. Taureans can be theatrical, but in matters of personal importance their feelings are cloaked behind a matter-of-fact public mask.

Prince Philip was born on 10 June 1921 on the Greek island of Corfu. His exact time of birth is unknown, although it was some time in the early evening. This uncertainty is quite important, for during the hours of dusk the Ascendant moved from adventurous Sagittarius to conservative Capricorn. Capricorn is the more likely, for anyone who has attained the lofty position of Prince Consort clearly has the staying power represented by this sign. However, we can gain enough information from the rest of Philip's horoscope for a slight uncertainty over his time of birth not to matter too greatly.

The most telling comparisons are between Philip and the Queen's father George VI, for these tell what kind of man she was looking for. The relationship between the Prince's horoscope and the King's is extremely close, and reveals their differences more than their similarities. The two men's birthdays are almost exactly six months apart: George was born on 14 December and Philip on 10 June. This means that their Suns were in opposite degrees: George's was at 19° in Sagittarius and Philip's is at 19° in Gemini. In other words, Elizabeth was attracted to Philip because in many ways he was the polar opposite of George.

Sagittarians and Geminians have various traits in common; both signs are happy in the realm of ideas, often book-lovers and fond of learning. In addition to this, these signs tend to dominate the media. However, Sagittarians are attracted to principles and ideals and are great ones for devoting themselves to creating a better world. Geminians, on the other hand, are more likely to enjoy the cut and thrust of debate, arguing over contentious issues, raising questions and giving instant opinions on almost every subject you care to mention. George, afflicted by his stammer, was very much the quiet Sagittarian idealist, pursuing principled aims in private, while Philip – as we know so well – has a ready opinion on any and every question

137

under the sun. In the 1960s his controversial outbursts made regular headlines. Wildlife conservation became his regular theme, but he was also outspoken on social affairs. Often he came close to exceeding the bounds of what was considered right and proper for a member of the royal family. Indeed, the notion that there were restrictions on what he might or might not say only seemed to drive the Prince to still further outbursts. It was as if he was damned if he was going to allow anyone to cramp his Geminian freedom of speech.

Both men had Mercury, which rules the mind, in opposite signs. While George was born with Mercury in Capricorn, in Philip's horoscope this planet is found in the opposite sign of Cancer. Thus George was not given to expressing an opinion unless it had a direct practical purpose, whereas Philip is likely to respond readily to his emotions. If he feels that something is wrong he'll denounce it and only later will the facts be found to support his opinions. Philip was born with Mercury very close to Pluto, which explains why in the past he so often seemed to be courting danger with his public pronouncements, as if he were seeing how far he could push people before provoking them into a suitable reaction. He has, for example, always relished the controversy inspired by his simultaneous support of hunting and wildlife conservation. The differences between George and Philip go deeper still when we consider their Moons which, like their Suns, are in a very tense relationship. George's Moon was at 22° of Scorpio, exactly 90° away from Philip's Moon at 22° of Leo. The two men could not be more different. George's deep craving for privacy and instinctive secrecy stands in exact contrast to Philip's bombastic, powerful, publicity-seeking extraversion. While George shunned the public arena, Philip craves it.

We are now in a position to answer the question, why was Elizabeth so in love with Philip? The answer was that he appeared to be everything her father was not. George may have been a good father, but he hardly cut a dashing figure. Philip was strong. He let people know what he thought. He took control. He made decisions. He promised Elizabeth a new life.

There is one other very powerful planetary pattern which reveals Elizabeth's fascination for Philip, as well as his deep attraction to her. We have already remarked on Elizabeth's powerful and unusual

Mars–Jupiter alignment, and the difficulty she seems to have experienced in giving full vent to its true eccentricities. Well, Philip's Leonine Moon falls in exactly the opposite degree of the zodiac to Elizabeth's energetic planets. When we fit the two horoscopes together we can understand how she might have perceived him as someone who would help her develop her more unusual qualities and aspirations. He, meanwhile, felt a spark which he found truly exciting, and a million miles away from the normal staid Taurean front which Elizabeth presents to her subjects. Finally the couple would have experienced that unspoken mutual recognition we so often find between people who were born with the Moon in the same sign. He may have been a restless Gemini and she a cautious Taurean, but both were born with the Moon in Leo, and each would have sensed that they shared a very similar sense of fun and humour.

In other ways we can see a family pattern repeating itself. Philip, like George V, is blamed for being a bad father. As George V and Queen Mary were blamed for their inadequate upbringing of Edward VIII and George VI, Philip's alleged coldness to his children is judged to be partly to blame for the failure of their own relationships. The general allegation is that the royal parents failed to prepare their offspring for life in today's world. There seems to be a Geminian pattern at work here, which we can trace back to Queen Victoria, a Gemini who was blamed for her supposed failure to prepare Edward VII for his royal inheritance. George V and Mary were both Geminians – as is Philip. However, before we slander an entire sign of the zodiac as being poor parents, we should look at the deeper psychological processes.

Geminians tend to approach the world with preconceived ideas about relationships and the upbringing of children. This can be tremendously positive, and one of their greatest gifts is to offer children endless stimulation. They take great delight out of watching them learn, discovering new interests and encouraging them to develop their sense of curiosity. The drawback is that they often fail to sense when their ideas are unsuited to other people. How they respond depends entirely on what other signs are prominent in their horoscopes. Queen Victoria, born with both Sun and Moon in Gemini, was reasonably competent at understanding other people's needs, provided they were explained to her. George V had his own decided ideas but, with the Moon in Libra, was anxious not to offend his children. Queen Mary with her Moon in Pisces had perhaps the best combination, for Piscean intuition and sensitivity merge very well with the fact- and figure-dominated Geminian intellect. However, Philip has the Moon in Leo, so he finds it difficult to comprehend why anyone should disagree with his instant opinions. If they do, according to his logic, the fault lies in them, rather than in his ideas. Philip's tendency to shoot from the lip is confirmed by the close relationship between the Sun and Mars at his birth. This adds a healthy touch of aggression and a willingness to argue with anyone, no matter what their opinions. We can even imagine him disagreeing with people who share his ideas, expressly for the pleasure to be gained by the flexing of mental muscles. However, such is his impatience that he is all too ready to dismiss others' beliefs and feelings with a wave of the hand.

Unfortunately, Philip completely failed to notice that his three sons were born under sensitive water signs – Charles is a Scorpio, Andrew and Edward both Pisceans. Each has his tough side, and both Charles and Andrew have Leo rising, but essentially all three are sensitive and creative intellectuals. Even Andrew, who is widely perceived as a man of the people, fits this description. It must be said that Philip's understanding of Charles' and Edward's needs and natures was minimal. To send them to Gordonstoun, his old school, where the emphasis is on character building through physical struggle, was ill-advised; to encourage Edward to join the Royal Marines compounded his initial error.

Yet astrology seeks understanding, rather than attributing blame. Therefore to accuse Philip of being responsible for his children's failed marriages makes no more sense than to blame Victoria for Edward VII's philandering or George V for Edward VIII's abdication. Philip spent his childhood isolated from his mother, and was sent away from the family for his schooling. This was in many ways a normal upbringing for the sons of the British aristocracy, yet Philip, more than most, seems to have lacked any sense of being even remotely part of a loving family. Philip was born, like Elizabeth, under a very strong Saturn, and this made him more vulnerable than many people to the lack of affection he experienced early in life. Saturn encouraged him to set up powerful personal defences, and he came to realise that if he didn't expect affection he wouldn't be disappointed when it failed to be offered. His powerful Mars encouraged him in his belief, picked up at Gordonstoun, that physical fitness is the best way to overcome personal difficulties. We have to thank this particular element of the Prince's psychological make-up for the Duke of Edinburgh award scheme, which rewards young people for overcoming physical challenges. But we should still recognise that it was not a happy situation for the Prince to be in, to always have to prove himself worthy of love, or that he is capable of holding the post he acquired through marriage. These are the pressures which drive the Prince's argumentative relationship with the world at large. Unfortunately, he expected his sons to prove themselves to him in exactly the same way. They have done their best, but ultimately he has failed to understand that they are not mirror images of himself.

The psychological processes represented by Saturn are quite sophisticated, and it is possible to work through this planet's inhibitions by seriously tackling and coming to understand those early experiences which encourage us to erect defensive barriers against the world. Unfortunately for Philip, he has an extremely strong Saturn in his birth chart, and is in many ways a prisoner of circumstances. He comes from a generation in which it was considered a sign of weakness for men to show their feelings, especially in public. That Elizabeth and Philip both have powerful Saturnine characteristics is another reason for their mutual attraction; they offered each other security. Elizabeth offered Philip the family he had never had, and he offered her the stability and protection which she knew that she would need when the time came for her to ascend the throne. Saturn also provides Philip with a sense of duty, which was absolutely vital if he was to fulfil his role, walking two steps behind his wife, backing her to the hilt on every occasion and never, in his private behaviour, betraying her trust. Unfortunately, Saturn has also played a role in the separations which have kept them apart for long periods. In the early 1960s it was not unknown for Philip to be out of the country on overseas tours for up to six months. Yet they both understood the nature of royal marriage; that it serves a purpose beyond the purely personal and cannot be sacrificed without some danger to the status of the monarchy. That is, until the monarchy itself changes.

There is, as has often been remarked, a difference between the monarchy and the royal family. The monarchy is centred on the person of the monarch alone, who is believed to be in some way special, set apart from other people. Such residual beliefs date back to a time when the monarch was believed to be divine. Some of this divinity was shared by the monarch's closest relations, and from earliest times the concept of the royal family was central to the functioning of the hereditary system. However, our modern acceptance of an enormously extended royal family took root only in Victorian times. If we look back to a former era, we find that certain monarchs, such as Elizabeth I, had no family of their own. Others, like the Norman and Plantagenet kings, usually found themselves at war with their brothers and sisters, even their parents. George III enjoyed domestic life but argued bitterly with his father and was hardly on good terms with his successor, George IV. After Victoria, Edward VII and George V preserved the illusion of the royals as one big happy family. The concept took a battering with the abdication of Edward VIII and the subsequent rift between his younger brother and himself. Yet when George VI and Elizabeth set about polishing the monarchy's tarnished reputation they relied heavily on images of the whole family, including their daughters Elizabeth and Margaret. When she became Queen, Elizabeth followed their example. It came naturally to her, for with her Sun in Taurus, her Capricorn Ascendant and her Leonine Moon, she takes immense pleasure in tradition and loves family gatherings. As a true Saturnine person should be, she is immensely cautious, yet she is also a very generous mother. So strong is her love of family that she has always included her cousins and their children as part of the royal roadshow.

Another genuine aspect of the Queen's make-up is her modesty; one might say her 'ordinariness'. This is far from being an insult – for someone in her position not to give herself airs is admirable. This is naturally a quality common to a number of her predecessors, especially her father and grandfather, but with her Taurus–Capricorn combination, Elizabeth is more skilled at presenting an ordinary image than other members of her family. This is why her plan to bring

142

the monarchy up to date was based on encouraging the presentation of the Windsors as a typical British family. It was the device her parents used after 1936, and seemed a good example to follow. However, being such a Saturnine individual, Elizabeth jealously guarded the royal family's traditional privileges. Indeed, the central purpose behind her updating of the royal family's image was the preservation of the monarchy, complete with all its attendant ancient mystique. Here we find a basic contradition: royal weddings continued to be celebrated with great pomp, while at the same time an image was perpetuated of the Windsors as an ordinary middle-class family. Elizabeth's regal Moon in Leo and her thoroughly ordinary Taurean Sun pulled her in different directions, and the result of this contradiction was the crisis of 1992.

When Charles and Andrew, Diana and Sarah were shown to have feet of clay, questions were asked as to why the monarchy deserved certain of its privileges, such as exemption from payment of income tax on its private wealth. However, there had been royal scandals before; when Princess Margaret's marriage to Lord Snowdon disintegrated, no questions were asked about the relevance of the monarchy. The difference in 1992 was not just that it was the Prince of Wales' marriage which fell apart, but that Uranus, Neptune and Pluto were simultaneously making extraordinarily powerful movements over the Queen's horoscope. These three planets individually undermine the status quo; as a combination, they are capable of provoking revolution. If we ask the question whether the monarchy was lucky to survive in 1992, the answer must be yes. Certainly, the Queen will never again experience such powerful planetary transits. Once 1993 has passed, the pressure on her horoscope will begin to ease.

If we look at the relationship between the Queen's horoscope and that of the nation, a very interesting pattern emerges. The Queen was born with her Ascendant at 21° in Capricorn; when the United Kingdom was formed, at midnight on 1 January 1801, the Moon was at 19° in Cancer. This, being the opposite degree, is exactly the kind of connection we find in the horoscopes of married couples. We could say that the Queen is married to the nation. But the fact that the two positions are opposite means that, like many married couples, the Queen and her people tend to pull in different directions. This makes for a dynamic relationship, and is a major reason why Elizabeth has always been aware of the need to bring the monarchy up to date. Yet under certain planetary transits the contradictions emerge; that is what happened in 1992. Once 1994 is over this is unlikely to happen again, at least not with such force. The Queen may yet have to cope with the fall-out of 1992's upsets, but she can rest assured that no new crisis will be as deep or as threatening.

CHARLES, PRINCE OF WALES

Born at Buckingham Palace at 9.14 p.m. on 14 November 1948, with the Sun in Scorpio, the Moon in Taurus and the Ascendant in Leo.

When Prince Charles was born, the British astrologer Charles Carter wrote that while Charles' horoscope was 'rather favourable . . . whether it is of a royal character is possibly more open to question'. His main reason was that Jupiter was in a weak position. Carter was certainly picking up on a familiar royal pattern, for most recent British monarchs have been born under a powerful Jupiter. This is the reason why many British astrologers have considered that Charles will not become King. It may also be the reason why, prior to her separation from Charles, Diana came to believe that she would never be Queen. This is an idea she could easily have picked up from one of the astrologers she consulted in the late eighties, for Charles Carter's opinions are extremely well-known.

Charles is, and has always been, deeply confused about the nature of his royal role and the depth of his commitment to destiny. He was born with the Sun in Scorpio in an intense aspect of Pluto, and shares all the secrecy of the typical Scorpio, including a deep desire for privacy and a profound reluctance to show his feelings in public. There have been Scorpionic monarchs in the past; the Prince's grandfather, George VI, was born with the Moon in Scorpio, while his great-great-grandfather Edward VII had his Sun in Scorpio. Yet since their day there has been a technological and cultural revolution, which has meant that Charles has had to fulfil his royal duties under the constant gaze of the press and television. This is a truly difficult burden for any Scorpio to bear, and there must have been many times when he wondered why on earth he had been born to such a life. He has managed to find some Scorpionic escape routes in the form of spiritual retreats, sojourns in the wilderness and solo holidays, all vital in restoring and rejuvenating his Scorpionic life-force.

Most unfortunate for Charles, though, is that he has been held up to public ridicule for his active interest in a number of fringe theories and practices. While many of his concerns are easy to mock, some of them may well become tomorrow's orthodoxy. Even though it is known, for example, that plant growth is encouraged by soothing sounds, the Prince has been scorned for 'talking' to his plants. His active support of alternative methods of healing, such as homoeopathy, led to angry criticism by many doctors. Yet the treatment of cancer by improving a patient's psychological condition, of which Charles was an early advocate, is now being accepted in some orthodox medical circles. His attack on the 'carbuncles' of modern architecture received, on one hand, the support of the public, and on the other, the furious denunciations of many professional architects. All Charles' interests, from the promotion of organic agriculture to the regeneration of the inner cities, are based on a profound understanding of the deep processes underlying life, and the need to understand nature's cyclical patterns. Concerns such as these are typically Scorpionic. Astrologers often call this the sign of death and rebirth, and Charles seems to have intuitively brought out the essence of this deepest of signs.

Charles is the first male member of the royal family to develop a sincere interest in esoteric ideas since Edward VII. Interestingly, there are certain broad similarities between their horoscopes: Charles was born with his Sun in intense, secretive Scorpio and his Ascendant in outgoing, dramatic Leo, while Edward's Scorpionic Sun was contrasted with a lively and extraverted Sagittarian Ascendant. Each is therefore simultaneously torn between an inner need for secrecy and seclusion and the desire to live life to the full. For both men it is this central paradox, and the internal tensions it arouses, which encourages them to acquire personal understanding through any means possible.

Charles's astrological connections with his immediate family are extremely close. His Ascendant is at 5° in Leo, almost exactly the same degree as George VI's Midheaven and exactly opposite his great-grandmother Queen Mary's Ascendant. Such family connections indicate the web of relationships which tie family members more closely to some than to others. If we look at Charles' relationship with his grandfather, for example, we find the Leonine connection. We also find Charles' Sun in Scorpio in almost exactly the same degree of the zodiac as George VI's Moon. Taking these two contacts together, we can only assume that the relationship between the two was exceedingly close. It is often said that Lord Louis Mountbatten, Charles' great-uncle, was his true inspiration. That may well have been true for his later years, but for the first four years of his life Charles absorbed everything that was most admirable about his grandfather, the shy, intense, misunderstood philosopher. And this is precisely what Charles too has become.

Charles' horoscope shows very few connections with his father's. True, he has the Ascendant in Leo and Philip has the Moon in Leo, which gives them the competitive streak they find in their common love of polo. But Charles' Ascendant is separated from Philip's Moon by 15°, which means that although they share Leonine qualities, the personal bond between them is not close. It is not at all surprising that they misunderstand each other, that Philip has little sympathy with Charles' esoteric concerns, while Charles feel that his father has never made the effort to listen to his ideas or sympathise with his beliefs.

The intense bond is between Charles and his mother. His Sun in Scorpio is only 3° away from Elizabeth's Saturn and Midheaven in Scorpio. Even more powerful is the relationship between the Queen's Taurean Sun and Charles' Taurean Moon. They are so close as to suggest that mother and son are in almost telepathic communication. At least that's what we would conclude were their planets to be in an ethereal sign such as Pisces rather than solid, dependable Taurus. In Taurus they probably don't have telepathic experiences, as such. It's simply that they operate as a double-act, instinctively moving in tandem. There are obvious problems in such a relationship for, with her powerful Saturn, the Queen comes close to stifling Charles' creativity and emotional freedom. At her best, she channels him, encouraging him to move forward, gradually discovering himself and expanding his potential through experience. It is sometimes said that the Queen and all her immediate family operate as a single unit, and that it is difficult, even well-nigh impossible, for outsiders, even spouses, to break into this clique. Of course, this is an overstatement, yet in Charles' relationship with the Queen we can see a bond which could never be broken, not even by Diana. He shares a view of the world with his mother, a manner of behaving and a way of relating to other people. If it were not for this she would never be able to dominate him.

Charles' Taurean Moon and Leonine Ascendant are rather splendid – and much underrated. His Taurean qualities are expressed in his devotion to organic farming, which has been widely and foolishly ridiculed. Yet the Moon is also a guarantor of his public popularity, for it is very powerfully placed. The Prince is said to have become jealous of Diana's ability to arouse adulation at public events, and as a typical Scorpio he responded by withdrawing into anger and resentment. Yet, in truth, he needn't have worried. His horoscope indicates that public popularity is there for the asking. Perhaps he has never truly realised the depth of the admiration and support he roused in his assault on the architectural and medical establishments, together with his support of a number of other causes. People who had previously had no time for the monarchy began to feel that if Charles was to be king, royalty might be a force for the good after all.

One final point about Charles' horoscope concerns his creative skills. We know about his love of performance from his involvement in student revues at Cambridge, but he has also developed his talents as a writer, both of fiction and non-fiction, and as a watercolourist. His Leo Ascendant gives him an innate desire to show off, a confident feeling that he has something important to say. His creative powers are focused by his Sun, which is exactly on the cusp (the beginning) of the fifth house, the region of his horoscope denoting artistic potential. In any walk of life Charles would have found a way to paint, write or perform, and as he takes less of a part in competitive sport we will find him paying increased attention to his creative activities.

After 1993 the pressure of planetary transits in Charles' horoscope diminishes. Those powerful planets affecting his horoscope in 1994 are generally supportive. However, by the beginning of 1997 Charles will be plunged into an entirely new set of circumstances which threaten once again to cause havoc in royal circles. Intense pressure on the region of his horoscope signifying marriage confirms that relations with Diana must be settled for good. If Charles wants a divorce, but it has not been achieved, then have it he must. The real point at issue though, is that the prospect of remarriage comes up, and if Charles is to tie the knot again, that is the most likely moment. From then until the early years of the twenty-first century Charles' horoscope remains in a highly delicate state, and he will be susceptible to all sorts of pressures, including emotional appeals. With Neptune exactly on the degree of his horoscope signifying relationships in 2001, he will need to feel loved. And this perfectly understandable desire will shape all his behaviour, and will continue to do so through the whole of the next decade.

DIANA, PRINCESS OF WALES
Born at 7.45 p.m. on 1 July 1961 at Sandringham, with the Sun in Cancer, the Moon in Aquarius and the Ascendant in Sagittarius.

When Lady Diana Spencer became the wife of the Prince of Wales at seventeen minutes and thirty seconds past eleven on the morning of 29 July 1981, it was widely expected that she would be a dutiful wife, a model Princess of Wales and eventually a loyal Queen Consort. It was not anticipated that she might follow her own course, becoming perhaps a little like Prince Philip. It was not even thought that she had a mind of her own. Loyalists admired the shy young girl born with the Sun in Cancer. Anti-royalists poured contempt on the upper-class girl who appeared to have more money than brains. Yet Diana's horoscope contains a truly explosive planetary pattern; essentially she has the horoscope of a militant feminist.

There is a certain amount of confusion concerning her exact birth time, and the officially announced version, 7.45 p.m., may not be absolutely accurate. However, it was one of the key traditions of the ancient divine monarchy that, on assuming any royal status, a new horoscope was acquired. One ancient practice was to cast a horoscope for the moment the monarch entered the palace after his coronation; this then superseded his birth horoscope. When Buckingham Palace made the official announcement of Diana's birth they were unwittingly reviving this ancient tradition. The horoscope cast for this moment is then that for Diana the Princess, rather than Diana the private person.

At her birth Diana had strong Libran influences, expressed through her Ascendant. It is these which account for the shy charm with which the young Lady Diana Spencer emerged into the full glare of the public eye. Libra is a delicate sign which hates public arguments and needs to feel loved, and this is one reason why, years later, Diana suffered such pain during the public humiliation and tabloid exposures which accompanied her separation from Prince Charles. When Libran people are denied love, as Diana feels she was as a child, they begin to crave it. This is the secret of Diana's courting of the media. Her promotion of her public role is brilliantly successful, yet with exposure comes criticism, and the sort of prurient public interest which erupted in 1992, which in turn upset her again.

The official birth time released by Buckingham Palace gave Diana a Sagittarian Ascendant. This Ascendant represents the new Diana who came into being when she married Prince Charles. Gradually her innate, gentle, shy Libran qualities were replaced by Sagittarian spirit. By the mid-eighties Diana had fully developed the freedom-loving qualities associated with this sign, including the confidence to develop her regal duties in a manner not anticipated by Buckingham Palace. She began to express her private disappointment in Prince Charles through public competition, discovering that she, rather than him, was capable of arousing public adoration.

Essentially, Diana is playing two roles. The private woman remains Libran, a lover of peace and beauty who is dependent on others' approval. The public Princess has constructed a Sagittarian veneer, adopting the courage of this sign, developing a pioneering and independent face. When we examine Diana's Sagittarian Ascendant we are talking about everything in her character which has made her a Princess. Sagittarius also points to those adventurous qualities which Charles instinctively identified in her when they first met, but which he never imagined would become so powerful.

Diana's Ascendant varies depending on her correct time of birth, but her powerful planetary alignments would remain the same, with one exception – the Moon. This moved slightly during the afternoon and early evening of 1 July, but remained within one sign of the zodiac – Aquarius. At the moment of Diana's birth the Moon was in Aquarius, a sign denoting an independent spirit and people who are impatient with ties and conventions which appear to them to have little or no purpose. The effect of her increasingly Sagittarian nature has been to exacerbate and enhance the deeply combative qualities of the Moon in her horoscope. That, though, is only a small part of the story.

The Moon's powerful influence was compounded by its intense relationship with Uranus; these two planets were positioned in exactly opposing degrees of the zodiac. This stunning configuration reveals deep reluctance to accept pointless commitments or tedious routines. Diana cannot accept any imposition or restriction other than those which she has taken on of her own free will. There is no compromise in this position, and when we say that the Princess *cannot* tolerate unwanted restrictions, we mean just that. She has no choice. The intensity of this alignment was increased tenfold with the addition of Venus, which is exactly 90° away from both the Moon and Uranus. This adds an extraordinary obstinacy and emotional intensity which cannot be ignored. As soon as she faces restrictions the Princess must either turn inwards and attack herself (as she did when she developed a serious eating disorder and, so it is claimed, attempted to commit suicide), or else she must break out of those restrictions, even at the risk of causing chaos.

The Princess's frequent visits to astrologers in the late eighties are said to have helped her considerably. She was advised to channel her energy into positive activities, and that's exactly what happened when she began to take an interest in the hospice movement, paying special attention to sufferers from AIDS and leprosy. Her close contact with victims of both diseases surprised more cautious people, but all was grist to Diana's mill; Diana the superstar was replaced by Saint Diana, ministering to the sick and dying.

By following in the footsteps of Mother Teresa, Diana tapped into an ancient vein in popular adulation of the monarchy, one which finds its origins in archaic worship of the divine king or queen. In earliest times it was widely believed that the monarch had magical healing powers. In England, the tradition in which the monarch touched sufferers from the skin disease scrofula in order to heal them, died out almost three hundred years ago during the reign of Queen Anne. Diana, perhaps without realising it, has revived a religious quality which was central to ancient monarchy, and this in large part explains the depth of her popularity. To call Diana a revolutionary is to speak not in the familiar political terms. No, Diana is a true revolutionary in the sense that she possesses a rare ability to upset the status quo.

Prior to her transformation into an international superstar, Diana's maternal Cancerian instincts were channelled into her work, looking after young children in a smart London kindergarten. Here again, it was her powerful Neptune which provided a suitable image, and already her obvious kindness and gentleness foreshadowed the saintly role which was to emerge in the late eighties. Diana's Sagittarian Ascendant helped her project a sunny, casual image, and her Midheaven in Libra also contributed to her exceptionally polite public manner. When, before her marriage, she was being hounded by the press, she handled them with unfailing courtesy, even in situations in which many other people would have snapped. By contrast it is said that, in private, the Princess frequently behaved like an Aries, and will brook no opposition to her wishes. All that counts, however, in most peoples' eyes is the naturally gracious face which she presents in public.

Back in 1981, astrologers were aware of Diana's exceptional personality, for it was clearly revealed in the paradoxes and contradictions within her horoscope. The media, who had no such advantage, saw only a shy and inexperienced young girl. At that time Diana had experienced the destabilising effects of her Moon–Uranus alignment on her family only as a victim, through the trauma of her parents' divorce and her father's remarriage. Cancer is a complicated sign, for it is a mixture of exceptional sensitivity and deep ambition. Cancerians have a tendency to withdraw from the world, shutting themselves away as a simple protective measure; but when they emerge it is often with a ruthless determination never again to be exploited. In 1981, when Diana was still only twenty years old, she was still in the withdrawn phase. In addition, she was born with the Sun in a very close and harmonious alignment with Neptune. This is a pattern indicative of deep romantic ideals. She grew up believing in true love, and when Charles proposed she assumed automatically that she must be in love with him and he with her. Charles was undoubtedly fond of her, but inspired by his Saturnine parents, he was also doing his duty, acquiring a wife in order to provide a male heir. Nothing had changed since Henry VIII divorced and executed his wives for precisely the same reason.

Diana possesses a deep devotion to detail, and is capable of dealing with every single practical step necessary to achieve her goals. Her initial reaction to a situation may be emotional, but once she sets her heart on a chosen course, there is no changing her mind. The secret here is her Mars in Virgo, which convinces her that if a job is worth doing, it's worth doing properly. If nobody else can do it properly, she concludes, then do it yourself. People with Mars in Virgo often take up hobbies of a practical nature, and at their most extreme are to be found with screwdriver or spanner in hand, dismantling equipment. With the Princess' Mars also very close to Pluto, a planet of finality and endings, she's just the kind of person who is tempted to dismantle the TV set, only to find that she doesn't know how to put it back together again! The general trend of the Princess's chart inclines her towards intuitive and creative activities. Nonetheless, she has the potential of a champion tinkerer. Looking at this tendency in the broadest sense, the Princess has, in fact, tinkered with the inner workings of the royal family. By pressing her case for a separation from Prince Charles she challenged the mechanics of royal relationships in which, no matter how bad the relationship may have become, one's duty was to present a stiff upper lip and stay put. True, Princess Margaret separated from Lord Snowdon, but only after there was no longer any chance of her succeeding to the throne. Margaret, interestingly, also has very strong Pluto alignments. But when we see Diana carrying her challenge to the heart of the monarchy we see the deeper implications of her Mars–Pluto alignment.

This Mars–Pluto alignment was also found in the horoscopes of many of the Stuart monarchs. Out of the fourteen Stuarts who sat on the thrones of England, Scotland and Ireland, nine (including Mary, Queen of Scots) were born with powerfully disruptive Mars–Pluto connections and two others – among whom we find Charles I – with similar alignments which were slightly less difficult. If we examine the history of the Stuarts, every one of them was either on the receiving end of anarchy, like Mary, or helped to encourage it, like Charles I. It appears that half the monarchs born with a powerful Mars–Pluto alignment experienced difficulties not of their own making. In recent times, both George V and George VI were born with this combination, and while one led Britain through the trauma of the First World War, the other guided the country through the tragedy of the Second World War. The other half, born with every apparent advantage, appear unable to resist the temptation to create confrontation. We shouldn't judge them too harshly, for what drives them is an uncompromising desire to discover the truth. Diana's Mars–Pluto alignment actually falls in Virgo, a sign devoted to the principle of perfection. So great is her devotion to the truth that nothing less than 100% will do, even at the cost of pain and conflict on the way.

In the Plutonic mentality, sacrifice and healing, destruction and creation are opposites which invariably coexist. This is why it was so natural, while her own marriage was unravelling, for Diana to devote herself to Relate, the charity whose purpose is to reconcile estranged partners and try to save their marriages. Paradoxically, while she was saving other people's relationships, Diana was sacrificing her own.

When Charles met Diana they would both have experienced the pleasant reaction we usually find when any romantic Cancerian meets an emotional Scorpio. There's often a mutual recognition that each is a sensitive soul struggling to make sense of a rough and difficult world. Both signs have their secrets and find it easy to slip into sharing unspoken thoughts. Both Charles and Diana also have their Ascendants in extraverted fire signs; his is in Leo, hers is in Sagittarius. This makes for a second set of shared assumptions and a mutual appreciation of each other's adventurous qualities. However, while these astrological patterns may prompt an excellent friendship, they do not necessarily indicate a successful marriage.

The compulsive attraction between Charles and Diana was triggered not by their Sun signs or Ascendants but by the relationship between his Sun and her Moon. When we compare Charles' horoscope to Diana's, his intense Scorpionic Sun falls in an extremely powerful aspect to her explosive Moon–Venus–Uranus alignment. The answer to the compatibility question is therefore that, if their relationship is to work, it must be perfect. At the first indication that everything was not exactly right, Diana's explosive stars came into play. She then began the process by which small differences became exaggerated into large ones until the relationship lost all its meaning for her. Charles was clearly attracted to Diana by the easy relationship between their Sun signs and Ascendants, but was expecting a companionable marriage within the traditions set down by royal precedent. Diana was expecting perfection.

For Diana, Charles' Sun acted as a lightning rod, allowing her to discharge the incredible energy contained in her Moon–Venus – Uranus alignment. But, for the relationship to survive, Charles had to walk a tightrope. The moment he was found to have feet of clay Diana withdrew. First she retreated herself, becoming isolated as only a Cancer can, reliving the trauma of her parents' separation. Then she discovered her independence, living through her Aquarian Moon. And then, instead of Charles' Sun being the route for her to express her remarkable talents, he seems to have become the object of her pent-up anger. The Sun is a symbol of the father, and for Diana Charles came to represent a repressive parent against whom she eventually rebelled. The irony is that she needed to rebel in order to discover her more adventurous and powerful qualities, and had Charles not been there she would have had to have found someone else to fulfil his role. If she can ever look back on her disastrous marriage with genuine understanding she'll realise that she has a great deal for which to thank him. Without Charles, Diana might never have discovered her true potential.

Is there a chance of a reconciliation? Is there even any chance of Diana and Charles ever being on friendly terms? Unfortunately, there was a very inauspicious eclipse two days after their wedding. Charles and Diana were married on 29 July 1981 with the Sun at 6° in Leo, the same degree of the zodiac which was so important at Edward VIII's abdication. This in itself would not have mattered, but on 31 July, when the Sun reached 8° it was eclipsed by the Moon. This, being such a powerful royal degree, could only be considered inauspicious.

Any Cancerian has a good chance of being compatible with a Scorpio, and creating a civilised relationship with them. More interesting, though, is the relationship between Charles' Sun and Diana's explosive planets. Such is the magnetic power between their horoscopes that it can swing between compulsive attraction and repulsion without warning. For this reason, the future is unpredictable. From the original fairy-tale wedding, they have entered the kind of relationship so many couples get into where, even though they can't live with each other, nor, thanks to their shared history, can they live without each other. However, for a reconciliation to work there has to be a balance. Either Charles must be compulsively in love with Diana or she must accept that more casual, companionable relationship which makes sense to him.

The last word though, must lie with Charles; his Leonine pride has been offended, his Scorpio sensibilities wounded, and his Taurean sense of 'business as usual' has been disrupted by Diana's all too public revelations about their personal life. Plus, it is said, 'A Scorpio never forgets'. Both Charles and Diana have their most important planetary configurations in the stubborn 'fixed' signs – Taurus, Leo, Scorpio, Aquarius, and find it very difficult to forgive and forget. Charles, especially, will seek to make conditions, for he will wish to see Diana humble herself. But she on her part can never accept such limitations. In this sense, the prospects are bleak.

In theory, according to their horoscopes, there should be a great deal of mutual respect between Charles and Diana, based partly on their shared interests. Both are deeply attracted to esoteric beliefs, to religion and mysticism. The tragedy is, perhaps, that they married when Diana was too young. She had no more inkling of her true power than Charles did, and as she grew up and came to realise that power, the relationship collapsed. Instead of welcoming her assumption of regal powers, Charles resented it. Perhaps his proud Leonine ascendant was offended by sharing the limelight with his wife. After all, he was to be King. She was merely his consort.

The curious fact about Diana is that while she has only the one major astrological contact with Charles' horoscope, her official horoscope reveals contacts with the rest of the Windsor clan. It is almost as if, like Wallis Simpson, she was brought into the family to shake it up. Diana's Ascendant at 18° in Sagittarius, for example, is extremely close to George VI's Sun, which was at 22° of Sagittarius. This means that her Ascendant is also almost in the opposite degree to Prince Philip's Sun. Diana's Midheaven is also closely connected to other royal horoscopes. It is exactly 90° away from the Queen's Ascendant, indicating a powerful and tense relationship. Yet it is her

Moon which forms the greatest set of relationships, forming exact and tense alignments not only with Charles' Sun, but with George VI's Moon, the Queen Mother's Moon, the Queen's Midheaven, Prince Philip's Moon and Princess Anne's Sun. It even makes powerful alignments with Princess Anne's children's horoscopes, including Peter Phillips' Sun and Zara's Moon. We could go on. It is as if, with such powerful alignments, the royal family were a bomb waiting to explode and it took Diana to light the fuse. Before she married Charles, the monarchy had grown complacent. The Queen had attempted to modernise its image, but had failed to consider its substance. She had tried to make the Windsors appear ordinary, in the same way as so many of the modern European royal families. But this could not be done whilst at the same time retaining their privileges, together with all the attendant pomp and ceremony.

Diana's quest for personal independence is never going to diminish. Throughout the 1980s all her planetary patterns were difficult, with results of which we are all aware. Although from the end of 1993 onwards there is to be a temporarily lull in the pace of astrological change, she will meet great challenges later in the 1990s. And when this happens we will see her present a further challenge to the monarchy. It was the Queen who set out to modernise the Windsor dynasty, but she was too cautious to complete the task she set herself. It is almost as if she herself conjured up Diana as the future instrument of her policy.

Diana has passed through an astonishing series of planetary transits since her marriage. Throughout the 1980s one intense celestial alignment after another hit her horoscope, causing her to grow up far quicker than anyone expected. At the time of the wedding itself Pluto was passing across her Midheaven, the exact summit of her horoscope, bringing profound personal transformation. This was no young girl walking up the aisle of St Paul's, but an individual on the verge of the most total personal revolution. Soon afterwards, Pluto was joined by Saturn, bringing the intense pressures which, unrecognised, resulted in her eating disorder. The fairy-tale Princess, meanwhile, was the product of the passage of Neptune across her Sagittarian Ascendant. This planet always creates strange illusions, and in Diana's case it did a perfect job.

In 1985 Uranus reached Diana's Ascendant and she began to follow this planet's radical direction. This was when she began to separate herself from Charles' control. She set herself on the course which was to see her moving away from what she now experienced as the stifling role of glamorous Princess, the star of a thousand glittering balls, and began to wish that she could do something useful with her life. She began to rediscover the Diana who had enjoyed caring for young children and working in the kindergarten. Uranus seems to encourage rebellion, but only because it urges us to be more like ourselves, and less the product of other people's expectations. And so it was with Diana.

By 1989, as the rumours of her estrangement from Charles began to grow more intense, Uranus had moved on to Diana's Sun, where it was joined by Neptune. As Uranus encouraged her quest for her true identity, Neptune gave her the remarkable ability to effortlessly promote her image still further. The Princess has an uncanny knack for striking a pose, for hitting the right note, and in large measure this is due to the excellent relationship between the Sun and Uranus at her birth. Every time Neptune forms a new alignment in her chart, her innate skill is increased and enhanced.

In December 1992, when the split finally came, Pluto was once again the crucial planet. On the 9th, when the separation was formally announced, this intense planet was extending its uncompromising and emotional influence to Diana's Moon, completing the cycle in-augurated in 1981 when it passed over the top of her horoscope.

After 1994 Diana's horoscope enters a quiet phase, but one which lasts only a few years. 1997–8 are lively years for most members of the royal family, and January 1998 is an especially turbulent time for Diana. She'll be breaking free and defying convention for all she's worth. However, her next set of truly revolutionary alignments occur in the first years of the twenty-first century. For almost the whole of 2001 and 2002 Diana will be experiencing Uranus transits, triggering everything in her personality which is most individualistic, original and revolutionary. It is frankly difficult to know how the House of Windsor can contain the Princess' excitable presence. Throughout this period she will be experimenting with different ideas and lifestyles, not all of which will be conventional. The question of her remarriage will loom large, if it hasn't done so already, and she is likely to experience a number of serious relationships. She will be attempting to rerun the previous forty years, compensating for her failures and making up for lost opportunities. Among the unfinished business from the past with which she grapples will be her relationship with Prince Charles. There will be times when she attempts a genuine reconciliation, perhaps a meeting of minds, but there is no possibility of her compromising her freedom or independence. She cannot go to Charles as a supplicant, as the subject to her Prince. She can only go if she is accepted as his equal in every respect. This is the nature of Uranus!

The Princess will then move directly into another period which takes her from December 2002 to December 2004, during which time Pluto will be passing over her Ascendant. This period, which will truly get under way in February 2003, will be profound. Time and time again, events which might normally pass unnoticed will turn the Princess in on herself. There will be times when she craves the seclusion that Victoria sought when she went into mourning for Albert. There will be moments when she contemplates religious conversion. She may fall utterly, helplessly and passionately in love. She will also very likely spend large amounts of time abroad, as if travelling helps her escape from herself. The underlying psychological process will drive her to test her limits in every direction and at all levels of her being – physical, emotional, intellectual and spiritual. Having been born under a powerful Neptune, the Princess is a mistress of disguise and much of what takes place will be invisible to the public. But there will be times, as during February 2003, when it is clear that she is taking a new direction. She will emerge from this period with a new stature, with a wisdom and confidence which will be apparent in 2005. That's when Saturn makes a powerful aspect to her Midheaven, exuding authority, and Uranus once again lines up with her Sun, conferring a boundless optimism and faith in human nature. By 2009 Diana will be back on form, kicking over the traces, and once again being true to Uranus, her most independent-minded planet. But by then the world will be a very different place.

PRINCE WILLIAM

Born in London at 9.03 p.m. on 21 June 1982, with the Sun and Moon in Cancer and the Ascendant in Sagittarius.

During the royal crisis of 1992, many people questioned whether Charles would ever become King. Some said that the crown should pass directly from Elizabeth to William. Yet William himself is not an automatic candidate and, after looking at his horoscope, we are forced to conclude that there are serious doubts as to whether he will indeed one day succeed to the throne.

Prince William was born hours after a very powerful eclipse of the Sun. This was no ordinary eclipse, for it fell exactly at the summer solstice, one of the turning points of the year. At the precise moment of birth the degree of the zodiac at which the eclipse had occurred was setting over the western horizon. It is encouraging to speculate on the significance of such powerful alignments. We could expect that, if William becomes King, his reign will not be an easy one. This doesn't mean that he will necessarily be subject to problems not of his own making, for it will very likely be he who initiates change. However, such a powerful horoscope does allow us to pick out the major dates in William's life. For example, the period from 2008 to 2011 will be extremely important, and we might expect a passionate affair, a troubled succession or a threat to the monarchy itself. We can even be confident about picking out certain dates, and January 2008 will be a crucial month; that though, all lies in the future.

Does William have the chart of a king? The answer lies in a successful forecast made shortly before his birth by astrologer Charles Harvey. He received a call from the press in the middle of June 1981, asking if he could predict the day on which Diana would give birth. Harvey replied that he couldn't pick the date but that the expected heir to the throne ought to be born around 9.00 p.m. when Jupiter would be at its most favourable position, right on the Midheaven. William was indeed born just after 9.00 p.m. with Jupiter in the required position. This is the most powerful argument that William will one day become King.

William's Midheaven is 2° in Scorpio. This aspect represents his

159

most powerful connection with the rest of the Windsor clan, for it falls on the exact opposite zodiacal degree to Charles' Moon and the Queen's Sun. It follows that the monarch, the heir to the throne and the heir's successor will simultaneously experience identical planetary patterns. For example, in 1996 Elizabeth, Charles and Diana will experience a challenging 90° alignment from Uranus, planet of change. All three will have to respond to the same unsettling events at the same time. If we were to select important dates for them, in 1996 we would have to follow the passage of Mars over the Suns, Moons and Ascendants in all the royal horoscopes, which gives us early February, late April, the last week of May, the first week of June, the end of August, and late October as the sensitive moments.

Around these dates William will respond as his personality dictates. What do we know about this young man? With the Sun and Moon together in Cancer, he is quite clearly extraordinarily sensitive, and with Neptune, planet of inspiration, exactly on his Ascendant, he is a true romantic with a vivid imagination. He could take these talents in many directions. He could be a skilled musician or a painter. He will certainly be susceptible to the appeal of religion, and will inherit both his parents' fascination for mysteries and mysticism. He will also be a sensitive lover, and when the time comes, women will be charmed by his willingness to listen, his sympathy for their problems and his intuitive understanding of their feelings.

However, much depends on his relationship with Diana, his fellow Cancer. Fortunately, she seems to understand perfectly the Cancerian child's need of emotional security. William is even more naïve and trusting than most Cancerians. If his trust is betrayed, if he is wounded, or feels that he cannot cope with the harsh realities of the world, he will withdraw inside his Cancerian shell. This was exactly what Diana did when she responded to her parents' separation by hiding behind the mask of the shy young girl. Male Cancerians often retreat behind a cold and calculating façade. They are good at pretending they are unaffected by family problems, but nothing could be further from the truth. They pretend to a lack of concern for other people's feelings and human suffering, and an expression of solicitude is likely to be met with sarcasm and barbed comments. They can also appear aloof and snobbish. Such behaviour is the sign of the unhappy

Cancerian who has been hurt once too often and who has decided that the human race as a whole is not to be trusted. The only reason for pointing this out is that no Cancer, any more than any other sign, can entirely evade their negative qualities, and there will be times when William is accused of being unapproachable, cold and uncaring. But if we are forewarned with an understanding of the inner psychological processes represented by the Cancerian archetype, we will be able to understand and sympathise with his actions.

This is why Diana's relationship with William is so crucial, and why we can hope that he will have the confidence to show his softer side and the courage to be true to his feelings. Thankfully, today's world is, in some ways, a kinder place for sensitive men than it once was. However, William will find the unkind attentions of the tabloid press even harder to bear than Prince Charles did. At times the media will attack what they perceive as his arrogance, completely failing to understand that with Neptune, planet of illusion, exactly on his Ascendant and Jupiter, planet of expansion, exactly on his Mid-heaven, William will be compelled to explore activities which may not fit in with the media's view of what are fit pursuits and interests for a prince. William's horoscope is almost entirely devoid of practical planetary alignments. His natural *metier* is therefore the realm of ideas and feelings. He will grow up to be a philosophical man, and in this sense we're looking at a real case of 'like father, like son'. William has pronounced differences from Charles, but the general drift of their horoscopes is very similar, and we'll find him repeating many of Charles' familiar dilemmas: how to reconcile his ideals with the limitations placed on him by his birth, and how to carve out a meaningful role for himself beyond being a mere ceremonial figure-head.

William's Ascendant in Sagittarius confers an adventurous spirit, and when we see that he has a very powerful ninth house, and that this is the sector of his horoscope denoting long distance travel, it is clear that he has the horoscope of an explorer. Again this reminds us of Charles, although in William's case the desire to visit far-flung places is even greater. Neptune exactly on the Ascendant is ideal for sailors, and if it is proposed that William carries on the family tradition and has a spell in the navy, he is likely to leap at the chance. However, the ninth house is also connected to legal matters and, hence, the constitution. It is therefore extremely likely that during William's life, perhaps as a result of his own actions, there will be substantial changes in the monarchy's constitutional position. Because the planets which could affect his constitutional position are so spread out, it becomes almost impossible to pick out precise dates when such constitutional change is likely to take place. There are many possible dates which offer broad indications of major change in William's life, but the years 2008 to 2011, when he will be in his late twenties, should be watched closely.

William's entire horoscope is romantic, and he'll be extremely susceptible to emotional appeals. He is likely to misinterpret others' friendly advances as declarations of love, while his sympathetic and caring manner may often give a false impression that he is proposing marriage! William was born with Venus (signifying his ability to express affection) at 25° in Taurus. This is the exact degree held by the same planet when Diana was born, so it follows that the two have similar needs and desires. Like his mother, William places a high premium on loyalty. Having made a declaration of love, he will find it difficult to change his mind. Once he decides to make his move he will be exceedingly generous, to the point of theatricality. Ultimately, with his Venus so close to Diana's, William's relationships with women will be profoundly shaped by the lessons absorbed from his relationship with Diana.

William's godfather, Laurens van der Post, is perhaps Prince Charles' greatest spiritual mentor. Sir Laurens was a close friend of Carl Gustav Jung, the psychologist who did more than anyone else to give astrology a twentieth-century relevance. After William's christening Sir Laurens related the following curious story: 'It was a very simple ceremony – and a remarkable thing happened. The windows of the music room were open, the sun streaming in – and then the sky went grey, as a great storm gathered. Just as the Archbishop of Canterbury handed over a lighted candle, a violent gust of wind blew through the windows. The candle flickered – but did not go out.'

Sir Laurens recalled how his friend Jung once had an important dream, of standing in a great storm holding a lighted candle – how vital it had been that the candle should not be blown out, and how, when he awoke, he took great comfort from the fact that he had managed to keep the flame burning.

When asked whether he had told Prince Charles about Jung's dream, Sir Laurens said, 'Oh yes, of course. He understands these things.'

What would Charles understand by the event which both he and Sir Laurens regarded as a powerful omen? The candle symbolises not only life, hope and light, but William himself. And, as William is heir to the throne, the candle also represents the monarchy. The candle flickering indicated a grave crisis, but the fact that it wasn't blown out indicates that William will survive. Has the crisis already passed in the break-up of Charles and Diana's marriage? This has already provoked one constitutional crisis. But such omens tend to repeat themselves. I would therefore take Charles' and Sir Laurens' strange story as confirmation that William's life as heir or as monarch will be marked by further substantial constitutional change.

When we compare William's horoscope to those of the previous monarchs we find very few connections. True, his Midheaven is in the exact opposite degree to Prince Charles' Moon and the Queen's Sun. There's a powerful link there, but normally we would expect more than just this one connection. Indeed, when we take the four most important positions in William's chart – the Sun, Moon, Ascendant and Midheaven – and compare them to those in Charles', Diana's, Elizabeth's, Philip's, the Queen Mother's and George VI's, we find no more than those already mentioned. There is just one possible exception – a loose connection between his Midheaven and George VI's. One possible conclusion is that William's inheritance is that of a Spencer, not a Windsor. In other words, he has taken after his mother's side of the family.

However, if we look beyond George VI for comparisons to William's horoscope, we discover a very interesting fact: William has certain striking similarities with his great-great-uncle, Edward VIII. Edward, like William and Diana, was born with Venus in Taurus, in his case at 23°. That's one connection, but it is not the most important. The important pattern is based on their Sun and Moon positions:

* William was born with the Sun at 0° Cancer in an exact and powerful conjunction with Edward's Sun at 2° in Cancer.
* William was born with the Moon at 5° in Cancer in an exact and harmonious 'trine' aspect with Edward's Moon at 4° in Pisces.
* William was born with his Midheaven at 3° in Scorpio in a powerful and challenging 'square' aspect to Edward's Midheaven at 1° in Aquarius.

Those powerful contacts between planets in emotional Cancer and sensitive Pisces indicate that, had William and Edward ever met, they would have undoubtedly struck up an instant rapport and formed an enduring relationship. Edward would have taken William under his spiritual care, and the Prince would have found unlimited emotional support in Edward's intuitive understanding of his feelings, circumstances and purpose. Aside from these intense connections, Edward's emotional Sun and Moon were balanced by an independent Ascendant in Aquarius, while William's equally sensitive Sun and Moon are balanced by an adventurous Ascendant in Sagittarius. Both were born with exactly the same contrast between a longing for emotional security and a desire to break out, mixed in exactly the same proportions.

Yet there's more to these planetary connections than a mere similarity of temperament. Both William and Edward respond to the same planetary patterns within the overall history of the Windsor dynasty and the British monarchy. And Edward was the king who gave up his throne to follow his heart. William is therefore in exactly the same position; in 1936 he would have followed the same path as Edward. In the changed circumstances of the twenty-first century he may not have to face the same choice. But, should a dilemma similar to Edward's arise in William's life, it is possible that his feelings will take precedence over his sense of duty.

If we take a closer look still at William's and Edward's horoscopes we find an even stranger pattern emerging. William's Sun and Moon are both in Cancer, but if we want to find the most sensitive point, at which the power of the Sun and Moon is felt most powerfully, we look to the exact midpoint between the two. This falls at 2° 31 mins in Cancer. This is so close to Edward VIII's Sun at 2° 21 mins in Cancer as to be indistinguishable. When we then look back at the series of eclipses which in 1992 took the crisis between Charles and Diana along its tragic course, we discover that the final one was an eclipse of the Sun. This took place on 24 December at 2° 28 mins in Capricorn. This is the *exact* opposite degree to those positions shared by Edward and William. Poor William suffered as he faced the prospect of his first Christmas with embattled parents. But his inner pain at Charles' and Diana's separation was more than a personal matter; it concerned the life of the dynasty and the soul of the nation. It was as if the ghost of Edward VIII were stalking the corridors of Buckingham Palace. William will face very different circumstances from those which greeted his great-great-uncle in 1936. Edward was forced to sacrifice the throne for his feelings. William may therefore be the man who accomplishes what Edward could not, challenging royal convention and succeeding.

One important personality trait which will guide William through the pressures of being heir to the throne is his pride. When the pressure of being such a sensitive soul continually exposed to the glare of the cameras becomes too great, he will fall back on the knowledge that he must perform his task to the best of his ability. Jupiter at the very summit of his horoscope gives him the sense that he was born to fulfil a special destiny. However, in the final analysis the Prince's sense of theatre is greater than his sense of responsibility.

William has two examples to follow. He can follow that of his grandmother the Queen, and her father George VI, and put duty first; or he can follow in the footsteps of Edward VIII and Diana, and put his feelings above everything else. If William takes the second course of action around the year 2008, he will not become King. The choice is his.

PRINCE HENRY

Born in London at 4.20 a.m. on 15 September 1984, with the Sun in Virgo, the Moon in Taurus and the Ascendant in Capricorn.

Prince Henry is made in the image not of Prince Charles nor Princess Diana, but of his grandmother, Queen Elizabeth. It is as if the planets have skipped a generation. With his Sun in Virgo, his Moon in Taurus and his Ascendant in Capricorn, all the most important features in his chart are spread through the three practical 'earth' signs. In many ways, Henry is the polar opposite of William. Whereas William's first response to any situation is to ask himself how he feels about it, Henry asks, 'What use is it?' He is supremely businesslike and conservative, with a small c. That doesn't mean that he is dull. Far from it. It just means that if there are to be changes, they need to be for a very good reason indeed. There is absolutely no point in tampering with relationships, enterprises and processes which are operating perfectly well by themselves.

Henry's similarity to Elizabeth is intensified by the fact that, like her, he was born with Saturn in Scorpio, close to the Midheaven. In the Queen's horoscope this position is the ultimate guarantee that her commitment to duty is deep and unswerving. She simply cannot deviate from having accepted the responsibility of her position. Henry's Saturn is 5° away from his Midheaven, which makes it a less powerful factor than it is for the Queen, but in other ways his horoscope is more stable than hers.

Intriguingly, Henry's connections to the dynastic astrology of the Windsors and the national astrology of the British are stronger than William's. His Sun at 22° in Virgo is exactly 90° away from George VI's Sun (22° in Sagittarius) and Prince Philip's Sun (20° in Gemini). This locks him into the planetary patterns signified by both men. In addition Henry's Moon at 21° in Taurus is in the opposite degree to George VI's Moon (25° in Scorpio), the Queen Mother's Moon (20° in Scorpio), the Queen's Midheaven (25° in Scorpio) and Prince Charles' Sun (23° in Scorpio), and is 90° away from Prince Philip's Moon (22° in Leo) and Diana's Moon (25° in Aquarius). This is a truly astonishing set of astrological contacts, and is far more intense than anything in William's horoscope.

When we compare Henry's horoscope to the national astrology of Great Britain we find another set of connections. His Moon, at 21° in Taurus, is within 1° of the Sun's position on 1 May 1707, the day that England and Scotland formally declared their union as the Kingdom of Great Britain. His Ascendant, at 12° in Capricorn, is extraordinarily close to the Sun on the day that Great Britain then formally united with Ireland to create the United Kingdom – 11° in Capricorn. This is also very close to the degree occupied by the Sun when William the Conqueror was crowned and the modern English monarchy was created.

The only possible conclusion is that while William may love the pomp and ceremony of the monarchy, and may well be temperamentally suited to lead the royal family into a new era, Henry's planetary connections to the dynasty and the nation indicate that he would make an ideal monarch. Indeed, anyone seeking to put money on Henry succeeding to the throne would not be making a bad bet, and, if the bookmakers were to set odds on this, they should be short.

Henry is an overwhelmingly practical boy who needs to be set tasks which have a positive purpose. If he cannot see any reason for accomplishing a particular feat, he is unlikely to bother. This shouldn't be too much of a handicap, for all he requires is that he understands what use there is for him in doing something, or what benefit for others. Even pleasure can be a suitable goal for a child with the Moon in Taurus; and with the Sun in Virgo, any form of self-improvement is a worthwhile exercise. He will probably find much to offer in the country pursuits so popular with the Queen and Prince Charles, and is more likely to enjoy the rigours of a cold Balmoral summer than his more comfort-oriented elder brother, William.

Henry is also likely to inherit Prince Charles' love of dangerous sports for, in marked contrast to the caution of his Sun, Moon and Ascendant, he was born with a very close conjunction between Mars (sign of energy) and Uranus (the unusual) in Sagittarius (adventurousness). Any sport which relies on the latest technology will fascinate him, and if he can overcome his Virgoan reluctance to take risks, he will take to parascending, sky-diving or one of the other new sports which involves danger to life and limb by flying through the air.

The same Mars–Uranus conjunction gives him a love of unusual social gatherings and eccentric people; a party given by Prince Henry will be a party to remember. In love, the Prince will be attracted by old-fashioned manners and charm. He'd be happier in an age when gentlemen left their calling-cards and women wore white gloves. With his friends he will be brash and unreliable on occasion, but with anyone who is important to him he will be unfailingly courteous and eager to please. When he sets out to attract a woman no effort will be too great and no detail overlooked. The more he cultivates his sense of charm, the more fascinating and desirable he will become.

Henry was born with Mercury in Virgo, an indication that he will only ever say what he means. And Mercury's powerful relationship to Jupiter will make him a master of the white lie, always ready with a kindly word, to encourage other people and give them hope for the future. He also has great skill with money, and a career in business could beckon. Indeed, he would be the ideal candidate to take over as manager of the royal fortune.

Yet Henry's horoscope is more than that of a private individual; it is that of the third in line to the throne. We should remember that of the eighteen monarchs who have reigned over the thrones of England and Scotland since 1603, only five (Charles II, George III, George IV, Edward VII and Edward VIII) could have expected at their births to inherit the throne. When we consider the twenty-three monarchs who have reigned in England since the end of the Wars of the Roses, the list is increased by just one (Edward VI). More often than not, the heir to the throne does not succeed. In this case we must point out that, just as William was born with Jupiter in a region of the horoscope suitable for a king, so was Henry. If there is to be a change in the succession, then the years around 2008 bring the next possible dates. Until then we must wait and see.

PRINCESS ANNE, CAPTAIN MARK PHILLIPS AND COMMANDER LAWRENCE

PRINCESS ANNE

Born in London at 10.50 a.m. on 15 August 1950, with the Sun in Leo, the Moon in Virgo and the Ascendant in Libra.

Of all the Queen's four children, Princess Anne is by far the best at coping with the perils of growing up in the public eye. She combines the steely determination which comes from being born with the Sun in Leo, in a close conjunction with Pluto. It is in the nature of Pluto to bring confrontation, trauma and disappointment, but when the Leonine personality is functioning at its best, every crisis produces a resolve to do better next time. The Princess was born with the Sun and

Pluto prominent in her horoscope, an indication that she sets her sights high and aims for the top. Every time she has been insulted, slighted or put down she has quietly resolved never to be treated that way again.

As a teenager Anne channelled her Leonine energy into competitive riding, which was eventually to lead to selection for the Olympic team. This must make her almost the only member of the royal family ever to achieve any honour by merit alone, with no suspicion whatsoever of favouritism. However, it took some time to control the confrontational effects of her powerful Plutonic energy. No doubt the photographers she famously told to 'naff off' had provoked her, but this and other incidents earned her the reputation of being a truculent character. Through the sixties and seventies the Princess was hardly the most popular member of the royal family. Yet anyone looking at her horoscope would have observed the power of her Sun–Pluto alignment and acknowledged that here was someone who, rather than smile sweetly when hounded by the press, would give as good as she got. As a Leo she loved the adulation of the crowds, but she was not prepared to be treated like a fool.

Anne was born with her Ascendant in Libra, which means quite simply that she needs to be liked. Her unpopularity pained her and as she passed through her twenties she began to reveal the charming side of this sign rather more than her truculent Leonine Sun. Perhaps her Leonine desire to be accepted as a person in her own right rather than as the privileged daughter of the monarch was satisfied by her success in riding and showjumping. Perhaps she felt that she no longer had to fight for her identity. We may never know the true psychological processes which operated as Anne began to rely less on her Leonine willingness to fight and emphasise her Libran desire for peace. What we do know is that the two signs fed on each other, and being accepted as a champion sportswoman freed the Princess to express herself in public as charming, witty and thoroughly good company, an ideal mixture, in short, of Leonine sparkle and Libran charm.

The Princess's popularity is sustained by another extremely fortunate feature in her horoscope: her Moon in Virgo. Research in the early 1980s showed that nurses tend to be born with the Sun in Virgo. No investigation was conducted for Moon positions, but everything suggests that, if it had been, the results would be even clearer. For Anne to become active in the Save the Children Fund was therefore a natural step, and it is widely agreed that she has been extremely effective in her public duties. Like Diana, she has tapped into that ancient aspect of the divine monarchy in which the monarch was thought to have healing powers. The public's favourable reaction to her work is in part an unconscious reflection of this archaic belief.

Anne's first marriage was to **Mark Phillips**. Mark was born at 1.45 p.m. on 22 September 1948 in Tewskesbury. Interestingly, in a number of important respects, his horoscope is a repeat of Anne's. She has the Sun in Leo and Moon in Virgo, and he has the Ascendant in Leo and Sun in Virgo. They share in equal amounts the brashness and theatricality of Leo and the serious-minded attention to detail which is invariably associated with Virgo. Perhaps it was this which bound them, for their shared, passionate interest in sport and show-jumping combines extreme precision with a sense of theatre. However, while these planets are prominent in Anne's chart, indicating a love of public attention, Mark's planetary pattern indicates a resentment at public intrusion into his affairs. His most prominent planet is the Moon, and that is in the somewhat reserved sign of Taurus. Few people have ever seen the true passion suggested by his Venus–Pluto alignment in Leo. If they had done, they might have realised that his reputation for dullness was undeserved. Mark needs his privacy and is ultimately unable to play the game required of royalty in their public life. Despite the general similarities between Anne and Mark's horoscopes, we find none of the close connections between their Suns, Moons, Ascendants and Midheavens which we would expect in the horoscopes of marriage partners. The tight connections which brought them together were based on their 'progressions'. These are planets which move around the horoscope, helping create yearly changes in direction and mood. When two people's progressions make intense contacts, they often result in an intense relationship, but if the birth horoscopes do not show similar links the bonds will be temporary. This is what happened to Anne and Mark, and in the years following their marriage the planetary cycles which had brought them together gradually parted. There was nothing to keep them together, and the absence of contacts in their birth horoscopes began to show. There were no public traumas. There was no reason why there should be, for if there were few alignments in their horoscopes drawing them together, neither were there any driving them apart. It was a simple matter of two quite similar people discovering that they didn't have enough in common to sustain a marriage. Eventually Anne, true to her uncompromising Sun–Pluto alignment, decided that divorce was inevitable.

On 12 December 1992, three days after Charles and Diana's separation was announced, Anne married **Commander Tim Lawrence** in a quiet ceremony at Balmoral. Tim was born on 1 March 1955, with his sun in Pisces, a sensitive sign, and his Moon in lively Gemini. The combination of Pisces and Gemini is an exceptionally delicate one, revealing deep intuition, charm and a very pleasing manner. In many ways Tim is the opposite of the rather blunt Mark Phillips. While Mark believes that one should get on with the business in hand, Tim is a story-teller, a romantic, capable of using words to great effect to charm and seduce. Whereas in Mark, Anne chose someone who, in terms of the broad sweep of his personality, was similar to her, in Tim she has opted for her opposite. His Piscean Sun falls on the opposite side of the zodiac to her Virgoan Moon. Each of them was attracted by qualities they perceived in the other which they themselves lacked. Tim is captivated by Anne's efficient, down-to-earth, stable Virgoan qualities, while she is fascinated by his Piscean capacity to drift off to the far reaches of the imagination. If they become irritated with each other it will be because he is frustrated by what he regards as her pedantic lack of imagination, while she will resent his refusal to be pinned down, even for a second. However, when a relationship is based on opposite signs, such bursts of irritation form part of the dynamic which takes each partner forward, deepening their understanding of one another.

Ultimately, Tim must avoid Mark's mistake, which was to dispute Anne's position as boss. She is not a woman to take orders. She needs to feel in command, to be sure that there are no obstacles in her path. With Mark, whose temperament was similar to her own, this presented an irreconcilable problem. Yet Tim, being an imaginative Pisces–Gemini type to Anne's worldly Virgo–Leo, has his own world, which she can share but never control. He can therefore leave her to organise practical matters, while he provides the sense of fantasy and illusion which allows their relationship to breathe. As long as they can maintain this balance they will have a perfect match.

Looking ahead, Anne will enter an exciting period in 1997 which will take her through to about 2003. She'll experience a series of domestic changes, but also, by 2001, her entire professional persona will have moved on one very important step. She'll be looking for new ways to exploit her royal position, not for her own benefit, but to do good for others. The work she has already been performing with the Save the Children Fund, for example, could be taken in a radical new direction.

PETER PHILLIPS

Son of Princess Anne and Mark Phillips. Born in Paddington, London at 10.46 a.m. on 15 November 1977, with the Sun in Scorpio and Moon and Ascendant in Capricorn.

It is said that Peter Phillips, the Queen's first grandchild, has always been a favourite of hers. This would hardly be surprising for Peter was born with Venus, planet of grace, exactly on his Midheaven, and Jupiter, bringer of *bonhomie*, in an exact opposition to his Ascendant. These two planets are so important in Peter's public behaviour that, almost whatever else he does, he will be able to charm his way through life. It won't be what he says that causes other people to ply him with gifts and affection, just something very appealing in his nature which is irresistibly attractive. A pattern such as this might be simply described as lucky. There are other very powerful connections between Peter's horoscope and the Queen's. His Sun falls on her Midheaven and his Moon falls on her Ascendant. These links between the two charts indicate that, for the Queen, Peter is the living embodiment of some of the qualities central to her own existence, especially her loyalty, sense of responsibility and practical common sense.

In spite of Peter's magical ability to charm people, he is a deeply private person, and misunderstandings will arise if friends think his Venus–Jupiter charm is all there is to his character. As soon as they take him for granted, or offend him or, for that matter, anyone he loves, he will freeze them out. He may not say anything. He may not have to. He will merely put down invisible shutters and have nothing more to do with the individuals concerned.

He was born the day after Prince Charles' birthday, which means that his Sun is in intense, secretive Scorpio. In combination with the Moon in Capricorn this makes for an exceptionally serious character. It also indicates a slow developer, and it will be years before we see Peter's true potential. He is one of those people who flourish in their late thirties or early forties – that is, only after acquiring experience, and with it the confidence to take on a public role. However, Peter excels in sending out contradictory signals and the fact that he has Uranus in an exact conjunction with his Midheaven will make for dramatic changes and unusual twists in his career. These will confuse those who were deceived by the seriousness and loyalty of his Capricorn Moon and Scorpionic Sun. He will need a career which offers him independence and the chance to explore the latest ideas or work with the most advanced technology. In addition to this, he has a certain need to feel that he has a part to play in saving the world. If he is forced to do unsuitable work, as is all too likely, he will bear it for a while, and then cut loose. If he is forced into the wrong job again he will continue to break free. This pattern will be repeated until he finds an occupation in which he can use his own particular skills and talents, one where he is his own boss.

Like Prince William, Peter has a powerful connection with Edward VIII; Edward's Sun was at 2° 21 mins in Cancer, while at the very moment of Peter's birth the Ascendant was at 2° 27 mins in Capricorn, the exact opposite degree. The connection between Peter and Edward is weaker than that between William and Edward, but it is still strong enough to imagine that, had they met, the old King would have become a powerful role model for the Queen's eldest grandson. This also means that Peter and William have a powerful astrological connection, for Peter's Ascendant is also in a direct opposition to William's Sun. This means that they both respond to planetary movements over this degree at exactly the same time. They are, in effect, time twins. This means that, like William, Peter will experience powerful planetary transits in the year 2008. We begin to build up a picture then, that if the royal family is to experience dramatic changes in the near future, 2008 will be the year to watch.

173

ZARA PHILLIPS

Daughter of Princess Anne and Mark Phillips. Born in Paddington, London at 8.15 p.m. on 15 May 1981, with the Sun in Taurus, the Moon in Libra and the Ascendant in Scorpio.

Young Zara Phillips was born with the Sun and Ascendant in two stubborn signs, Scorpio and Taurus. The message is simple: woe betide the person who tries to change her mind for her. But wait. She was also born with the Moon in Libra, which means that she will be easily swayed by other people's opinions, completely unable to make up her own mind, and often agreeing with the last person she spoke to. When we consider her Moon's close conjunction with Pluto we find someone who is compulsively indecisive and obstinate, desperate to please and at the same time determined to do whatever she wants no matter what others may think. If Zara Phillips' horoscope is a muddle, it's an extremely creative and dynamic one, with the capacity to grab more headlines than most. Zara is saved by the fact that she will always make great efforts to ensure that other people are happy, and her own popularity is not in question. The only people who decide that they don't like her are those who expect her to be the kind of person she is not. People who take a one-dimensional view of her multi-dimensional personality will make the mistake of imagining that she is only a down-to-earth Taurean, or nothing more than an emotional Scorpio or simply a happy, companionable Libra.

Very much like her brother Peter, she may appear to be open and friendly to everyone, but her Scorpio Ascendant is the reservoir of great secrecy. There will be times when she has to withdraw from the social whirl in order to recoup her energy and spend time with a few close friends or relations. Those who intrude at such times will be decidedly unwelcome, although her charm is such that she will always appear to be welcoming.

Like anyone born with the Moon in Libra, Zara must have strong close connections with other people; whatever the experience, she requires a partner to share it. Yet at the same time she needs the freedom to change her course at a moment's notice. She also needs to be able to pursue her own passions rather than obey orders or perform tasks which may make sense to other people, but are frankly meaningless as far as she is concerned. In former times, when members of the royal family didn't do ordinary jobs, Zara would have become a notable socialite. In the twenty-first century she will be ideally suited to a career in the media or the arts.

When it comes to marriage she will have high standards. Any aspiring husband must conform to certain basic requirements; he must be utterly dependable, yet highly independent, deeply conservative, yet ready for change, discreet, yet passionate. The man who expects Zara to be predictable, to feel the same about him from one day to the next, or to explain herself to him, should not apply for the post. She has a horoscope well-suited to more than one husband, or to a series of intense, close relationships. The only way one man will stay the course is if he is willing to continually reinvent his and Zara's relationship, offering her the stimulation she requires and the incentive to stay with him.

The year 1999, when Zara will be eighteen, will be a perplexing one, and she may well embark on a course of action which is no more than a stopgap, using only a small part of her potential. After this, her next set of life-transforming planetary alignments occur in 2009–10, when she'll be twenty-eight, and hitting her fourth 'seven-year itch'. Under the combined influence of Mars, Jupiter, Uranus and Neptune, she may well decide to burn her bridges and start all over again!

PRINCE ANDREW AND SARAH FERGUSON

PRINCE ANDREW

Born in London at 3.30 p.m. on 19 February 1960, with the Sun in Pisces, the Moon in Scorpio and the Ascendant in Leo.

SARAH FERGUSON

Born in London at 9.03 a.m. on 15 October 1959, with the Sun in Libra, the Moon in Aries and the Ascendant in Scorpio.

Prince Andrew has had a number of public images over the last thirty years. From the joker who sprayed reporters with paint, through to

'Randy Andy' the sailor boy, to solid, dependable Andrew the loyal father and jilted husband. None of these changing faces is a true description of the real Andrew. None really touches the depths of the man born with the Sun in Pisces and the Moon in Scorpio, the emotional, intense and secretive individual driven by his feelings. Andrew was born with his Ascendant in Leo, so it became easy for him to find refuge in Leonine extraversion, becoming the jester, the clown always ready with a practical joke. This does not mean that there is anything contrived about his good humour and sense of fun. It's just that he is very skilled at putting on a brave face when deep inside he is drifting on a sea of uncertainty.

Both Pisces and Scorpio are known as 'water' signs, and Andrew has expressed both in a literal manner, making far more of his career as a naval officer than royal tradition required. Yet the psychological processes represented by these signs are the same for Andrew as for anyone else, and he has to cope with feelings which sometimes threaten to engulf him. He is capable of developing compulsive obsessions overnight but, in spite of his Leonine bluster, he has to face the intense fear of rejection. When everything is going swimmingly it's because he is following his instincts, moving effortlessly from one step to the next, often in unconscious telepathic communication with his partner.

Andrew, it is said, has always been the Queen's favourite child. This is hardly surprising, for every one of his four important degrees, the Sun, Moon, Ascendant and Midheaven, makes a powerful connection to the Queen's horoscope. His Ascendant in Leo, for example, occupies exactly the same degree of the Zodiac as the Queen's Moon. Compared to this, Charles' Leo Ascendant and Anne's Leo Sun are wide of the mark. Charles and Anne share a Leonine temperament with their mother, but between the Queen and Andrew there exists an unspoken bond. They have the kind of instinctive relationship that often occurs between twins.

Andrew's horoscope is undoubtedly highly creative. The combination of Scorpionic passion, Piscean imagination and Leonine flair is often found in performers. Apart from his clowning antics, Andrew has never taken up artistic activities, unlike his two brothers. However, he has in the past enjoyed a vicarious connection with the entertainment world through the women in his life. The actress Koo Stark seemed for a while to be his perfect partner, although she was deemed unacceptable as a royal wife in the eyes of his family. Andrew's affair with Koo took place during a long transit of Pluto across the degree of his horoscope symbolising home and family. From this we know that Andrew's relationship with Koo was a profound and intense experience which touched him deeply.

Venus, which indicates Andrew's ability to express affection, is in a very tight conjunction with Mars, which signifies his sexual desires. The tight link between the two is indicative of explosive passion. However, both planets are located in Capricorn, which suggests a tendency to be formal, somewhat inhibited and quite conservative. In other words, his passions are only able to express themselves with the right person in the right place at the right time. If the conditions aren't absolutely perfect, he'll withdraw into Scorpionic isolation. This is where Sarah Ferguson comes in. She may not have been a professional actress, but her boisterous manner certainly attracted Andrew's attention.

Opinions differ as to the true nature of Sarah's character. Those who don't like her and who are not personally acquainted with her think her rather vulgar. Those who do know her invariably regard her as extremely charming. Astrologically speaking, it is the latter who are correct. Sarah was born with the Sun in Libra and, as if this wasn't enough, the Sun was in a sector of her horoscope known as the eleventh house, which gives her a profound need to be part of a group. Sarah likes to be liked. She's a socialite. And rather than criticising her for this, we should recognise that part of her *raison d'être* is to cheer people up.

So where did Sarah's poor public reputation come from? And why was she demonised by the tabloid press as being the Ugly Sister to Diana's saintly Cinderella? Partly, she is her own worst enemy, for she has never truly learnt to reconcile her Moon in Aries with her Libran Sun. These two signs are opposites and much as Libra seeks agreement and harmony, Aries has a knack for stirring up even the most peaceful gathering. In any social situation the Sun in Libra begins by making sure that everyone else is happy and taking care of their requirements, whereas the Moon in Aries demands to be the centre of attention.

Libra asks, 'How are you?' while Aries shouts 'Look at me'. There's nothing inherently wrong with this. It's just that Sarah is not good at being an Aries because her Libran self doubts whether attention-seeking is really the proper thing to do. This is why, while her friends love her irrepressible sense of fun, to many her larking around looks more like the foolish antics of someone determined to discredit herself in public.

Even this does not explain why Sarah became the royal scapegoat. At the very top of Sarah's horoscope, exactly on her Midheaven, sits an intense conjunction of Venus and Pluto. At any other point in her horoscope this would indicate no more than her intense passions and her desire to take romantic attachments into total death-defying commitment. However, perched on her Midheaven, which is the single point in her horoscope describing her relationship with the world at large, it assumes a much greater significance. In many ways it can be seen as a symbol of emotional violence, and like all such Plutonic alignments it frequently offers a stark choice: either go on the offensive or else expect to be victimised. There is a third way, and that is to transform Pluto's destructive energy into a healing force, which should be possible, given that both planets are in Virgo, a sign closely connected to the healing arts. But before the emotional conflict symbolised by Venus and Pluto can be resolved, it has to be experienced.

When Sarah first became engaged to Andrew she was criticised for being overweight and having poor dress-sense. By the time she had kowtowed to public opinion and managed to lose weight her frequent holidays had become a source of complaint, not surprisingly, in a country slipping into the recession of the late eighties. She seemed incapable of altering her public behaviour. It is in the nature of Pluto to take any confrontation to its limit, and this is exactly what Sarah did in her conflict with the tabloid press.

There was one further interesting degree prominent at Andrew and Sarah's engagement, which takes us back to 1936 and the abdication crisis. When the royal marriages hit the rocks in 1992, it was as though the House of Windsor was being overtaken by a preordained fate; people began to talk about the Fall of the House of Windsor. Picking up on this theme, astrologer Patric Walker spoke of the curse of Wallis

178

Simpson, as if in some strange manner the Duchess of Windsor had returned to take her revenge for what she felt had been her shabby treatment at the hands of the royal family after the abdication crisis. Intriguingly, at the moment Andrew and Sarah's engagement was announced, the Ascendant was at 29° in Gemini, only one degree away from the Duchess of Windsor's Sun at 28° in Gemini. In other words, the Duchess's Sun had, only a few minutes earlier, risen over the eastern horizon. For the Duchess a new era had dawned, and indeed, just over a month later, on 24 April 1986, she died.

Such patterns are at first sight exceedingly strange. Yet astrology draws connections between people across time, suggesting that significant events in their lives are indeed connected by complex interlocking cycles. The same events are never repeated, but similar situations do recur and we keep returning to patterns we've experienced in the past.

What lies in the future? Andrew's next years of change are likely to be 1997–8, when Jupiter and Uranus meet in Aquarius. This happens to be the region of his horoscope symbolising marriage, so if he is to meet someone he would like to marry, that should be the first possible moment. For Sarah, 1998 is also due to be an intense year, but while it looks as if Andrew will be breaking free from his past, she has first to return to it and face her former mistakes before moving into the future with the confidence born from experience.

Sarah is, and always will be, a woman in search of a role; this is what being a Libran means for her. In 1998 and 1999 she'll probably be confronted with the painful fact that she doesn't have a worthwhile role, at least not one which she would recognise as such. This is when she may begin to regret the mistakes of her past, and devote herself to a noble cause. Hopefully this should do the trick, and she may imagine that she has found her true *métier* at the end of 2003, when she wins an accolade for work unconnected with her royal status. Yet in 2005 she'll be off again in search of adventure and new mountains to climb. As for remarriage, this is possible in 1998, for there are strong signs that she will be seeking emotional security. Yet, according to the best astrological advice, she should wait until after 1999, when she will have cleared the next hurdle set for her by Pluto.

PRINCESS BEATRICE

Eldest daughter of Andrew and Sarah. Born in Paddington, London at 7.18 p.m. on 8 August 1988, with the Sun in Leo, the Moon in Cancer and Ascendant in Capricorn.

Beatrice has inherited the royal family's powerful Leonine qualities via the Sun, which was in this sign on the day of her birth. This is almost the single sign which links the modern Windsors – Elizabeth, Philip, Charles, Anne and Andrew were all born with it occupying prominent places in their horoscopes. Beatrice also has her Ascendant in Capricorn, in exactly the same degree as the Queen. So does that mean that she's inherited her grandmother's natural reserve? Up to a point, she has. And there is no doubt that Beatrice is someone who will take a delight in all the trappings of tradition and ceremony. However, her Sun in Leo is matched by a Cancerian Moon and this is a combination which tends towards displays of self-indulgent emotion. People with this combination have a tendency to sulk, and make theatrical gestures. There's nothing wrong with this. It can just become a little wearing for others.

A career on the stage would be suitable, although often Leo–Cancer people spend so much time acting their way through real life that to work in the theatre seems a little too much like their everyday experience. Closer inspection of Beatrice's horoscope reveals that her compassionate Cancerian Moon is in a region of her horoscope connected to health and service, and that other important planets, mainly Uranus (which tends towards progressive ideas), connect with a sector indicating philanthropy. Add all these separate factors together and we have an individual who could become devoted to charitable causes.

Beatrice's connections with her cousins' horoscopes are powerful. In particular her Moon at 4° in Cancer and Venus at 1° in Cancer are close to William's Moon at 4° in Cancer and Sun at 0° in Cancer, and opposite to Peter's Ascendant at 2° in Capricorn. Quite simply, this indicates that they should all get on extremely well. The connection between Beatrice and William is exceedingly strong, and deep enough for them to develop a very special and enduring bond. Beatrice could become William's perfect confidante, the family member he turns to when he needs solace, support and advice. He in turn will be fascinated by her femininity, by that demonstrative and theatrical mix of Leo and Cancer.

Beatrice's connections with William and Peter mean that she is the third of the Queen's grandchildren who can look forward to a turbulent time between 2008 and 2111. She'll be twenty years old in 2008, and may well become embroiled in the changes in the royal family which are due to take place at that time. It looks, too, as if marriage is an extremely high probability at this point, or a turbulent relationship which makes her determined to follow her own idealistic, perhaps charitable path, before settling down.

PRINCESS EUGENIE

Younger daughter of Andrew and Sarah. Born in Paddington, London, at 7.58 p.m. on 23 March 1990, with the Sun in Aries, the Moon in Aquarius and the Ascendant in Libra.

The young Princess Eugenie was born with a horoscope which is at once extremely lively, yet private. If we can find a precedent in the royal family for such a curious set of planetary alignments, it must be George V. Eugenie's connections with George are more than a matter of shared temperament, for her planetary connections with her great-great-grandfather are extremely tight. Her Sun, for example, falls in exactly the same degree of the zodiac as George's Ascendant, and is exactly opposite to his Moon. So while her cousins William and Peter would have found an inspiring role model in Edward VIII, had Eugenie ever known George V, the two would have formed an instant and enduring bond.

This comparison will be a useful one to bear in mind for, as she grows older, the Princess will be accused of being, like her great-great-grandfather, a trifle dull. Such accusations will be levelled by people who completely fail to comprehend her horoscope. Her lively Aries Sun is extremely dynamic, but some people will persist in seeing her as a one-dimensional go-getter. Her Libran Ascendant will set out to be as pleasant as possible, but some people will mistake good manners and a friendly disposition for lack of ambition. Her Aquarian

Moon offers originality and a unique perspective on the world, but her defiance of convention may be misinterpreted as an absence of self-discipline and a lack of any sense of responsibility. If this sounds similar to the unjust allegations levelled at Sarah, there's a very good astrological reason – mother and daughter are very alike. Sarah has her Sun in Libra and Moon in Aries in a tight relationship with Eugenie's Ascendant in Libra and Sun in Aries.

Eugenie will therefore spend her life pondering exactly the same personal questions as her mother. She'll be unable to work out whether she is essentially an Arien pioneer, competing with everyone around her for first place, or a Libran teamworker, unable to operate unless backed by partners, lovers and anyone else who cares to offer support. She will send out confusing messages, sometimes demanding independence, while at the same time needing the closeness of partnership.

The contradictions in her horoscope can be resolved if she realises that there is no one lifestyle which absolutely suits her. For example, she needs a marriage partner who will be happy with long separations, and must understand that she also needs to spend time by herself. She requires a stable home, but as long as she has that base, she will be happy to wander the globe. She'll also be a very hard worker, but will find it impossible to take orders. As a child she needs careful guidance, for if her desires are blocked she will only fight all the harder, and her determination to succeed will be in no way diminished by her smiling Libran Ascendant. Behind that charm Eugenie possesses a steely determination. Rather than being blocked, she therefore needs to be encouraged and shown positive ways in which to channel her considerable energy. She is extremely bright and has a flair for seeking out new ideas. She is also highly impatient and opinionated and may dismiss others' suggestions out of hand. Her apparent lack of self-discipline is not what it seems, but will be the result of a refusal to perform tasks which she regards as useless. She therefore has very particular needs at school, and if her education suffers it will be the teachers, not she herself, who are at fault. The message to Andrew and Sarah therefore is that they have a daughter who is extremely special, and therefore likely to be misunderstood. She's a live wire who needs as much stimulation as can be offered.

The young princess will begin to grow up fast around 1996 when Pluto makes a powerful and harmonious aspect to her Sun. This is a planetary alignment which is likely to pass unnoticed by those around her, but the internal changes will be profound as the six-year-old girl begins to establish the direction which she will follow as a young adult. She will be very moved by the desire to help those less fortunate than herself. Yet it is the connections with her cousins William and Peter which are most noticeable; her Sun at 2° in Aries is 90° away from William's Sun at 0° in Cancer and Peter's Ascendant at 2° in Capricorn. This is a very powerful triple alignment and, quite aside from the fact that when all three get together they could have some splendid arguments as well as exciting adventures, it means that they respond in unison to the same planetary cycles. The years from 2008 to 2111, when Eugenie will be eighteen to twenty-one, will be powerful years for her. Simultaneous transits of Neptune to her Moon and Pluto to her Sun will herald the events one might expect at that age. She's likely to fall in love and consider marriage, but the ideal future she dreams of will prove an illusion. The result of this experience will not be domestic change, but an important move towards the world of work. However, the fact that she shares powerful planetary cycles at this time with William suggests that the headlines will focus not on her, but on the royal family as a whole.

PRINCE EDWARD

Born at Buckingham Palace at 8.15 p.m. on 10 March 1964, with the Sun in Pisces, the Moon in Aquarius and the Ascendant in Libra.

Out of the Queen's three sons, Edward takes the prize for being the most sensitive. The combination of Sun in Pisces and Moon in Aquarius provides a depth of imagination, an originality of mind and a rare sensitivity to feelings and ideas. The Sun in Pisces links with Edward's Ascendant in Libra to give a quite extraordinary desire to please. Edward doesn't just like to be liked; he *needs* to be liked. Without such support his confidence sinks and he lapses into indecision, paralysed by the fear that he will fail or make a fool of himself. He will do anything to be liked. He will be pleasant and good-mannered, avoiding any possibility of giving even the mildest offence. However, he will also take steps which go against his basic nature. The worst mistake he ever made was to enter the Marine officers' training course, quite possibly the toughest military schooling in the world. So anxious was he to prove to Prince Philip that he was indeed a real man, that he set out on a path which was utterly anathema to him. Nothing could have so graphically illustrated the gulf that exists between him and his parents as this.

It was to please Prince Philip that Edward decided to become a marine officer. That the Queen failed to realise that her youngest son was so unsuited to such a life is powerful evidence of her inability to see beyond the limitations and customs of royal tradition. These dictated that the monarch's sons went into the Navy, so Edward had to go. The Queen's powerful combination of Saturn with Capricorn and Taurus deserves respect for the stability it provides, but in her inability to recognise the need for genuine change, the Queen has provoked a series of royal crises. Her failure to understand Diana's extraordinary spontaneity is the most glaring and damaging example. Her almost total lack of comprehension of Edward's true nature precipitated trauma in his life and a minor public relations crisis, when Edward took the courageous decision that he didn't want to be an action man. His resignation from the marines brought more attacks on the royal family from those who resented its privileges.

The modern Windsors are, broadly speaking, a theatrical dynasty. Out of the entire family, only the Queen and Prince Henry have horoscopes which speak of a respect for tradition, a sense of authority and a willingness to endure the continual round of civic occasions. The rest of the family, from Philip and Anne to Beatrice and Eugenie, are, to one degree or another, creative people. Edward is about as far removed from being at ease with the rigours of royal life as we can imagine. Unlike the rest of his family, he lacks the strong Leonine configurations which enable them to cope with life under the constant scrutiny of the public. Even vulnerable, Scorpionic Charles and Piscean Andrew were born with their Ascendants in Leo, and are able to tackle the world head on. Not so their younger brother.

Edward has many talents, but they are of a kind which requires careful nurturing and encouragement from those whose love he craves

184

and whose respect he desires. Like both his brothers, Edward was born with the Sun in a 'water' sign – Pisces – so a maritime occupation seemed to present him with few difficulties. Indeed, his Libran ascendant would have relished the sense of community on board ship. However, Edward is, in his own quiet way, a philosopher and there is, too, something of the monk in him. In medieval times, when the Church was a proper political concern, the obvious job for Edward would have been Archbishop of Canterbury. He might even have been suggested as a potential Pope. He does, after all, have a powerfully placed Jupiter in Aries, and when the time comes to take control, he'll do his best. The only proviso is that he should take control in pleasant circumstances and with plenty of support.

What of Edward's future? The question of personal artistic talent aside, he has an overriding desire to be involved in creative pursuits. The obvious path for him would be to develop a wide-ranging role as patron and supporter of the arts. Head of the Arts Council, perhaps? His problems here are twofold. Firstly, in positions of responsibility he is almost chronically incapable of taking decisions. And if it comes to fighting for funding he is all too likely to agree that another organisation should be given the sponsorship he himself might be seeking. Secondly, we should note that he was born under the same Mars–Pluto alignment which repeatedly caused anarchy for the Stuarts. A ceremonial role would therefore be preferred to one of practical authority.

We can pick out two important periods for the Prince. One is 1996, when Uranus and Jupiter pass over his Moon. Venus and Jupiter will also be strongly aligned, indicating that during this year a major new development should occur in his domestic life. This is when he will discover the answer to the question as to whether or not he is to be a life-long bachelor. With the dawning of 2001 Edward could be the first member of the royal family to hit the headlines in the next century. If he has inherited an ability to create chaos from the Stuarts, that is the year when he launches his own personal assault on royal tradition. Edward will take almost any amount of personal criticism, but eventually he will react. It's his uncompromising Mars–Pluto alignment which shows his ability to fight back, and it's this which was triggered when he walked out of the Marines. And if anyone imagines that after 2001 Edward will calm down, they should wait for 2004, when Pluto passes over his Sun. Edward may be a late developer, but when he does come into his own, he will prove that there was always more to him than met the eye.

PRINCESS MARGARET AND LORD SNOWDON

PRINCESS MARGARET

Born at Glamis, Scotland at 9.22 p.m. on 21 August 1930, with the Sun in Leo, the Moon in Cancer and the Ascendant in Aries.

ANTHONY ARMSTRONG-JONES, EARL OF SNOWDON

Born in London at 6.15 a.m. on 7 March 1930, with the Sun in Pisces, the Moon in Gemini and the Ascendant on the cusp of Aquarius and Pisces.

The royal family appears to have a persistent need for a black sheep. Perhaps it's because, as an institution, the monarchy consistently emphasises conservative virtues. Given this, individuals who feel unable to conform to the established line automatically stand out. The young Edward VII, his eldest son Albert and Edward VIII all served their time as problem members of the royal clan. In the 1980s Sarah Ferguson reluctantly assumed this difficult role. Back in the sixties and seventies it was Princess Margaret, the chain-smoking, fast-living, theatre-loving naughty younger sister who caused raised eyebrows.

Margaret was born with the Sun in Leo and Ascendant in Aries. This is a combination not to be treated lightly, for each of these signs is capable of sticking to its own personal agenda regardless of what family, society or the church might decree. The warmth of the Aries–Leo combination has always been evident in Margaret's affectionate spontaneity and love of informality. She has been able to shed the burden of royal expectations in a manner beyond the comprehension of her conservative elder sister, Elizabeth. Yet Margaret's fiery aggression is strongly tempered by other planets of a more sensitive and inhibited nature. Her Sun is very close to Neptune, making it

186

difficult for her to deal with open confrontation. She would far rather bury her head in the sand, hoping that eventually any unpleasantness will simply go away. When we look closer, we see that the Princess's Moon is in emotional Cancer, very close to Pluto. This indicates an unconscious tendency to resolve emotional difficulties by having a fully-fledged blow-up. Put all these factors together and we find that the Princess allows confrontation to develop by allowing matters to drift, in other words, by abdicating control. Margaret's passive streak is encouraged by the one truly important planetary position she shares with the Queen. Like her sister she has Saturn, an indication of profound conservatism, placed at the summit of her horoscope. However relaxed and informal her public manner, she has always remained the Queen's younger sister, the daughter of a King, and has required due respect for that simple fact of birth.

It is often said that Margaret's happiness was irreparably damaged when her marriage to Group Captain Peter Townsend was forbidden by the Queen. Peter was an honoured member of the court, but he had divorced his first wife and was therefore, like Wallis Simpson, considered unfit for marriage to someone of royal birth. Margaret began her romance with Peter around the time of the King's death in early 1952, at which time she was under strong Saturnine influences. Peter was her senior by sixteen years, having been born on 22 November 1914. That made him a Scorpio, and no doubt the Princess was attracted by the sense of unfathomable wisdom which older Scorpios so often possess. However, their attraction was founded on a compulsive combination of Saturn and Pluto. At Peter's birth these two planets occupied a degree of the zodiac which for Margaret represented home and family. He expressed everything she could ever want from a man. He was so deep and intense that she felt as if she'd known him since the beginning of time; yet he was also older and wiser than her, as much a father as a lover. Margaret's passionate relationship with Peter is often presented as a rebellion against royal convention, yet in reality he appealed to the most conservative aspects in her horoscope.

Eventually Margaret's own conservative instincts were transferred from the love of the older, paternal man towards her regard for her elder sister's wishes, and for royal convention. On 31 October 1955 she silenced public gossip by announcing that she would not be marrying Peter Townsend after all. Jupiter and Pluto had by then positioned themselves exactly on top of Margaret's Leonine Sun. This is an indication of volcanic emotions and we can only conclude that, if Margaret had married Peter earlier, she might then have given him cause to regret it. She was making her bid for emotional liberation, for the only way to deal with such a powerful Jupiter–Pluto alignment is to demand total and complete personal freedom. Margaret may have looked back and regretted her failed romance, wondering what might have happened if she'd stayed with Peter. Yet, by the age of twenty- five, she was legally free to make her own decision without consulting the Queen, albeit at the cost of renouncing the succession. The decision was Margaret's alone, in spite of the subsequent mythology which has portrayed her as the romantic victim of a cold and unfeeling royal tradition.

Soon after leaving Peter, Margaret began to follow the artistic path favoured by her nephews. She didn't develop any personal creative skills but preferred instead to mix in theatrical circles. In the language of the 1950s, she became a true Bohemian. It was at this time that she met Anthony Armstrong-Jones, a photographer with a bright future and a rapidly growing reputation for his work. Her new love was born on 7 March 1930 with the Sun in Pisces and Moon in Gemini, one of the perfect combinations for such a career. Gemini provides an eye for detail and Pisces an ability to create and manipulate images; Neptune, which is also prominent in Tony Snowdon's birth chart is a planet powerfully connected with the invention of photography.

We're not quite sure what time he was born. It may have been at 6.15 a.m., which places his Ascendant in Pisces. However, if he was born only fifteen minutes earlier his Ascendant would have been in Aquarius and this, taken with other alignments involving Mercury and Mars, would give him an exceptionally incisive mind and a perceptive and original wit. Finally, the Moon in Gemini was very close to Jupiter. This is the exact opposite of Margaret's Moon–Pluto in Cancer. Whereas she is compulsively drawn towards emotional intensity and conflict, he is a born optimist. Face him with a difficulty and his first response will be to shrug his shoulders and get on with something else. Why create problems, he thinks, when there is so much to enjoy in life? His design of the aviary at London Zoo which, in contrast to traditional cages, allowed the birds to soar through the air, was the perfect outer manifestation of his inner love of freedom.

In many ways, Tony's horoscope is a fairly typical one for the Windsors. However, those born into the royal clan, from George V to Prince Philip and Prince Edward, have found their creative, freedom-loving natures trapped within the prison bars of their inherited positions. Tony Snowdon shows us what so many of the Windsors might have been like had they been born into different circumstances: optimistic, relaxed and able to fulfill their creative potential.

The most important planetary connection between Margaret and Tony placed her Sun in an exact opposition to his Ascendant and a conjunction with his Neptune. All this makes for a very strong bond. It also looks as if Margaret's attraction to Tony was partly the product of his chameleon-like ability to create impressions and conjure up magical images. His imaginative nature was a great attraction for Margaret, but ultimately she requires periods of emotional struggle and conflict in her life. Tony was never sufficiently intense, and eventually he failed to stay the course. In the mid-seventies, when Pluto had reached its opposition to Margaret's Ascendant, its first major stop since she left Peter Townsend, the couple drifted apart. His success in evading her desire to involve him in her personal battles might have undermined the relationship, but in the end it enabled the separation to take place with a minimum of rancour.

Margaret set a precedent when she left Tony, becoming the first member of the inner royal family to divorce since Henry VIII. She gave way to convention when she failed to marry Peter, but twenty years later she asserted the importance of her own feelings over the traditions of the monarchy. Finally, she had managed to shrug off the inhibition of Saturn and the sensitivity of Neptune, and was prepared to express the true power of Aries and Leo. In this respect we should point out one very important feature of Margaret's horoscope. Her Midheaven, which symbolises her public face and has a powerful, though indirect, significance for her home and family life, is exactly opposite her uncle Edward VIII's Sun. This is the degree of the zodiac which has come to represent rebellion within the Windsors. Margaret was therefore destined from birth to continue Edward's attack on royal tradition.

189

DAVID, VISCOUNT LINLEY

Son of Princess Margaret and the Earl of Snowdon. Born in London at 10.45 a.m. on 3 November 1961, with the Sun in Scorpio, the Moon in Virgo and the Ascendant in Sagittarius.

David Linley is a serious man who combines a sense of purpose with a desire to achieve goals which are both useful, worthwhile, and capable of elevating the human spirit. His horoscope provides an excellent mix of detail with vision, and imagination with practical skill. His Ascendant in Sagittarius gives him the overall perspective and optimism necessary to pursue his particular goals. His Sun, which falls in Scorpio and is very close to Neptune, provides him with an intense conviction that without beauty life is meaningless. Mercury, exactly on his Midheaven in Libra, provides him with an ability to communicate his ideas and the persuasive powers required to secure agreement from others. And his Moon–Pluto conjunction in Virgo has endowed him with a compulsive addiction to detail and an unwavering requirement that whatever tasks he takes on have a practical function. Put all these qualities together and we have the royal furniture-maker and part-time restaurateur.

David is extremely easy to get on with at first meeting, for he was born with Mercury and Venus together in Libra. His public manner is therefore pleasing, and he places a high premium on courtesy and good manners. His Sagittarian Ascendant lends a good-natured willingness to pass the time of day with anyone, no matter what their background. However, as soon as we take a step into his private life the situation becomes very different. The Sun conjunct Neptune is driven by impossible romantic dreams. In David's personal fantasy world the only true love is one which demands the ultimate sacrifice. His Moon–Pluto conjunction also denotes an obsessive personality. What is he obsessive about? Virgo gives us the answer – practical details, punctuality and hygiene. He may make a mess at home himself, but woe betide the person who disturbs his domestic order.

David will enter an intense phase in 1998 when Uranus poses a challenge to his Sun. The first signs will come in a very obvious desire to break out of what he will come to see as a rut, perhaps his furniture designing. This doesn't mean that he will abandon his business, but that he must personally find a dramatic new direction. This is then followed from 1999 to 2001 by simultaneous transits from Neptune and Pluto. These are alignments of unremitting idealism and passion, under which David will come to question his independence. He may then search for new people who are capable of living up to his sky-high standards and can share his life.

LADY SARAH ARMSTRONG-JONES

Daughter of Princess Margaret and the Earl of Snowdon. Born in London at 8.20 a.m. on 1 May 1964, with the Sun in Taurus, the Moon in Capricorn and Ascendant in Cancer.

Sarah Armstrong-Jones was brought up, like her brother, to regard any advantages gained by possessing royal status as purely secondary to her own interests and talents. She has therefore been free to develop her artistic skills, and has had the honour of having her paintings selected for the Royal Academy. She was born with the Sun in Taurus and Moon in Capricorn, an excellent combination for solid, practical achievement. Although Taurus can appear to be a rather dull sign, Sarah was born with Mercury and Jupiter in prominent positions, very close to the Sun. This indicates a lively and optimistic mind and a friendly social manner. Sarah's pleasant disposition is enhanced by the location of her Ascendant in Cancer and the Moon in the exactly opposite degree, in Capricorn. If we could sum up this horoscope in one word, it would have to be 'sensible'.

Depth is added by a powerful alignment between both the Sun and the Moon and Uranus and Pluto. These patterns lend a creative depth which is considerably less intense than that which we find in her elder brother's horoscope, but still strong enough to give her sufficient confidence in her own talents and beliefs.

In some senses Sarah is her brother's opposite. She was born with the Sun at 10° in Taurus, whereas in his horoscope the Sun is at 10° in Scorpio, the exact opposite degree. As much as he is driven by his intense passions, she is motivated by what she perceives to be practical necessity. However, both of them have the Sun in a powerful aspect with Neptune, planet of the imagination, and it is this which provides their shared artistic talents. Sharing such close contacts means that Sarah and David will experience powerful planetary movements at the same time. Like him, she will try and break out of a rut and create a new creative direction and lifestyle around 1998. However, it will be in 2008, as Pluto begins its passage over her Moon, when she turns her life upside down. This is the transit under which her mother and father split up. Will Sarah repeat the pattern or, hopefully, break it by coming to terms with her parents' divorce?

THE MINOR ROYALS – THE FAMILIES OF KENT AND GLOUCESTER

RICHARD, DUKE OF GLOUCESTER

Grandson of George V, cousin of the Queen. Born at 10.15 a.m. on 26 August 1944, with the Sun in Virgo, Moon in Scorpio and Ascendant in Libra.

BIRGITTE, DUCHESS OF GLOUCESTER

Wife of the Duke of Gloucester. Born on 20 June 1946, with the Sun in Gemini and Moon in Pisces.

Alexander, Earl of Ulster

Son of the Duke of Gloucester. Born early in the morning of 24 October 1974, with the Sun in Scorpio and Moon in Aquarius.

Lady Davina Windsor

Eldest daughter of the Duke of Gloucester. Born on 18 November 1977, with the Sun in Scorpio and the Moon in Pisces.

Lady Rose Windsor

Youngest daughter of the Duke of Gloucester. Born on 1 March 1980, with the Sun in Pisces and Moon in Virgo.

Richard, Duke of Gloucester is not just a Virgo. At his birth the Sun was joined in this sign by Jupiter, Venus, Mercury and Mars, all of which contribute to a thoroughly genial, sensible personality. And these are qualities which are enhanced by his charming Libran Ascendant. Richard's chosen career was in architecture, which is typically Virgoan in its attention to detail. However, he was born with Pluto exactly on his Midheaven, indicating the possibility of dramatic career changes. This is precisely what happened in 1972 when Richard's elder brother William died, leaving him to inherit the title and take over the family estates.

Richard is ably supported by his wife, Birgitte, whose Geminian Sun and Piscean Moon is one of the most refined combinations known. The couple's two daughters were born under emotional water signs – Scorpio and Pisces – but it is their son Alexander who has the most remarkable horoscope. He was born with a multiple conjunction of the Sun, Mercury, Venus, Mars and Uranus, all five planets being squashed into seven degrees of the zodiac. Alexander is extraordinarily independent in both thought and action and has the capacity to deliver shocks which could send his friends and family reeling. From 1995 until the end of the century he will have first Uranus and then Neptune passing over his horoscope, creating one surprise after another. January 1996 and January 1997 are two months to watch, and if he stays out of the headlines it won't be for want of trying.

EDWARD, DUKE OF KENT

Grandson of George V, cousin of the Queen. Born on 9 October 1935, with the Sun in Libra and the Moon in Pisces.

KATHERINE, DUCHESS OF KENT

Wife of the Duke of Kent. Born on 22 February 1933, with the Sun in Pisces and Moon in Aquarius.

George, Earl of St Andrews

Eldest son of the Duke of Kent. Born at 2.00 p.m. on 26 June 1962, with the Sun in Cancer, Moon in Aries and Ascendant in Libra.

Lady Helen Taylor

Daughter of the Duke of Kent. Born on 28 April 1964, with the Sun in Taurus and Moon in Sagittarius.

Lord Nicholas Windsor

Second son of the Duke of Kent. Born on 20 July 1970, with the Sun in Leo and Moon in Taurus.

The Duke and Duchess of Kent are known for their amiability, and both have an impeccable sense of what it means to be part of the royal dynasty. The Duke has the Sun in Libra and the Moon in Pisces. The Duchess has the Sun in Pisces and the Moon in Aquarius. The Pisces–Libra combination is exceedingly pleasant, while Pisces–Aquarius is very imaginative, so it's hardly surprising that the Kents have an untarnished record as well-behaved members of the royal family. Of their three children, Lady Helen Taylor is the best-known, being the most vivacious. Helen was born just four days before her second cousin, Lady Sarah Armstrong-Jones, whom she closely resembles. Both girls, being sensible Taureans, have provided a model of good behaviour when compared to the disasters which have visited the Queen's children. Helen was born with the Moon and Ascendant together in Sagittarius, one of the most relaxed, casual and confident configurations possible. Her Sun is in the creative fifth house, which has taken her towards a career in the arts. Her marriage to art dealer Tim Taylor in July 1992 provided a rare happy moment in the royal family's most difficult year since 1936.

Helen's elder brother George, Earl of St Andrews was born with the Sun in Cancer in the ninth house, the sector of his horoscope signifying higher education. As forecast when he was still a child, he has taken up a career in academe, and is determined to shun the limelight. Like Helen, he has a very powerfully placed Moon and has no trouble turning on the charm. It's just that, with his Ascendant in Libra, he'd rather have a quiet life. George's younger brother Nicholas is a much tougher proposition. He has the Moon in Taurus (in exactly the same degree as Helen's Sun), but the solid qualities of this sign are taken in a very expressive and powerful direction by a tight group of planets in Leo – the Sun, Mercury and Mars. Nicholas is a fighter, and not afraid to create drama. He'll be making waves in 1996 when a powerful Uranus alignment encourages him to rebel against his background.

PRINCE MICHAEL OF KENT

Grandson of George V, cousin of the Queen. Born on 4 July 1942, with the Sun in Cancer.

PRINCESS MICHAEL OF KENT

Wife of Prince Michael. Born on 15 January 1945, with the Sun in Capricorn and Moon in Aquarius.

Lord Frederick Windsor

Son of Prince Michael. Born on 6 April 1979, with the Sun in Aries and Moon in Leo.

Lady Gabriella Windsor

Daughter of Prince Michael. Born on 2 April 1981, with the Sun in Aries and the Moon in Pisces.

Prince Michael of Kent is known as a pleasant fellow. He was born with the Sun in Cancer, close to Jupiter, which makes for a generous disposition and hospitable behaviour, but for a while in the seventies and eighties his family's image was tarnished by media attention focused on his wife. Marie Christine von Reibnitz, Princess Michael, is a Capricorn with the Moon in Aquarius and strong Mars–Saturn and Pluto alignments. This is a pugnacious combination, and the Princess made a series of public pronouncements in which she seemed to be competing with other members of the royal family for attention. Accordingly, between Princess Margaret's divorce and Sarah Ferguson's arrival on the scene, Princess Michael became royal scapegoat number one, proof that the public requires, at any one time, at least one member of the royal family to be offered up for ritual abuse. Both the couple's children are Ariens, and thus quite capable of giving as good as they get. The elder, Frederick, is the more likely to follow in his mother's combative footsteps, for he was also born with the Moon in Leo and a Sun–Pluto alignment which gives him an extraordinarily competitive streak.

PRINCESS ALEXANDRA

Granddaughter of George V, cousin of the Queen. Born at 11.20 a.m. on 25 December 1936, with the Sun in Capricorn, the Moon in Taurus and Ascendant in Pisces.

ANGUS OGILVY

Husband of Princess Alexandra. Born at 3.40 a.m. on 14 September 1928, with the Sun, Moon and Ascendant in Virgo.

James Ogilvy

Son of Princess Alexandra. Born at 12.20 p.m. on 29 February 1964, with the Sun in Pisces, Moon in Libra and Ascendant in Cancer.

Marina Mowattt

Daughter of Princess Alexandra. Born at 7.00 p.m. on 31 July 1966, with the Sun in Leo, the Moon in Aquarius and Ascendant in Capricorn.

If the Duke and Duchess of Kent are the amiable royals, Princess Alexandra and her husband Angus Ogilvy are the sensible ones. She was born with the Sun in Capricorn and the Moon in Taurus, and he was born with both Sun and Moon in Virgo. She was also born with an extremely powerful and restrictive Saturn, just like the Queen. In fact, out of all the royal couples, the Queen has the most in common with the Ogilvys. As the Queen's personal business manager, Angus Ogilvy is largely responsible for increases in the Queen's personal wealth over the last thirty years, putting his businesslike Virgoan qualities to excellent use.

The couple's eldest son James has sensitive planetary alignments similar to so many of the other Windsor horoscopes. His Sun is in Pisces, his Moon in Cancer and his Ascendant in Libra, and his only requirement is that he be left alone to get on with his life. He will eventually rise to prominence in his career through his own efforts, but he will do anything to avoid hurting other people along the way.

His sister, Marina, is very different. She was born at the Full Moon, with the Sun in Leo and the Moon in Aquarius, and has developed all the pride of the former sign and the radical notions of the second. Interestingly, her Ascendant occupies exactly the same degree of Capricorn as the Queen's, and in some senses it was Marina who opened the floodgates to the royal family's crisis-ridden year of 1992. She became the first royal woman to conceive a child out of wedlock, and her marriage to baby Zenouska's father, Paul Mowatt, was accompanied by the hurling of public insults at her parents and the selling of family secrets to the tabloid press. Marina's battle with Alexandra was a rehearsal for the problems the Queen was later to face with Diana and Sarah.

However, there is a strange message in Marina's horoscope for the Queen. Not only are the two women's Ascendants in the same degree, but Marina's Sun at 8° of Leo is very close to the Queen's Moon at 12° of the same sign. If we consider these two simple factors, their horoscopes are identical. The woman who holds the Windsor traditions together and the one who launched the most bitter assault on its conservatism, were, in terms of their broadest astrological patterns, one and the same. The astrological message to the Queen is therefore that, rather than blame other people for the royal family's disasters, she should look to herself and her own responsibility. She, after all is the monarch, the bridge between heaven and earth.

The Future

The horoscopes of the Queen and her family are connected by very powerful patterns. The direct result is that they tend to experience the same powerful planetary cycles at the same times. This makes it easy to pick out the periods of greatest significance, but more difficult to distinguish the individual importance for various members of the family. From the present perspective, the most important coming years include 1997–2000 and 2008–13. This second period culminates in a period of massive instability for the United Kingdom. It will be comparable to the years 1981–2, which featured inner city riots, the Falklands War . . . and the royal wedding. A closer parallel might be the years 1990–3, with the Poll Tax battles, the fall of Margaret Thatcher . . . and the Queen's Annus Horribilis.

1994

Planetary transits in 1994 are powerful, but the royal family is in the waning phase of the series of cycles which brought the crisis of 1992. There is a good deal of uncertainty, but no resolution of the difficult relationship between Charles and Diana and its implications for the succession. The most powerful transits occur from June to November, bringing great tension in the Queen's and Diana's horoscopes in particular. The eclipse on 18 November is the most important date and coincides with a major attempt by the Queen to gain the initiative and assert her undisputed leadership at the head of the royal family. Charles is generally recovering his direction, but Diana is likely to make a major bid for freedom and independence, also in November.

1995

The horoscope with the strongest alignments in January is Sarah Ferguson's; she makes a major attempt to present herself as a responsible and caring person. Around May, Diana faces new restrictions, Charles achieves additional responsibility and Edward accepts a position of authority. Anne begins to take a more public role as a royal representative after March. The major new long-term cycle involves Uranus, which now makes very powerful aspects to three members of the royal family – the Queen, Charles and William. This cycle lasts from April 1995 to December 1996 and indicates continued debate over the succession. For Charles, it also means several changes of home as he moves his base between different royal properties. For William, the events which happen now shape his attitude to his role, and could incline him against accepting the crown.

1996

Uranian pressures maintain uncertainty over the succession for the whole of the year, although both the Queen and Prince Charles take steps to transform the nature of the monarchy, staying one step ahead of events. Charles is especially confident during the summer. Diana attempts to take a more independent role in January, but in August she enters a critical period as it becomes clear that her precise constitutional position must be defined and restricted. The first week of August is a very tense time for her. William, who celebrates his fourteenth birthday in June, begins to perform a few royal engagements on his own account. Sarah recovers some of her personal popularity in the autumn by taking on a dignified public role.

1997

As Uranus moves into Aquarius it begins to exert a powerful destabilising role for the Queen, Charles, Andrew and Edward until the end of the decade. February brings extraordinarily powerful and positive alignments for Charles, and there are indications of a fresh start in his emotional life; he must now regularise his marital situation. He wishes to be free to remarry, precipitating a succession crisis which continues for three years. In April, November and December, Charles faces limitations on his public role, while Diana takes the headlines from July to October. Charles takes major new initiatives as a patron of progressive ideas, and his support of new educational institutions is more important to him than the state of the monarchy. Sarah contemplates remarriage and an emotional battle in October.

1998

Neptune now enters Aquarius, from where it makes powerful alignments to the Sun, Moon and Midheaven in the horoscopes of the Queen, Charles and William respectively. Charles assumes more power and asserts his role, not as the guardian of royal tradition, but as the guardian of the nation's soul, the philosopher Prince. Diana moves home in April, while the Queen faces mounting stress and her ability to organise the royal family comes under further question. Both Andrew and Edward face massive personal upheaval between March and August. Edward acquires a new home in May or November, amid massive speculation about his personal future. Sarah also acquires a new home, probably in April, although it's a difficult year and she is unlikely to feel settled until 1999. At the end of the year, the Queen, Charles and William come under simultaneous Saturn transits, indicating an urgent attempt, probably beginning in August, to re-establish the monarchy as the Queen sees it, as the guardian of national traditions.

1999

The Queen begins the year on a very uncertain note, probably because both Andrew and Edward are still facing continued instability. Prince Charles has a good year promoting his beliefs and acquiring stature as the promoter of a British cultural renaissance, rather than as heir to the throne. Prince Henry celebrates his fifteenth birthday in September, and begins to draw attention to himself as a young adult and third in line to the throne, rather than merely as Charles' and Diana's youngest child. After June he will begin to attract respect for his personal qualities. In October, both Andrew and Edward again come under very destabilising alignments, and these will continue until January 2000. However, they are now in a phase of consolidation, no longer alarmed by new developments, but clearly developing in a new direction. Andrew finds a replacement for Sarah, and considers remarriage.

2000

Appropriately, as the twentieth century merges into the twenty-first, planetary pressure arises for the end of Elizabeth II's reign. This pressure is maintained until 2002, but is most profound in 2000. The most intense month of the year is May, when Jupiter, Saturn and Uranus line up in exact opposition to Charles' Sun. In ordinary circumstances this alignment would cause a complete change in both personal and professional circumstances. We must therefore pick this date as a likely one for Charles to succeed to the throne. Interestingly, planetary alignments to Henry's horoscope are much stronger than those to William's, indicating that current events are of much greater significance for Henry than for his older brother. Throughout the year we find changes in the status of Anne (January, May), Edward (January–March, May), Andrew (January–March), Philip (May), Diana (May–July) and Sarah (May, September– October). However, the Queen's horoscope itself reveals a major shift of responsibility and authority in June.

2001

Pressure on the succession continues. From January to March, both the Queen's and Diana's horoscopes indicate great personal burdens. Both feel that they carry the weight of the world on their shoulders. By the middle of the year both of them switch simultaneously into a phase indicating the desire to escape and break out of restrictive circumstances. Diana is experiencing a phase known as her Uranus opposition, under which Uranus arrives at the opposite degree of the zodiac to that it held at her birth. She will be in a very intense and personally difficult period, reviewing her life, attempting to make up for mistakes and relive the past. If she should ever doubt the manner in which she handled her split from Prince Charles, this will be the moment. If she should attempt a genuine reconciliation, if only for her peace of mind, this is the most appropriate time. She also rebels against the life she has built up over the end of the 1990s, feeling it to be too restricting; she seeks a new and radical role. From September until the end of the year, the pressure for change switches from Diana to Charles, and he begins to feel the need to make dramatic gestures. In

April and May, William's horoscope is especially vulnerable. Physically, he should beware of accidents; psychologically, he will be burdened by pent-up anger. In June, July and September he begins to assert himself, but in August there is speculation concerning his possible marriage and his future role in general. In September and October Diana takes on a new position, one which may cause political waves.

2002

The pressure for personal liberation in the Queen's and Diana's horoscopes remains intense from January to March and September–December. Instability therefore continues, although by now we are seeing signs of a monarchy transformed for the twenty-first century. There are strong indications of pride in September and October, with Charles and Andrew being the main beneficiaries. Also in October, Edward is the subject of intense rumours concerning his romantic life.

2003

In January Diana becomes subject to a new and intense planetary alignment which is in operation for two years – until December 2004. This intense period begins with a sudden event around the middle of February. A period of profound emotional questioning could include a period of depression and seclusion, a religious conversion, involvement with strange beliefs or long periods spent abroad. Andrew also enters a period of intense change, although for him it is more lively and finds him experimenting with new interests and hobbies. He resents all restrictions, including domestic and professional responsibilities. Both he and Edward should be wary of accidents in the middle of May, taking extra precautions; both are also affected by a hint of scandal. Charles continues to thrive, and from January to June discovers more of his creative potential. Henry shares some of the same difficult moments as Diana, including mid-February, when both should act with extreme caution. By August–September both Henry and Diana will be sharing a brief quest for new and productive work, something of real practical value. The sharpest change is in William's horoscope and, in June, when he celebrates his twenty-first birthday, he begins to assert his own wishes. From then until January 2005 he

redefines his role in an independent manner, separate from his parents'
wishes. He is entering an eighteen-month phase of rebellion.

2004

The powerful long-term cycles in Diana's and William's horoscopes
continue from 2003. Henry is in an intense period of self-doubt and
introspection, much like Diana, and is desperate to make a life for
himself and develop a career. In August he takes his first great leap into
the adult world, possibly in a financial career. Andrew and Edward
pass under powerful Neptune transits, including a desire for a quiet
life, although Andrew still attracts attention for his new and news-
worthy activities. Sarah's horoscope will be in a very powerful
condition and she is now respected for her achievements other than as
a member of the royal family.

2004–2114

The ten years from 2004 to 2114 are noticeable for the steady build-up
of important alignments in William's horoscope. In 2006 Pluto begins
to approach a conjunction with his Ascendant; in 2007 it reaches the
conjunction, which in 2008 overlaps with an opposition to his Sun.
Pluto then moves on to an opposition to William's Moon which lasts
until 2111. These are transits of extraordinary intensity, and to
experience all three in such quick succession is indicative of a most
remarkable period. Emotionally, William packs as much experience
into these six years as most people manage in sixty. Nothing about his
life can be understood until he has passed through this phase, and this
is why we must be open to the possibility that he will not accept the
crown. There are times during this long process under which Henry
experiences profound planetary alignments, such as between
November 2008 and March 2009, focusing on the eclipses of 26
January and 9 February. In addition, examination of the United
Kingdom's horoscope indicates that in the years 2112–14, the entire
nation will be rocked by intense social and political instability with a
peak around September 2013. We must consider the possibility that
William passes the throne to Henry, or that those are the dates when
the existence of the monarchy is finally called into doubt.

The Kings and Queens of Europe

Belgium

The Kingdom of Belgium proclaimed independence from the Netherlands on 4 October 1830, with the Sun in Libra and the Moon in Taurus.

LÉOPOLD I
1831–1865

Born at 1.30 a.m. on 16 December 1790, with the Sun in Sagittarius, Moon in Aries and Ascendant in Libra.

Léopold I was born with the Sun in Sagittarius, a sign which often brings an interest in philosophy. When we take into account his charming Libran Ascendant it is hardly surprising that he was known as a highly cultured man. At one time he had been expected to sit on the throne of Great Britain as consort to his wife, Charlotte, the daughter of George IV. She, however, had died in childbirth in 1817. Léopold was also uncle to Queen Victoria. He was born with the Moon in Aries, so he had all this sign's powerful ambition. The combination of Aries, Sagittarius and Libra is an exceptionally goodnatured one, indicating an individual who is naturally lucky – or so it appears to those who have to struggle for every reward.

Having been deprived of the crown of Great Britain, Léopold was elected the first King of Belgium on 4 June 1831. He was then forty years old and experiencing an alignment known as his Uranus opposition. This event occurs when Uranus reaches the exact opposite degree to that it held at birth and always brings dramatic changes in lifestyle. In Léopold's case, he suddenly found himself King of Europe's newest country.

The horoscope for the date of the election is not only that for Léopold's reign, but for the Belgian monarchy as a whole. This can be demonstrated by looking forward to future events. For example, on the day of Leopold's election the Sun, the most important planet, was at 13° in Gemini. When, in 1944, Léopold III was sent into exile as a punishment for having ordered the surrender to the Germans in 1940, Uranus, indicating revolutionary movements, was passing over this very degree of Gemini. Léopold III himself was born with Uranus at the opposite degree of the zodiac, in Sagittarius.

LÉOPOLD II
1865–1909

Born at 10.15 p.m. on 9 April 1835, with the Sun in Aries, Moon in Virgo and Ascendant in Scorpio.

Léopold II, Léopold I's son, was born with the Sun in Aries, indicating that he had inherited his father's ambition. However, the Sun was in exactly the opposite degree of the zodiac to Saturn, indicating a deep sense of duty and a rare ability to handle authority. His organisational abilities were complemented by a Virgoan Moon, always an indication of great efficiency and attention to detail. His Ascendant was at the end of Scorpio and about to pass into Sagittarius, endowing him with a profound imagination. It is no surprise that Léopold was known as an able, energetic, strong-willed ruler and a man of vision.

However, when we add Mars to Léopold's planetary equation the picture becomes a little more intense. His precise alignment between the Sun, Saturn and Mars is an exacting one and denotes an individual capable of pushing himself to the edge, working harder than is healthy or sensible. Unfortunately, Léopold's exacting demands in the Congo Free State in Africa, which he ruled as a separate kingdom, were so great that rubber tappers were subject to harsh punishment, including mutilation, if they failed to meet their quotas. In the ensuing scandal, Léopold was forced to hand control over the Congo to the Belgian government. He died a year later, in 1909, and his reputation has never recovered.

ALBERT I
1909–1934

Born at 4.50 p.m. on 8 April 1875, with the Sun in Aries, Moon in Taurus and Ascendant in Virgo.

Like his uncle, Léopold II, Albert I was born with the Sun in Aries. In fact the two were, in a sense, astrological twins, for Albert's birthday was the day before Léopold's. Also like Léopold, he was born with the Moon in an earth sign, in his case, Taurus. This is normally a very stable and helpful position. However, the Moon was was within a degree of Pluto and in a very difficult alignment with Saturn, a pattern which often brings violent incidents in personal or domestic affairs. But Albert being King, his horoscope applied to the whole nation. He was therefore destined to be on the throne during the traumatic years of the First World War and the German occupation of 1914–1918. Curiously, when Albert died on 17 February 1934, this same alignment was prominent. What had signified upheaval for the nation in 1914 now had its full effect in Albert's horoscope.

LÉOPOLD III
1934–1951

Born at 3.05 p.m. on 3 November 1901, with the Sun in Scorpio, Moon in Leo, and Ascendant in Aries.

Léopold III was born with the Sun in emotional, secretive Scorpio and the Moon in proud, theatrical Leo. This is an extraordinarily stubborn combination, and he would have found it very difficult indeed to listen to advice from almost any quarter. His Ascendant in Aries gave him a heightened sense of his own importance and he had a deep conviction that, even in a constitutional monarchy like Belgium, he had a right to rule. Léopold made his biggest mistake on 28 May 1940 when he ordered the Belgian forces to cease fighting against the invading German troops. If he'd consulted his horoscope that week he would have noticed that Saturn had reached the degree of the zodiac directly opposite his Sun. This was an indication of obstinacy almost beyond belief. Although Léopold remained on his throne under German protection, the Belgian government in exile declared him deposed. When Belgium was liberated on 2 September 1944 Pluto, the planet which always causes us to face our past mistakes, was passing over Léopold's Leonine Moon, and he was sent into exile. He returned to the country in July 1950, but so great was the hostility that his son Baudouin was invested with the royal powers on 11 August. Léopold abdicated on 16 July 1951 with the revolutionary planet Uranus in an exact, though harmonious, alignment to his Sun. The change in rulers was thus accomplished peacefully.

CHARLES
Prince Regent, 1945–1950

Born at 11.10 p.m. on 10 October 1903 with the Sun in Libra, Moon in Gemini and Ascendant in Leo.

While Léopold III was in exile his younger brother Charles ruled as Prince Regent. Charles was born with the Sun in Libra, which always makes for public popularity, mainly on account of an effortless ability to charm other people, no matter what their background. Charles' image gained further from his Moon, which is not only in Gemini but also in the best relationship possible to the Sun. Charles was a gifted communicator and was well-fitted to soothe anti-monarchical sentiments after Léopold was sent in exile. His regency came to an end when Léopold was allowed to return on 22 July 1950.

BAUDOUIN
1951–1993

Born at 4.25 p.m. on 7 September 1930, with the Sun in Virgo, Moon in Pisces and Ascendant in Capricorn.

Prince Baudouin inherited the throne on the abdication of his father, Léopold III. Léopold abdicated on 16 July 1951 and Baudouin became King on the following day while the Sun was in Cancer and the Moon in Capricorn. This is an excellent combination for a man whose purpose was to restore the monarchy's credibility; Cancer, a sign famed for its maternal qualities, has enabled Baudouin to function as a good king should – as a kind of parent to the entire nation, while

Capricorn encourages respect for tradition. The only difficulty lay in powerful difficult alignments sent from the Moon to four planets: Mars, Jupiter, Uranus and Neptune. This suggests scandal, corruption and the domestic tensions we have seen in divisions between the predominantly Protestant Flemish and mainly Catholic Walloon communities. This alignment was very powerful when this simmering problem erupted into riots in 1966.

Baudouin himself was born with the Sun in Virgo and Moon in Pisces. This presents us with an interesting pattern, for he was born just hours before a Full Moon, and became King shortly before another Full Moon. Baudouin is thus a man whose task is to reconcile opposing forces. His Sun in Virgo supplied him with common sense and organisational skill in abundance, while his Moon in Pisces lent him a sympathetic manner. He was capable both of analysing questions scientifically and arriving at an answer using pure intuition.

He was also a man who took his responsibilities extremely seriously, for he was born with Saturn very closely aligned to his Capricorn Ascendant. He shared this pattern with the British Queen Elizabeth II. However, he also had Mars very powerfully placed, and was not one to rely exclusively on tradition; he was far more likely to take the initiative to preserve his position. It must be said that Baudouin's horoscope was a very stressful one, and every time his difficult planetary alignments were activated some political problem blew up, often the perennial dispute between the Flemings and Walloons.

On 15 December 1960 Baudouin married Doña Faviola de Mora y Aragon of Spain – Queen Fabiola. This was a romantic moment for a wedding, for the Moon in passionate Scorpio was very close to Neptune, planet of romance. In addition, the Moon was in a very helpful alignment with Baudouin's own horoscope. The positions of the Sun and Moon at the marriage indicated the King and Queen's roles in their relationship. He was represented by the Sun in Sagittarius, so his role was to take the relationship forward, always searching out new experiences and adventures. Faviola's role, represented by the Moon in Scorpio, was deeper and more intense, providing a stable bed of emotional security and love. The couple had no children, partially due to Baudouin's powerful Saturn, which often brings emotional limitations. In addition, in Baudouin's case a complex pattern linked Saturn to the sector of his horoscope which indicates children.

Baudouin died suddenly at about 9.30 p.m. on 31 July 1993 while away on holiday at Motril in Southern Spain, leaving his brother Albert to succeed to the throne.

ALBERT II
1993–

Born on 6 June 1934, with the Sun in Gemini and Moon in Aries.

Albert II, is Baudouin's younger brother. There are four years separating the brothers' births, although their horoscopes show some striking connection. Albert was born on 6 June 1934, with the Sun at 15° in Gemini. This was exactly one quarter of the zodiac away from Baudouin's Sun at 14° in Virgo. Any planet forming an alignment with one brother's Sun therefore simultaneously contacted the other's Sun. Like Baudouin, Albert has an analytical mind and is capable of sifting the evidence very carefully, but also has powerful intuitions. Albert's Moon is in Aries, which gives him a tough and argumentative edge, impatience and a desire for action.

On 2 July 1959 Albert married Doña Paola Ruffo di Calabria. The marriage horoscope tells us about their relationship, with Albert, represented by the Sun in Cancer, being happy to allow Paola, signified by the Moon in Taurus, to run day to day affairs.

The Belgian government chose Albert as Baudouin's successor at about 6.00 pm on 1 August 1993. Intriguingly the Ascendant was at that moment exactly in the middle of Sagittarius, the opposite degree of the zodiac to that occupied by the Sun at Albert's birth. Once again we see a pattern unfolding with uncanny accuracy. Like his older brother Albert also succeeded to the throne under a Full Moon, suggesting that the lunar cycle will be significant in future developments in the Belgian monarchy.

Albert's horoscope enters a powerful phase in 1998 when Pluto begins to make a very powerful alignment to his Sun, moving on to link up with his Sun in 2001.

PRINCE PHILIPPE

Eldest son of Albert II. Born at 8.40 a.m. GMT on 15 April 1960, with the Sun in Aries, Moon in Sagittarius and Ascendant in Cancer.

Prince Philippe Léopold Louis Marie, Albert II's eldest son, is first in line to the Belgian throne. His horoscope is quite clear on one point – that in spite of widespread doubt he could be an inspiring monarch. The Sun in Aries and Moon in Sagittarius is about the best combination possible for sheer optimism and enthusiasm, and as he matures he will become even more skilled at encouraging the Belgian people to follow a particular line, or perhaps just to support the status quo. When he was born the Moon made two ideal alignments. One was to the Sun, and this is additional evidence of Philippe's essentially optimistic and outgoing personality. The Moon's other harmonious alignment was with Uranus. This is a powerful indication of an independent personality. Some people born with Uranus so power-fully placed feel obliged to fight for their freedom, and often engage in battles in which they lose more than they gain. Philippe, on the other hand, has an effortless ability to maintain his individuality and to stand apart from the fray without compromising his position. The Moon is strongly associated with the Prince's domestic life, and in the sixth house of his horoscope it links up with his work. We can therefore expect him to create unusual family circumstances and bring innova-tions to the monarchy. In particular, he will see himself as the direct representative of the people rather than as a figurehead limited by constitutional convention. There may even come a time when he will appeal to the Belgian people over an important constitutional matter, bypassing the government.

Philippe's Cancer Ascendant introduces a slightly more inward-looking side to his character. As much as Aries and Sagittarius give him an abundance of confidence, so Cancer provides a softer edge, giving him deep intuitions and a sense of the importance of home and family. The combination of emotional Cancer with his extraverted Sun and Moon signs is a difficult one, partly because it leads to excessively vulnerable emotions; hurt pride is perhaps the major problem. However, excessive vulnerability leads to deep secrecy, mainly as a means of self-protection; the Prince will believe that if he keeps his feelings to himself he can't be criticised. His behaviour will also be somewhat contradictory, for while there will be times when he gives way to emotional outbursts, his real feelings will remain deeply buried. Other indications in Philippe's horoscope show that such outbursts should be few and far between. Jupiter and Venus are both very strong, indicating that he is excessively aware of the need for correct behaviour and will do everything in his power to avoid causing offence. Venus indicates that he likes to be the centre of attention, and for many people this can lead to problems. For the heir to the throne, who naturally has all the attention he requires, this can be seen as a rather fortunate position.

The planets indicating marriage in Philippe's horoscope are restrained and conservative. Perhaps we should make a distinction here between love and marriage. Philippe can be a passionate lover, and once he feels an attraction for somebody he will throw everything into achieving his ends. However, any long-term partner must provide him with security; even though Philippe may be quick to fall in love, commitment is for him a very different question. One particular position in his horoscope, conservative Saturn in the cautious sign of Capricorn in his house of marriage, indicates that a successful union can only take place late in life.

When we look at Philippe's future, one fact becomes instantly apparent, and that is that his Moon is due to be aligned from 1998 onwards by the very same planets which suggest a change of monarch in his father's horoscope. The pattern, which has emerged most forcefully since the Second World War, can be traced back to the beginning of the Belgian monarchy with the election of Léopold I on 4 June 1831 and involves planets in the middle of the four 'mutable' signs. These are Gemini, Virgo, Sagittarius and Pisces, and any planets occupying these degrees are very powerfully linked with each other:

* Election of Léopold I: Sun at 13° in Gemini.
* Baudouin: Sun at 14° in Virgo.

212

★ Albert: Sun at 15° in Gemini.
★ Philippe: Moon at 12° in Sagittarius.

If we look back at past events we see other interesting patterns emerging connected to these degrees. For example, when Léopold III went into exile in September 1944, Uranus was at 13° in Gemini. This is exactly what we would expect, for Uranus is a planet of shocks, surprises and sudden changes in circumstance.

When, from 1998 onwards, Pluto begins its intense alignment to Albert's Sun, it will simultaneously align with Philippe's Moon. So intense is this series of planetary patterns that it would be astonishing if Albert were not to hand over the crown. The question is whether Philippe will succeed. In view of the prolonged nature of Pluto's transits, which are not due to end until December 2001, one further possibility must be considered, and that is that the institution of monarchy itself is dramatically undermined, as it was in 1944. Philippe himself will be certain that he will accept the crown. According to his birth horoscope he is not one to willingly turn down the chance to be King but, from April 1998 to December 2001, a period of three and a half years, he will be pulled in different directions. An initial commitment to fulfil his responsibilities, which will be very strong from June 1998 to May 2000, overlaps with an alternative feeling beginning in December 1999 that his personal future is about to take priority over the nation's. Given the over-lapping of planetary influences between Albert's and Philippe's horoscopes we cannot make a hard forecast. We can only point out the most likely options, the most dramatic of which is that the monarchy itself passes through a major crisis comparable to that in 1944–50 when the King was sent into exile. All we can guarantee is that the headline writers will have plenty of copy.

PRINCESS ASTRID

Daughter of Albert II. Born at 11.20 p.m. GMT on 5 June 1962, with the Sun in Gemini, Moon in Cancer and Ascendant in Aquarius.

Princess Astrid was born on 5 June 1962. This means that she was born with the Sun in the lively, restless and inquiring sign of Gemini. Intriguingly, this was the day before her father's birthday, so the Sun was occupying the same degree of the zodiac at her birth as at his. This then links her into the same astrological pattern as both Albert and her brother, Philippe, so the years 1998–2001 will be as powerful for her as for the rest of the family.

Astrid manages to combine restless and unusual planetary influences with cautious and conservative ones in a very pleasant and balanced manner. Her Sun is very close to Mercury, which gives her forthright opinions, especially about domestic and family matters. Her Ascendant is in Aquarius, and this can only add to her sense of curiosity and fascination for new ideas; she is always interested in looking at life from a fresh perspective. However, Saturn, the planet of conservatism, is very close to her Ascendant so, in spite of her curiosity, she'll think long and hard before finally changing her mind. In addition, the Princess' Moon is in Cancer, which gives her a deep desire for emotional security and family stability.

Astrid's sensitive Cancerian Moon is powerfully affected from 1995–7, so this period brings intense changes in mood. These are bound to affect her family life, mainly because she wavers between trying to assert her freedom on one hand, and create the ideal, loving, secure home on the other. The Princess's powerful Pluto transits from 1999 to 2001 could bring further changes in her personal life, but in view of the fact that the monarchy as a whole is affected, she may be implicated only indirectly and as a result of the changes which take place in the lives of her father and brother.

PRINCE LAURENT

Youngest son of Albert II. Born at 10.20 a.m. GMT on 20 October 1963, with the Sun in Libra, Moon in Scorpio and Ascendant in Sagittarius.

Prince Laurent was born with the Sun in Libra and the Ascendant in Sagittarius. This is an excellent combination, for Libra is charming and good-natured, and Sagittarius is spirited and adventurous. His Moon in Scorpio brings similar qualities to those found in Philippe and Astrid's horoscopes, providing him with deep sensitivity and an underlying need for emotional stability. All three of Albert's children therefore possess temperaments which, according to the broadest patterns in their horoscopes, are similar, combining a dominant inquisitive, extraverted and lively nature with a deep desire for family security.

If we consider Laurent's talents, it is clear that he has a penchant for business. However, there are indications of scandal in his horoscope, and he should be advised never to bend the rules, not even in ways normally considered acceptable to most businessmen. If he does, he will be caught. He is also an extremely careful public communicator, skilled at considering every word before he speaks. For some people this can make him seem boring, but this is far from the truth. In relationships with the opposite sex he is very anxious to please, but reluctant to be tied down.

Looking ahead, 1995 is a powerful year for Laurent, one which finds him growing in confidence and building up his public role. However, in 1996 he enters an intense Plutonic period which lasts for two years and foreshadows that which the rest of his family enters in 1998. These are the years when Laurent strikes out and makes a life for himself, eager to prove that his talents are based on more than being merely a royal Prince.

Denmark

The Danish monarchy can be traced back to Harald Bluetooth, son of Gorm the Old, King of Jutland. Harald's reign is dated from 940. His son, Sweyn, conquered England, and his grandson Canute was one of the most famous of English kings. The story of the modern Danish kings and queens began just over a hundred years ago.

CHRISTIAN X
1912–1947

Born in Copenhagen at midnight on 25–26 September 1870, with the Sun and Moon in Libra and Ascendant in Leo.

Christian X was born under planetary alignments indicating great charm and courage. His Sun and Moon were together in Libra, and above all Christian needed to be liked; in fact he needed to feel loved. He therefore had an instinctive knowledge of what was needed to court public popularity. In addition, he was born with Mars close to the Ascendant in the royal sign, Leo. This is one of the toughest positions Mars can occupy, and the King earned the loyalty of his people by showing great courage during the Nazi occupation from 1940 to 1945.

In his private affairs Christian had all the shyness conferred by Venus, the ruler of emotion, in the reserved sign of Capricorn. With the Moon in Libra, his overwhelming desire was for a quiet home life and a peaceful environment. He married Alexandrina of Mecklenburg-Schwerin and had two children. He died on 20 April 1947 and was succeeded by his eldest son, Frederick.

FREDERICK IX
1947–1972

Born on 11 March 1899, with the Sun and Moon in Pisces.

Frederick IX's temperament was as pleasant as his father's. While Christian had been born under a New Moon in charming Libra, Frederick was born under a New Moon in sensitive Pisces. This gave him a vivid imagination and a love of peace and beauty. However, both his Sun and Moon made powerful alignments to Uranus, Saturn, Neptune and Pluto. This was a very stressful alignment, bringing a profound threat of violence and confrontation. Yet this was an historic alignment, present in the horoscopes of many of the young men who died in the First World War. In Frederick's horoscope it was given additional force by its connections to his New Moon.

In his personal life Frederick was a romantic. With his Moon in idealistic Pisces and Venus in Aquarius in addition to his powerful Saturn, he believed in the perfect marriage, and was capable of feeling profound love together with a deep sense of loyalty and responsibility. In May 1935 he married Ingrid, daughter of the Crown Prince of Sweden. She was born on 28 March 1910, with the Sun in Aries and Moon in Virgo. Aries loves to take decisions and Virgo is an excellent organiser, so in many ways Ingrid was Frederick's opposite. She would certainly have taken charge of the household, leaving him to daydream.

Frederick died on 14 January 1972, and was succeeded by his daughter, Margarethe.

MARGARETHE
1972–

Born in Amalienborg at 9.10 a.m. on 16 April 1940 with the Sun in Aries, Moon in Leo and Ascendant in Cancer.

While her grandfather and father were born with peace-loving temperaments, Margarethe has the horoscope of a true queen, full of courage and pride. Had she succeeded to the medieval throne Margarethe would have joined that select band of women who managed to control and outsmart the rebellious barons. Her Sun is in Aries in a very close alignment with Jupiter, indicating great self-confidence. Her energetic Arien qualities are reinforced by a dramatic Leonine Moon, while an emotional edge is added by an Ascendant in Cancer. This is also an excellent combination, for her powerful Moon links up with her Cancerian Ascendant and both are indications of strong maternal qualities. Margarethe is therefore able to project herself as mother of her people, a useful skill for a successful monarch.

She was born with Venus and Mars in Gemini, a powerful indication that she is both lively company and requires that close partners offer her plenty of stimulation. When she married Count Henri de Monpezat on 10 June 1967 the Sun itself was in Gemini. Indeed, there had been a New Moon in this sign only two days earlier. From the marriage horoscope it is clear that Margarethe offers the relationship independence, change and excitement, while Prince Henrik, as he is now known, provides emotional depth and security. From 1997–8 Uranus occupies the opposite degree to Margarethe's Leonine Moon, indicating that these are years of domestic change and uncertainty. One possibility, for example, is that she becomes a grandmother by 1999.

217

CROWN PRINCE FREDERIK

Born on 26 May 1968, with the Sun in Gemini and Moon in Taurus. Son of Margarethe, Queen of Denmark, and Prince Henrik.

Prince Frederick was born just one day before a New Moon in Gemini. However, at his birth the Moon was actually in Taurus, giving him his sense of stability and love of order. In addition, the Moon is powerfully aligned with Neptune and Pluto, and he is therefore a true romantic. His relations with the opposite sex are dominated by deep passions and a tendency to place women on a pedestal, but he also has a romantic view of the world as a whole, and a profound sense of future possibilities, of how the world could be changed for the better. Indeed, we can imagine him developing a very deep friendship with Prince Charles, with whom he has strong planetary connections.

Frederick's Sun is in Gemini, together with Mars, and this gives him energy and restlessness; in this he resembles his mother. His next set of powerful planetary alignments occur from 1997–9, when Pluto moves across the degree of the zodiac opposing his Sun. This is an intense phase, during which he may rebel against his royal role, but is also likely to come one step closer to the succession, beginning to take on an increasingly royal role.

PRINCE JOACHIM

Born on 7 June 1969 with the Sun in Gemini and Moon in Pisces. Younger son of Margarethe, Queen of Denmark and Prince Henrik.

Like his elder brother, Joachim was born with the Sun in restless Gemini. He also has the Moon in sensitive Pisces, and this is a gentle, poetic and imaginative combination which often confers an interest in the arts, a love of beauty and a natural affinity with mysticism. However, intensity is added by a very powerful Pluto, and Joachim is capable of profound changes of personality, or so it seems. In fact it will be his behaviour which shifts as unconscious pressures build up and push him towards rebellion against his past.

With friends and lovers Joachim is naturally very loyal and dependable, for Venus, indicating his romantic attachments, is in conservative Taurus and very close to Saturn. However, when between 2002 and 2005 Pluto activates his desire to revolutionise his life, his relationships are likely to be swept away along with everything else. These are the years when Joachim will discover his purpose, and until then anything he does is in the nature of preliminary training.

France

Nobody can say for sure when the French monarchy came into being. One date commonly used is that for the conversion of Clovis, the first Christian King of the Franks, on Christmas Day, 496. The Sun on this day was in Capricorn and very powerfully aligned with Saturn and Pluto, indicating many trials but great persistence. For fifteen hundred years France has survived invasion and civil war and time and again returned to the centre of the European stage.

The power of the cycles connected to the French monarchy are revealed in the astonishing connection between this chart and that for the crown's greatest trauma, the execution of Louis XVI at the hand of the French revolutionaries in 1793. The connections lie in repeating planetary patterns in Aquarius, itself a revolutionary sign. When Clovis was baptised and welcomed into the Church of Rome, a revolutionary moment for his people, the Moon was in Aquarius. When we move forward thirteen hundred years to 21 January 1793, the day Louis was taken to the guillotine, Pluto and Mars, the most violent combination possible, had moved over the exact same degree of Aquarius as that occupied by the Moon in 496. It was as if the monarchy instituted by Clovis had a life of its own, and that on that fateful day in 1793, an ancient destiny was unfolding.

Our astrological examination of the French kings begins as we enter the modern age, with Louis XIV, the Sun King himself.

LOUIS XIV
'THE SUN KING'
1643–1715

Born at St Germain-en-Laye at 11.10 a.m. on 5 September 1638, with the Sun in Virgo, Moon in Leo and Ascendant in Scorpio.

Louis XIV was the most splendid of all European monarchs. We are fortunate to know his time of birth to the nearest minute, since the royal astrologer, Morin de Villefranche, was present in the Queen's bedchamber at the time. It is perhaps not surprising that Louis was born with the Moon in Leo, the royal sign, and the glittering theatricality of his court is a testimony to this sign's love of show and colour. The Moon's close relationship with Venus, the planet of love and beauty, further enhanced the reputation of Louis' court as a centre of pleasure and decadence. Still more fascinating is the Moon's powerful relationship with Saturn, the planet of conservatism, for in spite of the opulence of Louis' court at Versailles, a strict code of discipline ruled every aspect of day-to-day affairs. Each minute of Louis' day, from waking to going to bed, was conducted with a precise series of rituals, and every one of the hundreds of nobles required to live at Versailles was subject to similar rules. The centre of this spectacle was Louis himself. It is often said that Leonine people create dramatic surroundings in which they then see themselves reflected. It is fitting then that Louis' most memorable achievement is the great Hall of Mirrors, the centrepiece of the palace at Versailles. The Sun was in Virgo at Louis' birth, and in this sign's legendary attention to detail we see further evidence of the King's precise regulation of every aspect of royal life. Louis' Moon in Leo endowed him with a magnificent sense of theatre, but the myth of the Sun King also owes a great deal to the sheer thoroughness with which the courtly spectacle was organised. Louis' Ascendant was in Scorpio, adding an intensity to his personality and indicating that he was driven, not just by a Leonine love of theatrical display or a Virgoan need to organise, but by a Scorpionic belief that he was absolutely above criticism. Scorpio people are not always so arrogant, but in combination with Leo and Virgo it is the most likely outcome.

220

He succeeded to the throne at the age of nearly five, just as Uranus was passing over his Ascendant. Under any circumstances this planet signifies profound upheaval, but in Louis' case its powerful movements coincided with the death of his father, Louis XIII, and his succession to the oldest throne in Europe.

Although Louis was married to Maria Theresa of Spain, he is perhaps better known for his mistresses, Louise de la Vallière, Madame de Montespan and Madame de Maintenon. With Venus in Leo and Neptune, planet of illusion, on his Ascendant, Louis was extremely susceptible to any display of affection, yet, thanks to his powerful Saturnine influences, even in the boudoir a strong sense of propriety ruled. One of Louis' mistresses, Madame de Maintenon, was a devout Catholic, and after Maria Theresa's death she became the King's wife. Her influence over him was boundless, for Louis' strong Moon/Venus alignment in Leo gave him a love of powerful women.

Louis reached the peak of his power in 1679 when, after a long war, he dictated terms to the other European powers. However, after 1692 the English gained control of the seas and he began to face increasing difficulties. Finally, when Pluto, a planet which always brings people face to face with the consequences of their actions, began to pass over his Midheaven, Louis' empire began to collapse. The British victory at Blenheim in 1704 was followed by others, yet once Pluto had moved on Louis recovered. However, by 1715 this uncompromising planet had commenced its approach to Louis' Sun, and he died. His reign, seventy-two years, was one of the longest in the history of hereditary monarchy.

LOUIS XV
1715–1774

Born at Versailles at 8.45 a.m. on 15 February 1710, with the Sun in Aquarius, the Moon in Virgo and the Ascendant in Aries.

Louis XIV outlived both his eldest son and grandson, who died in 1711 and 1712 respectively. The Sun King was therefore succeeded by his five-year-old great-grandson, Louis XV. Like Louis XIV, the young King was born with powerful Virgoan influences, although in his case it was the Moon rather than the Sun which fell in this sign.

Louis' Sun was in Aquarius, always an independent-minded sign, and his Ascendant was in Aries, the most assertive sign. This is a combination which brings erratic behaviour, and the King tended to fluctuate between Arien–Aquarian impulsiveness and a Virgoan regard for the virtues of routine day-to-day government. The contrast between these two halves of his personality was revealed in his marital affairs. He was originally betrothed to the Infanta of Spain, daughter of Philip V, and had this marriage gone ahead it would have been an extremely important dynastic union. However, Louis decided he'd rather marry the daughter of the ex-King of Poland and sent the Infanta back home, much to her father's indignation.

Louis was born with Venus in Aries in almost exactly the same degree of the zodiac as his Ascendant. It is difficult to imagine a more powerful placement for this affectionate planet, and its strength was revealed in his love of tough women. This was a trait he shared with his predecessor, as well as with his son, the ill-fated Louis XVI. In fact, Louis' most famous mistress, the Marquise de Pompadour, exerted a considerable influence over matters of state from 1745 until her death in 1764. Towards the end of Louis' reign another strong woman, the Comtesse du Barry, controlled the government, though she was totally lacking in de Pompadour's political skill.

LOUIS XVI
1774–1792

Born at Versailles at 6.24 a.m. on 23 August 1754, with the Sun in Leo, Moon in Scorpio and Ascendant in Virgo.

QUEEN MARIE ANTOINETTE

Born in Vienna at about 7.30 a.m. on 2 November 1755, with the Sun and Ascendant in Scorpio and Moon in Libra.

Were Louis XVI to have had his horoscope analysed by any eighteenth-century astrologer, he would have been told that excessive pride would be his undoing. Louis was born with the Sun in Leo, the sign of pride. Admittedly, the Sun was only two hours away from moving into Virgo, which added an element of Virgoan pedantry to his personality. On the other hand, his Leonine pride was reinforced by a tight conjunction between the Sun and Jupiter, which were occupying exactly the same degree of the zodiac. The Sun was also very close to Mercury, the planet ruling Louis' mind, and which was just over the border into Virgo. This was an indication of such arrogance that Louis would have found it virtually impossible even to acknowledge the existence of other points of view, let alone listen to them.

It is said that Louis had a lack of energy and was unable to understand the complexities of his situation. This is true to an extent, but tells only half the story. His real problem was more to do with a rare capacity to do the wrong thing in the wrong place at the wrong time, and sabotage every advantage he was given. This was because, at the time of his birth, the Sun, Jupiter and Mercury were occupying a sector of his horoscope known as the house of self-undoing. This same sector also indicates deception, subversion and all places of seclusion and incarceration, including prisons, hospitals and monasteries. In a curious way, Louis' horoscope thus substantiates his executioners' accusation that he was no more than a criminal with a crown. It also indicates that the perfect career for Louis would have been a bishop. As the horoscope of a king, his was a total disaster.

Louis' Ascendant was in Virgo and his Moon was in Scorpio. When combined, these two serious signs often indicate a love of formal behaviour and a devotion to strict morality. True to his horoscope, Louis possessed none of the decadence associated with his predecessors, and was a devoted family man, loyal husband and dutiful father. However, Marie Antoinette, his beloved Queen, undid any improvements he made to the monarchy's reputation by her love of dances, theatres and parties. She was easily painted as a greedy and callous woman; in reality she was merely tactless, possessing little concept of life in France and no understanding of the popular pressure for reform. Her famous response to the crowd of hungry people who marched from Paris to Versailles during the opening stages of the revolution, 'Let them eat cake', may have been a later invention, yet as far as people as the time were concerned she might as well have said it. Her heartlessness was contrasted with Louis' good-natured agreement to let the angry mob have as much bread as they wanted.

Marie Antoinette was born with the Sun in Scorpio in a very close alignment with Venus, a planet often strongly connected to self-indulgence. This is a powerful indication of the Queen's love of pleasure. Yet, more importantly, it is the sector of the horoscope occupied by the Sun – the twelfth house. This duplicates Louis' horoscope, and if pride was his downfall, pleasure was Marie Antoinette's. She was born with the Moon in Libra, denoting a love of beauty, and the Ascendant in Scorpio, indicating surprisingly deep emotions. Intriguingly, her Ascendant was in almost exactly the same degree of the zodiac as Sarah, Duchess of York. In addition, Sarah's Sun in Libra is very close to Marie Antoinette's Moon.

For two people whose marriage was a matter of dynastic importance rather than personal preference, Louis and Marie Antoinette had extremely compatible contacts between their horoscopes. His Moon at 7° in Scorpio fell in almost exactly the same degree as her Sun at 9°. The classic marriage indication in any pair of horoscopes is for the man's Sun to be in the same degree as the woman's Moon. It was rather strange to find this pattern reversed in Louis' and Marie Antoinette's horoscopes, suggesting that in terms of the typical eighteenth-century marriage, she was the boss!

Marie Antoinette's influential and destructive role at the French court is often blamed for the tragedy of the revolution. However, it was Louis' stunning astrological connections with the horoscope for Clovis' baptism which reveal the approaching cataclysm. Remarkably, his horoscope also reveals the manner in which planetary cycles draw connections between events separated by hundreds or even thousands of years. When we take the planets forward to Louis' execution, at just after 10.15 a.m. on 21 January 1793, a very strange pattern becomes apparent. If we look at the Moon, the most important planet, along with the Sun at Clovis' baptism we find the following connections:

* Clovis baptised: Moon at 26–28° in Aquarius.
* Louis XVI: Sun and Jupiter at 29° in Leo, in the opposite degrees to Clovis' baptism Moon.
* Louis XVI executed: Pluto at 22° in Aquarius, Mars at 29° in Aquarius, Uranus at 22° in Leo.

Firstly, we see Louis' horoscope with his Sun–Jupiter alignment, indicating his pride, in the opposite degrees to the Moon at Clovis' baptism, as if Louis was primed to wreck Clovis' legacy. When Louis was executed revolutionary Uranus was joined by Pluto, the planet of final confrontations, and Mars, ruler of violence, on these same degrees of the zodiac. Louis was no longer King when he was sent to the guillotine. On 21 September 1792 the National Assembly, controlled by revolutionaries, had already proclaimed the Republic, and the French monarchy – the legacy of Clovis – had met its final end. Or so it seemed.

LOUIS XVII

Born at Versailles on 27 March 1785, with the Sun in Aries and Moon in Libra.

Louis XVII, the dauphin, was recognised as King by French royalists the moment his father, Louis XVI, was beheaded. At the time he was a child of eight years old, held in prison with his mother Marie Antoinette.

Louis was born with the Sun in Aries and the Moon in Libra. There is no surviving official horoscope for him, but we know that later astrologers cast his horoscope for 7.30 p.m., and that placed his Ascendant along with the Moon in Libra. Had he lived he would therefore have possessed the impulsive power of Aries together with the balanced charm typical of Libra. However, this is a difficult combination, often leading to erratic judgment, and therefore not the perfect indication for a king. More serious was a very close alignment between Mars and Pluto in Aquarius. This linked the planet of war with that of intense, final and ultimate confrontations. In any circumstances it brings a warning of potential violence, and to one whose childhood was spent in the midst of revolution, it brought profound danger. In a fascinating repetition of this cycle, Louis' father, Louis XVI, was sent to the guillotine under another Mars–Pluto alignment in Aquarius. As for the young Louis, he escaped revolutionary justice when he contracted tuberculosis of the bones during his incarceration. He died on 8 June 1795, strangely when Mars had once again formed a powerful alignment with Pluto. The destiny carved out at his birth had brought his short life to its end.

NAPOLEON I
1804–1815

Born on the island of Corsica on 15 August 1769, with the Sun in Leo.

We are not sure what time Napoleon was born, for, being of lowly parentage, his birth was not recorded. We cannot therefore even be sure what sign the Moon occupied. However, the astrologers of the day believed that he was born some time around 10.00 to 11.00 a.m. That would give him a Moon in conservative Capricorn, fitting for a man who turned the clock back, not only by restoring the monarchy, but by proclaiming the French Empire. With such a vague horoscope it is impossible to determine an Ascendant for Napoleon. It is thought that when he was Emperor he might have visited the Parisian fortune-teller Mme Le Normand, but if she cast a horoscope for him, it has long since been lost.

We do know though, that Napoleon's horoscope was connected to Louis XVI's in a number of strange ways. For example, when Louis was guillotined, the planetary situation had been dominated by a revolutionary opposition between Uranus at 22° in Leo and Pluto at 22° in Pluto. This was the major planetary alignment which coincided with the trauma of the revolutionary terror. Napoleon himself was born with the Sun at 22° of Leo. In this sense he was the man, above all others, whose task was to avenge Louis' execution. There were other planetary connections, especially ones linking the Moon and Saturn in Napoleon's horoscope to the chart for Louis' death, all of which build up a picture in which his birth locked into the same planetary cycles evident at Louis' death.

Napoleon is remembered as a man of action above all else. He was very loyal to his brothers and sisters, whom he installed on many of the thrones he conquered, but was never regarded as a family man. He is known for his marriage to Josephine de Beauharnais, yet he always had more time for war than for love. It is therefore fascinating to find that Napoleon was born with the three planets most important in historical cycles, Uranus, Neptune and Pluto, perfectly aligned in the three practical signs of Taurus, Virgo and Capricorn. This profoundly important triple alignment was in operation for many years and signified the entire generation which matured in the French revolution and believed that their historical destiny was to create a new world. Napoleon had two very important planets connected with the triple alignment. These were Mars, planet of war, and Jupiter, planet of growth and expansion. Napoleon had a special relationship with the triple alignment, and for him it was to be quite simply an excuse to fight.

He seized power in an event which has gone down in revolutionary legend known as the Coup of the Eighteenth Brumaire. This was 9 November 1799. He then put an end to the revolutionary chaos which had wrecked France over the previous decade, and on 18 May 1804 proclaimed himself Emperor. The monarchy was restored, greater than ever. A Leo, like Louis XVI, he restored the splendour of the French Golden Age. On 18 May the Sun was at 27° in Taurus, and this tells us that Napoleon's purpose was practical, his purpose relentless. Yet what is truly important is that this was exactly the degree of the zodiac occupied by the Moon at Louis' election. Once again, we find Napoleon's planetary cycles continuing directly those central to Louis' life and death. It was as if the man was almost irrelevant; it was the office of king, or emperor, which was important, seeming through the planetary alignments almost to have its own life cycles. The monarchy was proclaimed dead on 21 January 1793 when Louis XVI was executed, and reborn just over ten years later when Napoleon was proclaimed.

At Napoleon's birth Venus, indicating his emotional relationships, was in Cancer strongly aligned with Neptune. This is a position combining shyness with a romantic view of women. However, bearing in mind Cancer's need for emotional security, this is a fitting description of his reliance on family support; three of his brothers, Joseph, Louis and Jerome were made kings, while his brother-in-law, Joachim, was given the kingdom of Naples. Napoleon was also devoted to Josephine, and showered the same favours on her children by her previous marriage as on his own family.

The Emperor's decline began soon after he came under the influence of Saturn, a planet whose cycles often bring great limitations, and which tends to indicate the worst problems for those who have overreached themselves. The cycle became active in late 1812, while Napoleon was in Moscow, having reached the limits of his power. By the time the cycle was over he was about to abdicate. The victorious allies exiled him to the island of Elba, off the Italian coast, but on 1 March 1815 he returned to France, landing at Cannes, and attempted to restore his empire. The Sun in Pisces and Moon in Scorpio indicated the depth of his conviction that he was destined to reconquer, but he had landed too late to benefit from an ideal alignment between these two planets. On 22 June 1815 he abdicated for a second time and was sent into exile on the island of St Helena, which is where he died.

NAPOLEON II
1814

Born on 20 March 1811, with the Sun in Pisces and Moon in Aquarius.

When Napoleon saw that his empire was disintegrating, he attempted to salvage something from the ruinous situation by having his four-year-old son recognised as Napoleon II. On 6 April 1814 he abdicated in favour of the young Prince, but the allies saw this, quite rightly, as a ruse by which Napoleon hoped to retain his power, and on 11 April forced him to abdicate unconditionally. Napoleon II therefore occupied the throne for five days, which must be one of the shortest reigns in history.

The young Emperor was born with the Sun in imaginative Pisces and the Moon in independent Aquarius. No official horoscope remains, but a tradition has survived that he was born with his Ascendant in restless Gemini, which complements the curiosity and artistic qualities inherent in Pisces and Aquarius. This is an excellent combination for an aspiring philosopher, but almost useless for a claimant to an imperial throne. His mother, Marie-Louise, was the daughter of the Austrian Emperor Francis I, so his life and security were never in doubt. The exiled Emperor was therefore allowed to live out his days in peace, pursuing his various interests, away from the pressures of high European politics. In France it was the Bourbons, not the Bonapartes, who were restored to the throne.

LOUIS XVIII
1814–1824

Born at Versailles at 3.00–3.30 a.m. on 17 November 1755, with the Sun in Scorpio, Moon in Taurus and Ascendant in Libra.

After Napoleon was overthrown, the victorious allies searched around for a new king. They considered several candidates, including Count Bernadotte, who a few years later was made King of Sweden instead. It must have been humiliating for Louis not to have been the automatic choice, for he was Louis XVI's younger brother and therefore the next in line to the succession. Louis had already proclaimed himself King on the death of his nephew, Louis XVII, on 8 June 1795, but when he had to flee Paris during Napoleon's brief restoration in 1815, his credibility was almost permanently damaged.

Yet Louis' horoscope included suitable indications of monarchical power and, had he been born in more peaceful times, he would have been a competent ruler. His Sun in Scorpio gave him sufficient intuition to be able to stay one step ahead of his rivals. In turn, the Sun's powerful alignments to Venus, Mars and Saturn endowed him with the charm, determination and discipline representative of these three planets. His powerful Jupiter is a factor often found in the horoscopes of those who achieve great power. An eighteenth-century astrologer observing this at his birth might well have concluded that Louis had an excellent chance of becoming King.

However, the relationship between Mars and Saturn in his horoscope is one more often found in the horoscopes of those who function best when second-in-command. This is precisely what happened to Louis. Under ordinary circumstances he would never have become King. Yet when he was placed on the throne he was imposed on by the allies and never managed to control the competing factions which were still in danger of tearing the country apart. For ten years he survived, and his greatest achievement was that he avoided another revolution. In September 1824 Louis became the last French monarch to die in office.

CHARLES X
1824–1830

Born at Versailles at 7.00 p.m. on 9 October 1757, with the Sun in Libra, Moon in Virgo and Ascendant in Gemini.

When Louis XVIII died he was succeeded by his younger brother, who ascended the throne as Charles X. Charles was born with the Sun in Libra and the Moon in Virgo, and when we compare the charm of the former sign with the care and caution of the latter we find a personality which is at once very pleasant but very formal. Above all, Charles loved order. He longed for the old days before the revolution and did his best to recreate the original absolute monarchy. Charles' Ascendant was exactly on the cusp, or dividing line, between Taurus and Gemini, and by all accounts he seems to have possessed Taurean obstinacy in a greater amount than Geminian flexibility. He managed to alienate both the middle-classes and the workers, and in 1830 he provoked revolution. This time the revolutionaries were kinder and Charles was allowed to live out his days in peace, dying in 1836.

He was born with Venus, ruling his emotional life, in Scorpio, indicating depth and intensity, and very close to Jupiter, bringing great passion. He married Maria Teresa of Savoy, and the couple's eldest son, the Duke of Angoulême, was recognised by his supporters as Louis XIX. His nephew, in turn, claimed the throne under the name Henry V. However, the throne now passed to a different branch of the family.

LOUIS PHILIPPE
1830–1848

Born at 9.40 a.m. on 6 October 1773, with the Sun in Libra, Moon in Gemini and Ascendant in Scorpio.

When it appeared that the revolution of 1830 was in danger of sweeping away not only Charles X but the monarchy as a whole, the liberal royalists decided to save the day by choosing a king from a different branch of the ruling Bourbon family. On 7 August they proclaimed Louis Philippe, Duke of Orléans, sixth in descent from Louis XIII, the King of the French people.

At first, Louis Philippe was a popular choice. He was born with the Sun in Libra in an exact harmonious alignment with the Moon in Gemini, one of the most graceful and charming combinations possible. His Ascendant was in Scorpio, combining that sign's intensity with his Libran charm. However, had the King's revolutionary supporters cast his horoscope they would have noticed that he was born with the Sun in the same awkward sector as Louis XVI, in the twelfth house. This is an excellent position for revolutionaries who set out to undermine the existing order, but very difficult for those who are trying to hang on to power. As soon as he had been transformed from hero of the liberals to successor to the Sun King, Louis Philippe altered his priorities from constitutional reform to preservation of the monarchy.

Eventually, in 1848 another wave of revolution swept Europe and Louis Philippe succumbed to the pressure for change. On 24 February 1848, only two days after disturbances broke out in Paris, the King abdicated in favour of his grandson, the Count of Paris. But it was too late. That evening the revolutionaries proclaimed France a Republic for the second time, and the Bourbon dynasty, which had ruled France since 1589, finally came to an end. The current claimant to the throne, supported by some romantically inclined French royalists, is Henry, Count of Paris.

One of the dominant planetary patterns in Louis Philippe's horoscope was the harmonious Sun–Moon alignment, which accounted for his personal charm and easy circumstances. It was fitting that when he was swept to power and when he abdicated the Sun and Moon had once again formed exactly the same pattern. After the revolution of 1848 the King, like his predecessor, was not punished but left alone to lead a quiet life until his death in 1850.

Emotionally, Louis Philippe's character was dominated by a tight alignment between Venus and Mars in Scorpio, indicating intense passions. He married Marie Amélie of Sicily and the couple had eight surviving children. Louis Philippe was not the last member of his line to occupy a European throne and through his children's marriages he is a direct ancestor of both Queen Beatrix of the Netherlands and King Juan Carlos of Spain.

NAPOLEON III
1852–1870

Born in Paris at 1.00 a.m. on 20 April 1808, with the Sun in Aries, Moon in Aquarius and Ascendant in Capricorn.

Within two years of the proclamation of the second republic by the revolutionaries of 1848, the French elected Prince Louis Napoleon as their President. The Prince was the son of Louis, King of Holland, Napoleon's younger brother, and the current standard bearer of the Bonapartist cause. Only four years later, on 2 December 1852, the anniversary of the first Napoleon's coronation, the President proclaimed himself Emperor Napoleon III.

The new Emperor was born with the Sun in Aries; that endowed him with ambition. Yet there was more, for the Sun was in exactly the same degree of the zodiac as Mars, planet of war, an indication of unstoppable, irrepressible ambition. He was also born with his Ascendant in Capricorn and a powerful Saturn, indicating deep conservatism, and the Moon in Aquarius, suggesting great independence of spirit. Nothing could be more unusual, yet more reactionary, than the revival of Napoleon's empire. And nothing could do more to satisfy Napoleon III's desire for power.

Like Charles X, Napoleon III wanted to restore the absolute powers of the eighteenth-century monarchy, and in this aim he was supported by his wife, the beautiful Eugénie de Montijo. She was a devout Catholic and did much to engineer the restoration of church power and privilege. However, she is also associated with the decadence of the second Empire. The contradiction between Napoleon and Eugénie's authoritarian Catholicism and the image of a court which gave free rein to licentiousness was embodied in the horoscope for the Emperor's proclamation. A bold Sagittarian Sun and dramatic Leonine Moon encouraged a return to the theatrical show of Louis XIV's court. Yet the Moon was also strongly aligned to Saturn, indicating an underlying conservatism and fear of change.

Napoleon's powerful Mars in Aries gave him a warlike nature and in turn he fought the Crimean War against Russia, attacked Austria and occupied Mexico. However, like his uncle Napoleon I, he gradually over-extended himself. When in 1870, Bismarck and the Prussians invaded France, this rang the death knell for the second Empire, and in the ensuing revolutionary chaos the Republic was restored. It was the horoscope for Napoleon's proclamation which revealed the crushing of his hopes, for Saturn, which often brings unbearable burdens, had become the most important planet. On 4 September 1870 Napoleon was overthrown and France's monarchical traditions were brought to an end. The final humiliation, on 18 January 1871, was the proclamation in the Hall of Mirrors at Versailles not of a French king or emperor, but of the first German emperor, Kaiser Wilhelm I.

However, in a sense the cycle had come full circle, for Clovis, the first Christian King of the Franks, was himself a German chieftain. At Wilhelm's proclamation at Versailles Saturn had now come to the exact degree of the zodiac occupied by the Sun at Clovis' baptism. One cycle had ended, but a new one had begun.

Germany

From 800 to 1806, with occasional interruptions, the supreme monarch in Germany was the Holy Roman Emperor. The empire was founded on Christmas Day 800 with the coronation of Charlemagne, and originally covered all of Germany as well as France and most of Italy. However, the emperors gradually lost most of their power to the many princes who carved out their own territories. Eventually, in 1806 the empire was snuffed out by Napoleon, who saw himself as the true successor of Charlemagne. Napoleon didn't know it, but Saturn had by then assumed a dominant role in the horoscope for Charlemagne's coronation. Just sixty-five years later, when Saturn had achieved a dominant position in the horoscope for the foundation of the Christian French monarchy by Clovis, the imperial crown passed back to Germany. Soon after midday on 18 January 1871, with the Sun in Capricorn, the Moon in Sagittarius and the Ascendant in Gemini, Wilhelm I, King of Prussia, entered Louis XIV's Hall of Mirrors at Versailles, and was proclaimed the first Emperor of Germany.

WILHELM I
King of Prussia 1861–1888
Emperor of Germany 1871–1888

Born in Berlin at 1.45 p.m. on 22 March 1797, with the Sun in Aries, Moon in Capricorn and Ascendant in Leo.

Wilhelm I was born with a horoscope which was thoroughly suitable for an aspiring emperor. His Ascendant in Leo gave him a healthy dose of pride, the Sun in Aries gave him a belief in his own right to lead others, while the Moon in Capricorn made him suitably conservative. When found together, Aries and Capricorn often create an intense belief in the maintenance of order.

Although Wilhelm himself was the first German Emperor, the Empire was not his creation, and in many ways he was the puppet of the true leader of Germany, his Chancellor, Otto von Bismarck. Being born with Mars in Taurus, a sign averse to change, and Venus in Pisces, Wilhelm could see little point in stirring up trouble and causing possible war, and was a reluctant partner in some of Bismarck's foreign adventures. Mercury in Pisces also gave Wilhelm a dislike of unnecessary arguments and an inclination to agree with the last person he spoke to. His rule began in 1858 when he was appointed Regent for his elder brother Frederick William I, who had been judged insane. Wilhelm was sympathetic to demands for liberal reform, and when faced with a tide of protest, he contemplated abdication. It was only Bismarck, who became Chancellor in September 1862, who toughened Wilhelm's resolve and encouraged him to act more like a typical Aries–Capricorn.

In his family life Wilhelm was dominated by the sensitivity of his Venus in Pisces and the conservatism of his Moon in Capricorn. A stable existence was not merely a matter of social convention, but a deep psychological need. Wilhelm married Augusta of Weimar and had two surviving children, a daughter, Louisa, and Frederick, his son and heir.

FREDERICK III
1888

Born at Potsdam at 10.00 a.m. on 18 October 1831, with the Sun in Pisces, Moon in Libra and Ascendant in Scorpio.

Frederick III occupied the throne for just over three months, succeeding his father on 9 March 1888, when he was already ill from cancer of the throat. He died on 15 June.

Frederick had a pleasant horoscope. His Sun was in Libra and his Moon in Pisces, combining the charm of the former sign with the sensitivity of the latter. His Ascendant was exactly on the cusp, or dividing line, between Scorpio and Sagittarius, so he had a little Scorpionic intensity, but a healthy dose of Sagittarian optimism. His sensitivity was reinforced by Neptune, planet of illusion and, had he not been born to reign, Frederick would have enjoyed a quiet life as an artist. He was born with only one difficult planetary alignment, a tricky opposition between Venus and Pluto, which indicates a deep streak of impatience. This would have surfaced mainly in his private life, but although he was not above losing his temper with his family, he would immediately have regretted any harsh words.

Frederick married Victoria, Queen Victoria's beloved eldest daughter, reinforcing the already close links between the British and German royal houses. He was survived by seven of his children, including his heir, Wilhelm II.

WILHELM II
1888–1918

Born in Berlin at 3.00 p.m. on 27 January 1859, with the Sun in Aquarius, Moon in Scorpio and Ascendant in Cancer.

Wilhelm II was born with the Sun in Aquarius and the Moon in Scorpio. Aquarius is an intellectual sign, Scorpio an emotional one, but what both have in common is obstinacy. There was worse to come: Wilhelm's Sun was in an exact and very destructive alignment with Saturn and Pluto, and in any country or class he would have sought confrontation. He was born with an unconscious desire to push arguments to the limit and a total inability to compromise. Wilhelm's Moon was in a powerful though harmonious alignment with Mars and Neptune, but a very dangerous one to Uranus. This indicated that he was capable of tearing his environment down around him.

He was known by his family as a potentially difficult character, and his grandmother Queen Victoria gave him a sound ticking off after he wrote a letter to her that she thought rude and insensitive. When Wilhelm picked a fight with his family it assumed global proportions, for he was related to most of the crowned heads of Europe – the British King George V and the Russian Czarina Alexandra were his cousins. If any world leader can be blamed for the outbreak of the First World War, then, from a study of all their horoscopes, it must be Wilhelm. Other nations were also ready to fight, and although the war was launched by the Austrians, Wilhelm's horoscope was by far and away the most difficult of all the European leaders. When the war broke out at the beginning of August 1914, his horoscope was under the most stressful alignments.

In his personal life Wilhelm's affections were indicated by Venus in Sagittarius and Mars in Pisces. This indicates romantic ideals, but a weakness in dealing with close human relationships and a desire to avoid commitment. He married Augusta of Schleswig-Holstein and the couple had seven children. Their eldest son, William, the Crown Prince, was born on 6 May 1882, with the Sun in Taurus, in a very close alignment with Saturn. This indicated a character who was unlikely to achieve much early in life, but would come into his own after middle age. However, William was never given the chance to prove himself, for in 1918 revolution broke out in Germany and his father fled into exile.

Shortly after midday on 9 November 1918, the socialist leader Scheidemann proclaimed the Republic in front of a vast crowd in Berlin. A month later, at about 6.30 a.m. on 10 December, Wilhelm slipped across the border near Maastricht and went into exile. In 1914, when Germany had gone to war with such hopes, Uranus, planet of sudden change, had been making a stressful alignment with Wilhelm's Moon. By November 1918 Uranus had switched its attention to his Moon and the cycle came to an end. When Wilhelm eventually crossed into exile on 10 December the Sun was at 17° in Sagittarius. It had returned to the degree occupied by the Ascendant when Charlemagne became the first Holy Roman Emperor, over a thousand years earlier. This was more than the end of a reign. It was the end of an era, the end of empire in Europe.

Greece

Greece proclaimed its independence from Turkey in 1821, and nine years later the Kingdom of Greece was internationally recognised. The first King, Otto I, son of Ludwig I of Bavaria, was appointed in 1832. He was deposed in 1867, setting a pattern which has been maintained until the present day. Of the eight kings since independence, five have been deposed.

GEORGE I
1863–1913

Born in Copenhagen at 7.30 p.m. on 24 December 1845, with the Sun in Capricorn, Moon in Scorpio and Ascendant in Leo.

George was the son of Christian IX of Denmark. With the Sun in Capricorn and Moon in Scorpio, his character was serious and conservative. Venus close to Saturn and Neptune in Aquarius gave him deep ideals, especially in the conduct of human relationships. Mars was strong, and in a very difficult alignment with the Sun, and was at its strongest shortly before the First World War. This was when the Balkans was consumed by the struggles which later grew into the European war. George died, though, one year before the final outbreak of war.

CONSTANTINE I
1913–1917, 1920–1922

Born on 2 August 1868, with the Sun in Leo.

Constantine I, George I's son, proved an inadequate king and was deposed after only four years and his son Alexander was placed on the throne. He was then restored in 1920 and deposed again in 1922, dying the following year. His Sun was in Leo in a difficult alignment with Pluto, indicating pride, obstinacy – and his short and interrupted reign.

GEORGE II
1922–1923, 1935–1947

Born on 20 July 1890, with the Sun in Cancer and the Moon in Virgo.

George II, Constantine I's son, was deposed in 1923, restored in 1935 and exiled from 1941–6. He was born with the Sun in Cancer and the Moon in Virgo, indicating a careful, punctilious and serious personality. The Moon was in an exact alignment with Neptune and Pluto, indicating possible violence and death. In fact, George channelled this alignment into a deep interest in spiritualism. While he was in exile in London, he is thought to have conveyed communications from the beyond to George V. What the British King thought of these messages, we are not told.

PAUL
1947–1964

Born on 14 December 1901, with the Sun in Sagittarius.

Paul succeeded his brother George in 1947 and, like him, was deeply involved in spiritualism during his exile in London. Paul's Sun was in Sagittarius, indicating an expansive and optimistic spirit but, like George's Moon, was closely aligned with Pluto. He also possessed a very stable and practical alignment of Mars, Jupiter and Saturn in Capricorn; the Moon may also have been in this businesslike sign. Paul had a greater appreciation of practical realities than his predecessors and survived longer than any monarch since George I.

CONSTANTINE II
1964–1973

Born on 2 June 1940 with the Sun in Gemini.

Constantine succeeded his father Paul in 1964 at the age of twenty-four. Only four years later the Greek colonels seized control and, by his failure to condemn their dictatorial rule, Constantine was widely discredited. As a result, when the Republic was proclaimed in 1973 he had lost public support, and when democracy was restored in 1974 he was not invited back. Instead he became one of Europe's many wandering ex-monarchs.

He was born with the Sun in Gemini, indicating a lively and restless personality. In addition, his Moon was passing from Aries into Taurus, and his mishandling of the colonels' dictatorship reflected the arrogance of Aries and the stubbornness of Taurus. As we look ahead at Constantine's horoscope it is clear that the years 2000–1 will be very powerful, with a great deal of personal change. Could he be restored? In the current circumstances in which republicanism is so popular, this seems an unlikely prospect. However, in Constantine's horoscope profound developments will take place as the twenty-first century begins and, even if restoration is out of the question, he should be open to questions of a similar magnitude.

Italy

The Kingdom of Italy was proclaimed on 16 March 1861, with the Sun in Pisces and the Moon in Taurus. It was ten years later that national unity was achieved when at 12.30 p.m. on 2 July 1871 the King, Victor Emmanuel II, entered Italy to a rapturous reception.

VICTOR EMMANUEL II
1861–1878

Born in Turin at 1.00 a.m. on 14 March 1820, with the Sun and Moon in Pisces and Ascendant in Sagittarius.

Victor Emmanuel succeeded to the Kingdom of Sardinia in 1849 and would have remained King of a small Italian state had not the revolutionary leader Garibaldi decided to unify the entire peninsula in 1861, and place him on the throne. The King was born with the Sun and Moon in Pisces, an unambitious sign, so it is unlikely that he would ever have achieved such high honour by himself. In addition, his Ascendant was in Sagittarius, a sign which resists formal ties and commitments as much as Pisces does. Victor Emmanuel's historic role is signified by his Sun's close relationship with Uranus, Neptune and Pluto, the three planets most responsible for long-term historical cycles. He was, quite simply, the right man in the right place at the right time.

UMBERTO I
1878–1900

Born in Turin at 10.30 a.m. on 14 March 1844, with the Sun in Pisces, Moon in Capricorn and Ascendant in Gemini.

Umberto succeeded Victor Emmanuel, his father, on 9 January 1878. Like his predecessor, Umberto was born with the Sun in Pisces. In fact he was born on his father's birthday, so they would have shared many qualities, chiefly the deep personal sensitivity which Pisces always confers. Umberto could also be extremely stubborn, for Venus and Mars were together in Taurus, and the Moon in Capricorn was close to Saturn. All these factors indicate a high regard for practical routine, but also a deep inflexibility. This contrasts totally with Pisces, which is utterly flexible. Umberto therefore had the worst of both worlds, finding it difficult both to make decisions and to stick to a course of action. In his private affairs, as in public, he was instinctively conservative, though his close Mars–Venus alignment is an indication of intense passions. On 29 July 1900, while this alignment was being aligned by the Sun, he was assassinated by an anarchist at Monza, leaving his son to inherit the throne.

VICTOR EMMANUEL III
1900–1946

Born at Naples at 10.20 p.m. on 11 November 1869, with the Sun in Scorpio, Moon in Aquarius and Ascendant in Leo.

Victor Emmanuel was born with the Sun in Scorpio, which makes him similar in many respects to his father and grandfather. Like them, he was deeply sensitive and governed by his emotions. Also, like

Victor Emmanuel II, his Sun made very powerful alignments, in his case to Jupiter, Uranus and Pluto, which indicated that he was destined to be swept up in historical forces beyond his control. With Pluto so heavily implicated, these forces were to be dark and require confrontation and conflict. First he led Italy against Austria and Germany in the Great War, in alliance with Britain, France and Germany. Then in 1922 Mussolini and his fascist Black Shirts took power, ruling Italy until their defeat by the allies in 1944. The darkest period of all took place in 1943 when Italy was ravaged by war, and the Nazis took direct control of the north.

Victor Emmanuel was a difficult man to categorise, for at his birth the planets were spread around the zodiac. He could be conservative and shy in love, yet he was also a man of action, independent-minded yet tied to convention. In the event, for almost half his reign he was effectively Mussolini's prisoner. After the war it was felt he was tainted by that association with Mussolini, and on 9 May 1946 he abdicated in favour of his son, Umberto.

UMBERTO II
1946

Born at Racconigi at 11.00 p.m. on 15 September 1904, with the Sun in Virgo, Moon in Sagittarius and Ascendant in Gemini.

Umberto II was born with the Sun in Virgo and the Moon in Sagittarius, so he always found himself pulled between the caution of the former sign and the adventurousness of the other. This gave him a very strong family connection with his grandfather and great-grandfather, for while the Sun in their horoscopes was at 22° in Pisces, Umberto's was in the exact opposite degree – 22° in Virgo. It was as if the heavens were saying that he stood in opposition to their achievements, that he was to bring them to an end. Like many kings whose reigns are short, Umberto was also born with the Sun in a close alignment with Pluto. And so it was that at 6.00 p.m. on 10 June 1946, after only four weeks of Umberto's reign, the Italian government proclaimed the end of the monarchy and the beginning of the Italian Republic. On that very day the Sun was passing over the same degree of the zodiac occupied by Pluto at Umberto's birth. Once again, a monarchy came to an end at the exact moment decreed by the major planetary cycle.

Liechtenstein

Before Napoleon's conquests, Germany consisted of hundreds of principalities, many as small as a single town. All have disappeared except one: the Principality of Liechtenstein.

FRANZ JOSEPH II
1938–1989

Born on 16 August 1906, with the Sun in Leo and the Moon in Cancer.

Franz Joseph II ruled Liechtenstein for over fifty years. He was born with his Sun in Leo, conferring pride and self-confidence, exactly the qualities needed in a prince. His Moon, though, was in Cancer, an emotional sign, and extremely close to Neptune. This was a profoundly sensitive and romantic alignment, indicating that in the final analysis Franz Joseph put his personal feelings first, family interests second and national welfare third. Fortunately, the nature of the tiny Principality was such that he, his family and the state were inseparable.

If we look at the horoscope for Franz Joseph's succession, 9.45 p.m. on 25 July 1938, we find four planets, including the Sun and Moon, in a sector indicating pleasurable, competitive and speculative activities; Venus and Neptune, also indicating leisure and extravagance, were powerful as well. It is therefore not surprising that under Franz Joseph's control the principality became renowned for two activities – banking and skiing.

ADAM II
1989–

Born on 14 February 1945, with the Sun in Aquarius and Moon in Pisces.

Adam II, who succeeded his father in 1989, was born with the Sun in Aquarius and Moon in Pisces. This is a likeable combination, for Aquarius brings an original character which is often attractive but can be abrasive, while Pisces adds softer and more sensitive qualities. Overall, this is a profoundly idealistic combination. In close personal relationships, Adam is likely to be quite demanding, for here the main combination is between Mars in Aquarius and Venus in Aries. Aries tends to exacerbate Aquarian abrasiveness and, while it can produce great passion, it also creates impatience and an inability to cope with delays. However, the sense of pent-up energy these planets generate can be most attractive, and to many people Adam appears an almost electrifying character. Yet he is a chameleon, capable of presenting different faces to different people, and to those who see his Piscean Moon he will always be deep, sensitive and caring to a fault.

Adam succeeded his father at 10.45 p.m. on 13 November 1989. It's an interesting fact that this took place during the fall of communism in eastern Europe, just days after the Berlin Wall was opened. Is Liechtenstein due to undergo its own revolution? The answer is that, in its own quiet way, it will. Powerful planetary alignments in the sectors of the horoscope signifying the country's foundations in general, its banking régime and working practices are all subject to immense change. This suggests that under Adam's rule Liechtenstein may abandon its role as a centre for tax avoidance and enter the European community, perhaps even surrendering its sovereignty. The most changeable years in Adam's life will be 2001–2, when Uranus passes over his Sun, creating a period of uncertainty during which he will be casting around for a new role, perhaps dissatisfied with what he will come to see as the dull routine of royal life.

Adam married Countess Marie Kinsky on 30 July 1967, and the couple have four children.

PRINCE ALOIS
Born on 11 June 1968, with the Sun in Gemini.

Alois, the heir to the throne, was born with the Sun in Gemini, a restless sign, and the Moon on the cusp, or dividing line, of Sagittarius and Capricorn. Most important, though, is the Sun's close alignment to Venus, Mars, Uranus and Pluto. This is a highly destabilising pattern which can create profound emotional swings and dramatic changes of opinion. It is an alignment found in the horoscopes of those who may either refuse the succession or, having accepted it, create the confrontations which lead to revolution. Such events are not inevitable, and if Alois channels his planetary energy positively he will take his life in a different direction. However, for this to happen his behaviour should be profoundly idealistic and not in the least self-interested. He is capable of sacrificing himself for a cause; the only requirement is that it be a worthwhile one. He is also capable of extraordinary leaps of imagination. The overriding consideration is that he should always concentrate on constructive action and positive results.

The most important years in Alois' future will be 2004–5. These years will take him through intense changes of a personal nature, including upheavals in his closest relationships. After then we'll know whether he is due to be Prince of Liechtenstein, or whether his destiny lies elsewhere.

PRINCE MAXIMILIAN
Born on 16 May 1969, with the Sun in Taurus and Moon in Sagittarius.

Maximilian was born with the Sun in Taurus and Moon in Sagittarius. This is a constructive combination, for Taurean caution and stability is contrasted with a typically Sagittarian love of adventure and freedom. Maximilian is therefore prepared to have the best of both worlds, pursuing a single path through life, while creating the space and excitement necessary to get the most out of other Taurean qualities, such as creative skills. He will find it difficult to settle into a single relationship, although he may be tempted to get married around 1997. Yet around 2002 he passes through a period of uncertainty very similar to that expected for his father, Adam.

PRINCE CONSTANTIN
Born on 15 March 1972, with the Sun and Moon in Pisces.

The annual New Moon in Pisces brings one of the most sensitive planetary alignments of the year, and Constantin, who was born under the Piscean New Moon of 1972, is nothing if not deeply and profoundly emotional. Indeed, everything he does will be shaped by his feelings. There will be times when, for reasons of self-defence, he wears a cool and confident public mask, but inside he will still be driven by his constantly fluctuating emotions. Fortunately, Venus and Mars were in Taurus at his birth, and this indicates a strong dose of practical application and consistency, qualities often lacking in true Pisceans. Above all, he will find deep satisfaction in helping other people. His major years of change will be 2005–7, when Pluto passes over his Sun and Moon, turning his personal life upside down.

PRINCESS TATIANA

Born on 10 April 1973, with the Sun in Aries and Moon in Cancer.

Tatiana was born with the Sun in energetic Aries and the Moon in emotional Cancer, always a powerful combination. This indicates not only a person who knows what she wants, but also how to get it. And with Mars in Aquarius, helpfully aligned with Jupiter, Saturn and Uranus, her methods will be a brilliant combination of the tried and tested together with the new and original. Emotionally, Tatiana's behaviour is indicated by Venus in Aries, revealing a powerful desire for affection and reassurance. If we look ahead, the years 2017–19 are extremely powerful ones for her. That's when Pluto passes over her Sun, and she'll revolutionise her home life and family relationships.

Luxembourg

The independence of the Grand Duchy of Luxembourg from the Netherlands was recognised on 9 September 1867, with the Sun in Virgo and the Moon in Capricorn. The current head of state is Grand Duke Jean.

JEAN
1964–

Born on 5 January 1921 with the Sun in Capricorn and Moon in Sagittarius.

Grand Duke Jean was born with the Sun in Capricorn, a suitable position for the ruler of a state which achieved independence with the Moon in this businesslike sign. Better still, are the Sun's positive alignments with Mercury, Jupiter and Saturn, all of which give him a deep sense of responsibility and authority, essential for one born to the duties of modern constitutional monarchy. When he succeeded his mother Grand Duchess Charlotte on 12 November 1964, Uranus and Pluto were the most active planets, exactly aligning his Sun and bringing out all that is most serious in his character. The Duke's personal charm lies in the combination of his Moon in adventurous Sagittarius, Venus in independent-minded Aquarius and Mars in sensitive Pisces. This adds a spark which helps him detach himself from his royal duties, avoiding taking them too seriously, and which allows others to see that he possesses unusual skills and qualities beyond his purely royal role. On 9 April 1953 Jean married Princess Josephine Charlotte of Belgium. As at his succession, the Moon was in Aquarius, indicating that however serious Jean becomes, he will always have his lighter side. Altogether the couple have five children, three sons and two daughters.

Jean passed through a personally testing time from 1989 to 1991, and aside from a possibly intense and unsettling period around 1995–6, his horoscope is reasonably calm until the next century.

PRINCE HENRI

Born on 16 April 1955, with the Sun in Aries and Moon in Aquarius.

Prince Henri, the heir to the throne, was born with the Moon in Aquarius, and has therefore inherited his father's lighter and more adventurous qualities. In addition, he was born with the Sun in Aries, and the combination of this sign with Aquarius is one of the most explosive possible. As if this were not enough, the Sun was also making powerful alignments with Jupiter, Uranus and Neptune, revealing a personality driven by dreams, ideals and a vision of the perfect future rather than practical reality. Henri has many wonderful qualities, not least of which are his dynamism and willingness to take risks, but if he is to achieve anything of substance he must listen very carefully to the advice of more experienced people; he must also cast around for practical support. In his private affairs Henri's feelings are dominated by Venus in Pisces and the Moon in Aquarius, a profoundly idealistic combination which gives him an inner longing for the perfect woman; he found his ideal partner in his Princess, Maria Teresa Mestre. The couple married on 14 February 1981, and have five children:

Guillaume
Born on 11 November 1981, with the Sun in Scorpio and the Moon in Taurus.

Felix
Born on 3 June 1984, with the Sun in Gemini.

Louis
Born on 3 August 1986, with the Sun in Leo and Moon in Cancer.

Alexandra
Born on 2 February 1991, with the Sun in Aquarius and Moon in Virgo.

Sebastien
Born on 16 April 1992, with the Sun in Aries and Moon in Libra.

The years 1994–5 will be unsettling ones for Henri, when he will be driven by romantic dreams which make it difficult for him to accept the routine of everyday life. Yet, if we look ahead, these influences are unlikely to recur in such a powerful form until around 2020, when he will be sixty-five.

Monaco

Monaco is one of the oldest principalities in Europe and has been ruled by the Grimaldi family since the thirteenth century. Since 1861 it has been under French protection, while retaining its own government and head of state.

RAINIER III
1949–

Born in Monaco at 6.00 a.m. on 31 May 1923, with the Sun in Gemini, Moon in Sagittarius and Ascendant in Scorpio.

PRINCESS GRACE

Born in Philadelphia at 5.31 a.m. on 12 November 1929, with the Sun in Scorpio, Moon in Pisces and Ascendant in Scorpio.

Rainier's horoscope is a lively mixture of adventurous and emotional influences. He was born with the Sun in Gemini, and that sign's restless qualities were enhanced by the Sun's close alignment with Mercury. The Moon was in Sagittarius, bringing all that sign's love of freedom. In addition, the Sun stood in a powerful alignment with Uranus, enhancing his love of unconventional behaviour. Rainier's Ascendant is in Scorpio, and it's this which provides him with his emotional depths and public dignity. There are two levels to the man: a public *bonhomie* represented by Gemini and Sagittarius, and an intensely private individual signified by Scorpio.

Perhaps it was Rainier's unconventional streak which led him to fall in love with and marry a Hollywood film star. Previously, European princes may have had actresses as mistresses, but they married from within the European royal circle. Rainier broke with centuries of convention when he married Grace Kelly, star of dozens of American movies. Grace was born with the Sun in Scorpio, so shared Rainier's intense and deep emotions. In addition her Moon was in almost the same degree of the zodiac as his Ascendant. This is the kind of astrological bond which often locks people into a close lifelong relationship. Even better prospects were indicated by the fact that

Grace's Sun was helpfully aligned with the Moon, in sensitive Pisces, and Pluto, a planet closely connected to Scorpio. Now, because of the closeness between Grace's Sun and Rainier's Ascendant, Grace's harmonious alignments were, in a sense, transferred to Rainier's horoscope. The upshot was that she helped him express everything in his character which is most sensitive, emotional, intense and passionate.

When Rainier and Grace married on 19 April 1956, the eyes of the world were on them. The wedding ceremony was televised and millions were swept along by this fairytale romance of the fifties and sixties – long before Charles and Diana seized the popular imaginations. Yet the horoscope of the marriage does not relate to the intensely emotional planets which linked Rainier's horoscope to Grace's. Perhaps this was fitting for two people who, in spite of their public situation, were intensely private individuals. The Sun was in very tight alignment with Uranus, indicating that Rainier was breaching centuries of royal convention. More importantly, it was in Aries, and the Moon in Leo was very close to Jupiter, planet of growth and expansion. This is a combination indicating the greatest possible theatrical show, and this was what the wedding became. From then on their marriage was presented in public in the most colourful terms, as the perfect union between one of the richest and oldest royal families in Europe and the new aristocracy of Hollywood. The idyll was shattered on 9 September 1982 when Grace was fatally injured in a motor accident. Five days later she died. Only days earlier Mars, indicating the possibility of accidents, had passed over Rainier's Scorpio Ascendant and Grace's Scorpio Sun.

Obviously, the future now lies with Rainier's children, but 1995–7 reveals profound planetary pressures in his horoscope. The two planets involved are Uranus and Neptune, and while they could bring upheaval in Rainier's public role, they are more likely to indicate an introverted phase, during which he is likely to engage in an almost mystical search for meaning in his life. This could be a very enlightening period for the Prince, one which helps him put his life in perspective.

PRINCE ALBERT

Born in Monte Carlo at 10.50 a.m. on 14 March 1958, with the Sun in Pisces, Moon in Capricorn and Ascendant in Gemini.

Albert was born with the Sun in Pisces and Moon in Capricorn. This is an excellent combination, for Piscean sensitivity and charm mixes well with the conservatism which is so typical of Capricorn. These two signs account for Albert's exemplary public conduct. His Ascendant is in Gemini, a sign which also combines well with Pisces and adds a healthy dose of charm.

Albert's romantic life is dominated by four factors. First there's his Sun in Pisces which gives him the typical shyness and reserve of that sign. Then there's his Moon in Capricorn, which craves a conventional marriage and secure family life. In addition, his Venus in Aquarius attracts him to partners who are slightly unusual and independent of spirit. Lastly, he was born with Saturn in a sector which indicates that for a marriage to be successful it should be made late in life, certainly after the age of thirty, perhaps forty.

If we look into the future we find that the years 2004–5 are among the most powerful in the Prince's entire life. In private he will be falling in and out of love, and in public he will be attempting to come to terms with his royal inheritance. It is unlikely that he will feel settled in any life he creates for himself until after then.

PRINCESS CAROLINE

Born in Monte Carlo at 9.27 a.m. on 23 January 1957, with the Sun in Aquarius, Moon in Scorpio and Ascendant in Pisces.

Princess Caroline was the *enfant terrible* of European royalty in the seventies and eighties. The teenage rebellion against her parents, her failed romances and her public antics were inexplicable to most people, and could be attributed only to adolescent high spirits. However, Caroline's horoscope explained her behaviour perfectly. She was born with the Sun in Aquarius, a sign which craves independence, in exactly the opposite degree of the zodiac to Uranus, the planet of revolution. So powerful is this alignment that if Caroline had not rebelled, there would have been something terribly wrong with her!

Her romantic adventures were symbolised by her intense, passionate Scorpionic Moon and romantic Piscean Ascendant. If any combination pushed her into falling in love, this was it. The Moon was also very close to Neptune, planet of illusion, which explained why she was for so long seduced by glamour and incapable of realising when she was being exploited for her position. The reason why falling in love with unsuitable men played such an important part in her rebellion was that the Moon and Neptune, indicating her romantic hopes, were in a very difficult alignment with the Sun and Uranus, the planets revealing her revolutionary tendencies. The worst problems, and her most public failures, took place during the passage of, first, Uranus and then Pluto, through Scorpio, activating the sensitive points in her horoscope.

Caroline is an idealist and her teenage rebellion was the result of exactly the same quest for perfection which motivated thousands of student revolutionaries. The difference was that, rather than attacking her wealth and privilege, she made it seem ridiculous through her extravagant behaviour. She was unconscious of the deeper psychological processes in her horoscope, but the fact that she was stumbling through life, unaware of her deep motivation, makes her idealism no less real. In future her idealism will emerge in different ways, and she may even pass through a phase of religious devotion.

PRINCESS STEPHANIE

Born in Monte Carlo at 6.25 p.m. on 1 February 1965, with the Sun and Moon in Aquarius and Ascendant in Leo.

In her teenage years Princess Stephanie inherited Caroline's wild behaviour. In Stephanie's case, her conduct was explained by the position of the Sun and Moon at her birth; they were in exactly the same degree of Aquarius. Stephanie is therefore the Aquarian *par excellence* – independent, unusual, original, rebellious and idealistic. Her Ascendant in colourful Leo only compounded her tendency to attract attention by attacking tradition and convention.

Both sisters were born with Venus and Mercury in the conservative sign of Capricorn. This indicates that in their relationships, revealed by Venus, and ideas, represented by Mercury, they are conventional. This is why their rebellion did not take them away from their privileged backgrounds, but instead found them enjoying their status and wealth.

Stephanie is likely to find her true direction and establish a family life to her liking only after 1999, and the dramatic Uranus alignments of 1997–9. These will bring a deep craving for independence and change, and once she has broken free from what she still sees as emotional chains, she will be able to settle down.

The Netherlands

The Netherlands proclaimed independence from Spain on 26 July 1581, led by the Stadholder, William the Silent. The same family, that of Orange-Nassau, has ruled ever since, with a few interruptions. William III, Stadholder from 1672 to 1702, became King of England in 1689. In 1815 the Stadholders became kings, and the Netherlands has been a monarchy ever since.

WILHELMINA
1890–1948

Born in The Hague at about 6.30 p.m. on 31 August 1880, with the Sun in Virgo, Moon in Cancer and Ascendant in Pisces.

Wilhelmina was Queen of the Netherlands for fifty-eight years, five of them spent in exile, during the Nazi occupation. Her horoscope was a mass of contradictions, because deeply practical planets were mixed with others of great sensitivity. Her Ascendant was in sensitive Pisces and her Moon in romantic Cancer, so it is clear that she was driven by her feelings. However, her Sun in practical Virgo gave her an excellent grasp of detail and day-to-day reality; Venus and Mars in Virgo complemented her superb ability to handle routine business. Yet Uranus was also in Virgo, within a degree of the Sun. This confirms that, far from being a dull administrator, she was able to devise ways of accomplishing simple tasks which revolutionised daily routine. In other circumstances, Wilhelmina might have been a great inventor. Had she been born poor she might even have become a socialist or trades union leader.

Her powerful Uranus symbolised a revolutionary impulse which was in continual search of suitable expression. It eventually had its effect when, on 4 September 1948, she abdicated in favour of her daughter Juliana. (She eventually died on 28 November 1961.) There was a perfectly good reason, ill-health, but it was almost unheard of for a reigning monarch to abdicate unless forced; other monarchs remained on the throne even when insane. Wilhelmina established a precedent, which was later followed by Juliana. Perhaps Wilhelmina's greatest achievement, however, was her rejection of the mysteries and rites of the ancient divine monarchy. In the new era, members of the royal family were to be seen travelling by bicycle, like ordinary Dutch people. The revolutionary Queen Wilhelmina set a new standard for royal conduct which has been followed by most other royal families, with the exception of the British.

JULIANA
1948–1980

Born in The Hague at 6.49 a.m. on 30 April 1909, with the Sun in Taurus, Moon in Virgo and Ascendant in Gemini.

Queen Juliana shared many personal qualities with her mother. The Moon in Virgo at her birth indicated a businesslike approach, great skill with practical details and a high regard for order and stability. In addition the Sun and Moon were both making very harmonious alignments to each other, as well as to Venus and Jupiter. This is an indication of enormous charm and generosity, together with an ability to arouse intense loyalty and support.

Juliana's Ascendant tells a different story; this lies in Gemini, adding a restless streak to her character. However, her Ascendant's importance lies in the fact that it occupies exactly the same degree of the zodiac as Pluto, a planet which always brings emotional confrontation. Although Juliana is capable of exuding charm, the person who oversteps the mark and takes liberties will experience the full force of her anger and contempt. Other factors, including a close Mars–

Mercury alignment, reveal an incisive mind and a sharp tongue, and the person who underestimates her soon regrets it.

Juliana's husband, Prince Bernhard, was born at 2.45 a.m. on 29 June 1911, with the Sun in Cancer, Moon in Leo and, like Juliana, the Ascendant in Gemini. Although they share the fundamental curiosity and desire for intellectual stimulation which is always associated with Gemini, their other planetary alignments are very different. Juliana's desire for order contrasts with Bernhard's volatile emotions and moods. The initial attraction between the pair was largely due to the fact that Juliana saw him as a dramatic and colourful figure, while he saw her as a source of order, offering him the possibility of a stable home life.

Following her mother's example, Juliana abdicated on 30 April 1980. At the same time Venus, Neptune and Saturn were in a rare and powerful alignment, indicating that this was an ideal moment to put dreams of future happiness into effect.

BEATRIX
1980–

Born in The Hague at 9.47 a.m. on 31 January 1938, with the Sun and Moon in Aquarius and Ascendant in Aries.

If her mother and grandmother were born with conventional horoscopes livened up with a dash of revolutionary fervour, Beatrix is an out-and-out rebel. She has no time for outmoded rituals or meaningless convention and has continued the reshaping of the monarchy as a twentieth-century institution. Beatrix was born with the Sun and the Moon within a few degrees of each other in Aquarius, so she's what we might call a 'double Aquarius'. She is therefore determined to set her own course, stamping her individual seal on Dutch affairs as the country enters the twenty-first century. The Queen's Ascendant is in Aries, further confirmation of her dynamism and energy. Beatrix also has great social powers. Her Sun and Moon are extremely close to Venus and Jupiter, two planets which indicate boundless charm and optimism. In addition, all four planets are in the sector of her horoscope representing friendships. This is the horoscope of the perfect social catalyst and, were Beatrix to have been born in other circumstances, she might have become a professional party organiser. However, this same alignment is also ideal for a political career and Beatrix's ideal alternative profession would have been as the Netherlands' first woman prime minister.

Beatrix married Prince Claus on 10 March 1966, when the Sun in Pisces was making intense alignments to five planets: conservative Saturn, optimistic Jupiter, intense Pluto, revolutionary Uranus and romantic Neptune. The relationship is therefore extraordinarily intense, complex and deep. The couple have three children.

The years 1998–9 are powerful ones for Beatrix, for that will be when Uranus passes over her Aquarian planets. She'll be anxious to adapt the monarch's role once more, perhaps as a result of political changes within the country. The years 2003–4 could find the monarchy affected by a scandal, although Beatrix herself will be moving in a mystical direction, perhaps becoming more interested in religious matters.

PRINCE WILLEM

Eldest son of Beatrix. Born on 27 April 1967, with the Sun in Taurus and Moon in Sagittarius.

Willem, Beatrix's eldest son and heir, was born with the Sun in Taurus and Moon in Sagittarius, an intriguing combination, suggesting that he can combine a Taurean sense of order with a Sagittarian love of adventure. He can therefore follow a steady course without becoming stodgy, and experiment with new ideas and lifestyles without sacrificing his achievements. Emotionally, Willem is dominated by Venus in Gemini and Mars in Libra, planets which suggest that, no matter how charming he can be, he prefers to maintain his independence and will be careful about committing himself. If he does make a commitment but then changes his mind, he will not hesitate to seek a separation.

If and when Willem succeeds Beatrix to the throne, he will have to control his tendencies to be swept away by his feelings and act on impulse. This is a personal task he will have accomplished by 2005, for in 2003–4 he will abandon every personal commitment. Some, those which truly suit him, will be remade but others will not, so he cannot feel settled or confident of his purpose until then.

255

PRINCE JOHAN

Second son of Beatrix. Born on 25 September 1968, with the Sun in Libra and Moon in Scorpio.

Johan was born with the Sun in charming Libra and the Moon in emotional Scorpio, an intense combination indicating a willingness to please and a seriousness of purpose. The Sun is also very close to Uranus, indicating an independent spirit and an ability to break out of restricting circumstances. This makes for an interesting and unusual life. His personal manner is revealed in his close alignment of Mercury and Venus in Libra, conferring a high regard for polite behaviour and pleasant environments. With his friends and lovers he is likely to be slow to make the initial advance, but nevertheless very loyal and reliable.

PRINCE CONSTANTIJN

Youngest son of Beatrix. Born on 11 October 1969, with the Sun and Moon in Libra.

Constantijn was born under a New Moon in Libra, which means that both his Sun and Moon are in this sign. He is therefore the perfect Libran, charming to a fault though perhaps over-concerned with appearances. In addition, Jupiter is so close to the Sun and Moon as to suggest not only the great generosity signified by this planet, but also a degree of impatience. Constantijn's weakness is that he wants perfection – and wants it immediately. If he can cultivate genuine patience, rather than just a façade of Libran good humour, he could become an artist or designer of great skill, with remarkable achievements to his credit.

Norway

Norway had its own kings as long ago as the ninth century, but the modern Kingdom of Norway came into being in 1905, when independence was gained from Sweden.

HAAKON VII
1905–1957

Born in Copenhagen at 4.05 p.m. on 3 August 1872, with the Sun and Moon in Leo and Ascendant in Sagittarius.

Haakon VII, first King of modern Norway, was the son of Frederick VIII of Denmark. He was born with excellent credentials for a king, particularly the Sun and Moon Leo, the royal sign. His Ascendant was in adventurous Sagittarius, confirming his energetic character. In addition, Venus, planet of love and affection, was close to Jupiter, planet of optimism and expansion, and Uranus, the most unusual of all the planets, in Leo. The end result was a larger than life character who led his country ably for over fifty years.

In 1896 Haakon married Maud, daughter of the future British King Edward VII, inaugurating the close relationship between the two royal houses which survives to this day. Haakon died in 1957, and was succeeded by his son, Olav.

OLAV V
1957–1991

Born at Sandringham on 2 July 1903, with the Sun in Cancer and Moon in Libra.

Olav V was born with the Sun in Cancer, an indication of a character driven by deep and powerful emotions. But when we consider that the Sun was extremely close to Neptune, we see how romantic he was. Olav was a dreamer, wanting only the best for those around him. He was also born with the Moon in Libra, which adds to the impression that here was a man whose mission in life was to spread goodwill. He was not above arguing with his family or fighting his corner, for Mars was closely aligned with his Moon and in a difficult relationship with his Sun, but he was anxious that nobody should be hurt. His wife, Martha, was born on 28 March 1901, with the Sun in fiery Aries and Moon in emotional Cancer. This is a tough combination, and she had almost as much energy as Olav himself.

Olav succeeded to the throne at 4.35 a.m. on 21 September 1957, with the Moon and Mars occupying exactly the same degree of Virgo. This is about as businesslike a combination as is possible, combining great energy with attention to detail. Olav was a humble man who never stood on ceremony and was happy to mix with his subjects as an equal.

HARALD V
1991–

Born at Skaugum at 12.45 p.m. on 21 February 1937, with the Sun in Pisces and Moon and Ascendant in Cancer.

Harald V succeeded to the throne on the death of his father, Olav, at 10.20 p.m. on 17 January 1991. The Sun was then in Capricorn, together with Saturn, suggesting that the coming reign would be nothing if not businesslike. The Moon with Venus in Aquarius adds a touch of humour and pleasure, indicating that the new king will not lose his ability to enjoy himself. Harald was born with an extraordinarily sensitive and emotional horoscope, containing the Sun in Pisces and both the Moon and Ascendant in Cancer. He is a highly compassionate man, driven by deep emotions and anxious to do as much good as he can. Indeed, his powerfully placed Jupiter indicates that he is capable of great generosity, but that he is concerned to offer practical help rather than make sweeping but empty royal gestures.

On 29 August 1968, Harald married Sonja Haraldsen. At the time Jupiter, planet of growth and optimism, was aligned both to the Sun and Moon, and this is a very positive indication for a relationship in which both partners are determined to do their best. A heavy emphasis of planets in Virgo suggests that the relationship would be a discreet one, with neither partner prepared to discuss their feelings in public.

Changes in Harald's personal life will take place during 1996–7, although much that happens will be purely psychological. His moods will fluctuate and there will be times when he decides to give up the crown and find another job. However, he'll pass through such periods without implementing his decisions.

CROWN PRINCE HAAKON

Son and heir of Harald V. Born on 20 July 1973, with the Sun in Cancer and Moon in Pisces.

Haakon has inherited much of his father's sensitivity. Whereas Harald had his Sun in Pisces and Moon in Cancer, Haakon was born with the Sun in Cancer and Moon in Pisces. He is vulnerable, easily hurt and, consequently, can be shy in public, but is also considerate, compassionate and concerned to protect others' welfare. Haakon was born with Mercury very close to the Sun, an indication that his often reserved manner conceals strong opinions and a poetic nature. He was also born with Venus in Leo and Mars in Aries, indicating that when his Pisces–Cancer sensitivity is reassured, and when he feels comfortable and secure, he will behave in a most extraverted manner, the life and soul of the party. When in love he will pursue his quarry with unshakeable determination. The years 1995–7 will be romantic ones, during which Haakon falls in love, but also develops his vision of a better world and his part in creating it. He is unlikely, though, to find the confidence to promote his own ideas and develop a lifestyle to suit his personal interests until after 2005.

PRINCESS MARTHA

Daughter of Harald V. Born on 22 September 1971, with the Sun in Virgo.

Martha was born with the Sun in Virgo, sign of practical care and caution, yet in a very close alignment with Pluto, planet of emotional depth and confrontation. She will be driven by all the deep perfection associated with Virgo, finding it very difficult to accept second-best, and may decide that the only way to achieve her personal aims is to institute widespread changes in the world around her. Martha's Moon is on the cusp, or dividing line, between Libra and Scorpio. If she can develop Libra's ability to compromise, this will assist her considerably. The years 2002 and 2005–6 will be when Martha discovers her purpose and settles her private affairs and domestic life.

Russia

Russia traces its origins back to the medieval principality of Moscow. The first Czar was Ivan the Terrible, who reigned from 1533–1584. The last Czar, Nicholas II, was overthrown in the Russian revolution in March 1917.

NICHOLAS II
1894–1917

Born in St Petersburg at midday on 6 May 1868, with the Sun in Taurus, Moon in Aries and Ascendant in Virgo.

ALEXANDRA

Born in Darmstadt at 3.45 a.m. on 6 June 1872, with the Sun, Moon and Ascendant in Gemini.

Czar Nicholas II was the cousin of the British King George V through their mothers, both Danish princesses. His wife was a granddaughter of Queen Victoria and cousin of the German Kaiser Wilhelm II. Nicholas was born with the Sun in Taurus and Moon in Aries, an indication of great obstinacy and arrogance. When found in combination these two signs tend to reinforce each other's tougher qualities, with dire results in Nicholas' case. The Czar was utterly incapable of compromise over his belief in the divine right of kings. Like Charles I and Louis XVI before him, he believed that his duty was to maintain the monarchy's absolute powers. The close relationship between his Arien Moon and Jupiter added to his pride.

There's another significant reading of Nicholas' powerful Moon–Jupiter combination: the Moon indicates Nicholas' perceptions of his mother and the ways in which these shaped his relationships with other women. He was driven by a desire to treat all women as if they exerted a controlling and maternal influence over him, which explains why he was prepared to be so deeply influenced by his wife Alexandra. It was she who patronised the shamanic mystic Rasputin, encouraging his destructive influence over the entire royal family. Alexandra was born with the Sun, Moon and Ascendant in Gemini. This is an extraordinarily rare alignment and the only other known example in royal history occurs in Queen Victoria's horoscope. Alexandra then, was more than a recreation of Nicholas' mother. She was, in an astrological sense, her own grandmother!

Alexandra was also born with Venus and Mars in Gemini, and was therefore extraordinarily opinionated and egotistical. She was a single-minded person who had almost no capacity to consider any idea which she had not put forward. She might on occasion listen to other people's thoughts, which she would then reproduce as her own. Nicholas was overwhelmed by what he saw as her superior intelligence, and listened to her views on every single detail of government. Nicholas and Alexandra had five children:

OLGA

Born on 15 November 1895, with the Sun in Sagittarius and Moon in Aries.

TATIANA

Born on 10 June 1897, with the Sun in Cancer and Moon in Aries.

MARIE

Born on 26 June 1899, with the Sun and Moon in Cancer.

ANASTASIA

Born on 18 June 1901, with the Sun in Cancer and Moon in Sagittarius.

ALEXIS

Born on 30 July 1904, with the Sun in Leo.

The Russian Republic was proclaimed at exactly midnight on 28 February 1917, and from that moment Nicholas lost all authority, even though it was not until a few days later that he abdicated. Curiously, the planetary alignment at this moment was more significant for Alexandra's horoscope than for his. In an astrological sense it was she who was abdicating, just as it had been she who had always been seen to reign. On 16 July 1918, Nicholas, Alexandra and their children were murdered and the centuries-old Romanoff monarchy came to a bloody end. By this time Uranus, which brings sudden and often irreversible changes in fortune, had formed a very difficult alignment to the Sun in Nicholas' horoscope. Once again, a dynasty had been snuffed out under a dramatic planetary alignment, and a cycle in the affairs of the nation reached its final conclusion.

Spain

The Spanish crown dates back to the union of the kingdoms of Castile and Aragon on 19 January 1479. Philip II (1556–98) was briefly King of England when married to Mary I, but was never crowned. From 1873–4 Spain experienced its first brief period of Republican government. In 1931 a second Republic was proclaimed and it was not until 1975 that the monarchy was restored under the present King, Juan Carlos I.

ALFONSO XII
1874–1885

Born in Madrid at 10.30 p.m. on 29 November 1857, with the Sun in Sagittarius, Moon in Taurus and Ascendant in Leo.

Alfonso XII restored the monarchy following the Republic of 1873–4. He was born with the Sun in Sagittarius and the Moon in Taurus, a useful combination, for it combines common sense with an adventurous spirit. Appropriately, his Ascendant was in Leo, the royal sign.

ALFONSO XIII
1886–1931

Born in Madrid at 12.30 a.m. on 17 May 1886, with the Sun in Taurus, Moon in Scorpio and Ascendant in Aquarius.

Alfonso XIII began his reign as an infant, his mother ruling as Regent until 1902, and ended it in exile after the Republican party won the 1931 election. He was born with the Sun in Taurus, a stable and conservative sign, the Ascendant in Aquarius, which brings a capacity for independent thought, and the Moon in Scorpio, conferring deep emotions and intuition. Although this is a stubborn combination, Alfonso understood the weakness of his position and on 14 April 1931 he went into voluntary exile. The civil war followed, resulting in the dictatorship of General Francisco Franco. Alfonso died in 1941.

JUAN CARLOS I
1975–

Born in Rome at 1.15 p.m. on 5 January 1938, with the Sun in Capricorn, Moon in Aquarius and Ascendant in Taurus.

Juan Carlos, the grandson of Alfonso XIII, was born with the Sun in Capricorn and the Moon in Aquarius, combining the conservatism of the former sign with the independence of thought of the latter. He also has his Ascendant in Taurus, a sign which favours a businesslike approach to life and has a high regard for order. There is no point, in the Taurean world view, of changing anything unless there is a clear practical purpose. Juan Carlos has therefore proved himself to be a most sensible monarch. He is the only reigning European monarch since the war to have played a major part in a political crisis and survived. His brother-in-law, Constantine II of Greece, bungled very similar circumstances in Greece and lost his throne as a direct result.

Juan Carlos was put on the throne by the Spanish dictator, Franco, who saw in the young Prince a man who would preserve the conservative dictatorship under which Spain had languished for almost forty years. However, Juan Carlos was his own man, and proved that he owed allegiance not to the old authoritarian ways but to the new democratic Europe. By supporting the development of parliamentary democracy against a number of armed attempts to reinstate the old order, he won fresh support for the monarchy. In so doing, he transformed it from Franco's final fantasy into a central part of Spain's modern constitutional life.

The King was born with Venus and Mercury in Capricorn, indicating a high regard for formal manners, and Mars in Pisces, revealing a desire to please. These three planets account for his courteous and dignified behaviour, and this in turn is largely responsible for his continued popularity.

On 14 May 1962 Juan Carlos married Princess Sophie, the daughter of King Paul of Greece. She was born on 2 November 1938, with the Sun in Scorpio bringing her all the sensitivity, secrecy and intense emotions associated with that sign. On the day of the wedding the Sun was in Taurus in an exact and harmonious alignment with the Moon in Virgo. This is an excellent combination, indicating that both Juan Carlos and Sophie have a down-to-earth view of marriage, essential if the initial attraction is to become a mature long-term relationship.

Juan Carlos can look forward to major personal upheavals from 2000 to 2003. Family additions may include grandchildren, but the indications in 2002–3 also suggest political uncertainty in the country as a whole. Should the King ever contemplate handing on his crown to his son, Felipe, then the year 2015–16 would be perfect.

INFANTE FELIPE

Son and heir of Juan Carlos. Born on 30 January 1968, with the Sun and Moon in Aquarius.

Felipe is a double Aquarian, born with both the Sun and Moon in that sign. He is therefore quite capable of making up his own mind, regardless of what his father, the government or the country expects. However, given that Juan Carlos was also born with the Moon in Aquarius, the two men have a deep bond and a similar outlook on the world which will grow deeper as the years pass. The three planets which represent Felipe's personal relationships are spread through three signs, making for an interesting public manner. He is capable of appealing to different people and sections of the community by bringing out separate aspects of his character. Mercury in Aquarius gives him an ability to communicate and put across new and unusual ideas; Venus in Capricorn is shy and reserved, with a love of good manners and traditional social customs; Mars in Pisces gives him a sensitive approach, being careful not to offend people or damage their interests.

The years 1998–9 will be lively ones for Felipe, when Uranus, planet of sudden change, passes over first his Sun and then his Moon. First of all, he'll assert his own style and role as heir to the throne. Having done that, he'll create a family of his own in readiness for the day when he becomes King.

INFANTA ELENA

Elder daughter of Juan Carlos. Born on 20 December 1963, with the Sun in Sagittarius and Moon in Aquarius.

Elena's Sagittarian Sun and Aquarian Moon have given her a lively and rebellious personality, capable of going her own way no matter what the constraints of royal protocol. Yet Mercury, Venus and Mars in Capricorn add a healthy dose of caution. She rarely does anything without considering the consequences, and is therefore careful not to cause offence. Where necessary she'll curb her behaviour, waiting until she sees that she can obtain her ends with a minimum of fuss. In 2006 and 2007 Pluto will pass over her Sun, turning her life upside-down and setting her off on a new, idealistic course.

INFANTA CRISTINA

Younger daughter of Juan Carlos. Born on 13 June 1965, with the Sun in Gemini and Moon in Sagittarius.

Cristina was born with the Sun in Gemini and Moon in Sagittarius, a lively combination suggesting an adventurous personality, fond of competition and not afraid to fail in the short-term if she's confident she'll win in the end. She's a lover of freedom, resentful of all imposed ties and restraints. However, she will put up with restrictions for a long time before she attempts to shake them off. Cristina does have a strong Saturnine streak, indicating deep conservatism, so her goal should be to create her own limitations rather than accepting those from elsewhere.

Sweden

The Kingdom of Sweden can be traced back to the tenth century. The present monarch, the sixty-fifth in the line, is Carl XVI Gustave.

GUSTAVE V
1907–1950
Born on 16 June 1858, with the Sun in Gemini.

Gustave V was a Geminian, and possessed all the lively and intellectual qualities associated with that sign. His horoscope also included an extraordinarily lively conjunction of Uranus, Mercury and Jupiter in Gemini. A more creative combination is difficult to imagine; it is also an indication of profound independence of purpose. Gustave was therefore a fitting monarch to lead his nation through two world wars, supporting its neutral policies in both. He died in 1950 and was succeeded by his son, Gustave VI.

GUSTAVE VI
1950–1973
Born on 11 November 1882, with the Sun and Moon in Scorpio.

A New Moon in Scorpio is one of the most intense of all possible planetary alignments, and Gustave VI, who was born under such a pattern, was therefore a deep and secretive person with a profound desire for privacy. Mars, Saturn and Pluto were also powerfully connected to both the Sun and Moon, creating an alignment of extreme power. Gustave was deeply conservative, intensely romantic and very formal, and it is ironic that he was on the throne when Sweden acquired its reputation as the centre of the sixties' permissiveness. He died on 15 April 1973.

CARL XVI GUSTAVE
1973–
Born in Haga at 9.20 a.m. on 30 April 1946, with the Sun in Taurus, Moon in Aries and Ascendant in Leo.

Carl Gustave succeeded to the throne on the death of his grandfather in 1973 with the Sun in Aries and Moon in Virgo. This is a suitable combination for a new reign, combining Arien energy with the attention to detail typical of Virgo. The King was born with the Sun in

Taurus and the Moon in Aries, also combining a sense of order with energy and dynamism. His personal manner is represented by three planets: Mercury in Aries indicates strong opinions, Venus in Gemini adds a delightful social and romantic manner, and Mars in Leo contributes a theatrical and dramatic edge.

On 19 June 1976 the King married Silvia Sommerlath. The marriage horoscope is a lively one, with a Geminian Sun very close to Venus and strongly aligned with a Piscean Moon. The impressions which arise from this suggest tenderness and sensitivity.

The years 1998–9 find Uranus making a challenging alignment to the King's Sun, so this will be a time of change. He will be searching for new interests which take him away from his royal role, and also considering whatever reforms are necessary to take the Swedish monarchy into the twenty-first century.

CROWN PRINCESS VICTORIA

Eldest daughter of Carl Gustave. Born on 14 July 1977, with the Sun in Cancer.

Sweden is the only European country to give women equal rights with men in the succession to the throne, so Crown Princess Victoria is first in line, ahead of her younger brother, Carl. Victoria is a Cancer, and therefore has all the sensitivity of that sign, and she was born hours before a New Moon in Cancer, which makes that sign's emotional influence even stronger than normal. Mercury in Leo gives her strong opinions and Mars in Taurus gives her staying power. Once Victoria sets her heart on any practical goal it will take an enormous effort to change her mind. Socially she is more flexible, and capable of switching her affections at a moment's notice.

PRINCE CARL

Son of Carl Gustave. Born on 13 May 1979, with the Sun in Taurus and Moon in Sagittarius.

Carl was born with the Sun in Taurus, indicating a love of order and stability, yet he is also heavily influenced by a powerful alignment with the Sun and Uranus. He was also born with Venus and Mars in

267

Aries, an indication of great personal energy. He is therefore an extremely powerful person with set opinions and objectives. These extend to his personal life as well as his public role and professional standing. Carl will discover his purpose in 2001–3, when Uranus aligns his Sun. He will then develop a role which takes him beyond his royal roots.

PRINCESS MADELEINE

Youngest daughter of Carl Gustave. Born on 10 June 1982, with the Sun in Gemini.

Born with the Sun in Gemini, Princess Madeleine is one of the intellectual members of the family. However, the Sun's strongest alignments are with Saturn, Neptune and Pluto, so she's a deep thinker, and it may therefore take people some time before they realise how intelligent she is. Socially and emotionally she inclines towards stability and can be a faithful friend. In 2004 Pluto will occupy the opposite degree of the zodiac to Madeleine's Sun, inaugurating a period of change which will see her maturing rapidly and perhaps rebelling against her royal background.

Recommended Reading

Astrology

Campion, Nicholas, *The Practical Astrologer*. Cinnabar Books, Bristol, 1993.

Carey, Hilary, *Courting Disaster: Astrology at the English Court and University in the Later Middle Ages*. Macmillan, London, 1992.

Carter, Charles, *An Introduction to Political Astrology*. L. N. Fowler, London, 1951.

Elliot, Roger, *Astrology and the Royal Family*. Pan, London, 1977.

Greene, Liz, *The Astrology of Fate*. George Allen and Unwin, London, 1984.

Harvey, Martin, *Nativitas: Astrological Studies*. Triom, Sao Paulo, 1992.

Lilly, William, *Nativity of King Charles*. London, 1652.

Lilly, William, *Christian Astrology*. London, 1647; facsimile edition, Regulus Press, London, 1985.

Thomas, Keith, *Religion and the Decline of Magic*. Penguin, Harmondsworth, Middlesex, 1971.

Royalty

Andrews, Allen, *The Kings and Queens of England and Scotland*. Marshall Cavendish, London and New York.

Allison, Ronald and Riddell, Sarah (ed.), *The Royal Encyclopaedia*. Macmillan, London, 1991.

Brooke, Christopher, *The Saxon and Norman Kings*. Fontana Library, Collins, London, 1967.

Dale, John, *The Prince and the Paranormal: The Psychic Bloodline of the Royal Family*. W. H. Allen & Co., London, 1988.

Froissart, *Chronicles*. Translated Geoffrey Brereton, Penguin, Harmondsworth, Middlesex, 1968.

Fulford, Roger, *Hanover to Windsor*. Fontana Library, Collins, London, 1966.

Kenyon, J. P., *The Stuarts*. Fontana Library, Collins, London, 1966.

Monmouth, Geoffrey of, *The History of the Kings of Britain*. Translated Lewis Thorpe, Penguin, Harmondsworth, Middlesex, 1966.

Morby, John E. *Dynasties of the World*. Oxford University Press, Oxford, 1989.

Murray, Margaret, *The Divine King in England*. Faber and Faber, London.

Plumb, J. H., *The First Four Georges*. Fontana Library, Collins, London, 1966.